Discipline, Moral Regulation, and Schooling

Studies in the History of Education
(Vol. 4)
Garland Reference Library of Social Science
(Vol. 944)

Studies in the History of Education

Edward R. Beauchamp, Series Editor

Discipline, Moral Regulation, and Schooling
A Social History

Edited by
Kate Rousmaniere
Kari Dehli
Ning de Coninck-Smith

GARLAND PUBLISHING, INC.
New York & London
1997

Library of Congress Cataloging-in-Publication Data

Discipline, moral regulation, and schooling : a social history / edited by
  Kate Rousmaniere, Kari Dehli, Ning de Coninck-Smith.
      p.   cm. — (Garland reference library of social science ; vol. 944.
  Studies in the history of education ; vol. 4)
    Includes bibliographical references and index.
    ISBN 0-8153-1606-2 (alk. paper)
    1. School discipline—History—Cross-cultural studies.   2. Social
  ethics—History—Cross-cultural studies.   3. Moral education—
  History—Cross-cultural studies.   4. Teachers—Professional ethics—
  History—Cross-cultural studies.   I. Rousmaniere, Kate, 1958– .
  II. Dehli, Kari.   III. De Coninck-Smith, Ning.   IV. Series: Garland
  reference library of social science ; v. 944.   V. Series: Garland reference
  library of social science. Studies in the history of education ; vol. 4.
  LB3012.D568   1997
  371.5—dc21   97–11679
                                                                          CIP

Printed on acid-free, 250-year-life paper
Manufactured in the United States of America

Contents

Series Editor's Preface

Garland's Studies in the History of Education series includes not only volumes on the history of American and Western education, but also on the history of the development of education in non-Western societies. A major goal of this series is to provide new interpretations of educational history that are based on the best recent scholarship; each volume will provide an original analysis and interpretation of the topic under consideration. A wide variety of methodological approaches from the traditional to the innovative is used. In addition, this series especially welcomes studies that focus not only on schools but also on education as defined by Harvard historian Bernard Bailyn: "the transmission of culture across generations."

The major criteria for inclusion are (a) a manuscript of the highest quality and (b) a topic of importance to understanding the field. The editor is open to readers' suggestions and looks forward to a long-term dialogue with them on the future direction of the series.

Edward R. Beauchamp

Discipline, Moral Regulation, and Schooling

Chapter One
Moral Regulation and Schooling
An Introduction

Kate Rousmaniere, Kari Dehli, and Ning de Coninck-Smith

From their inception, formal schools in Western capitalist societies have been designed to discipline bodies as well as to regulate minds. A key purpose of modern state schooling has been the formation of conduct and beliefs, as well as the acquisition of prescribed knowledge. School discipline has frequently been overt and physically violent, with students most often the targets of teacher-administered punishment. But modern school discipline also encompasses conditions and practices that promote the self-regulation of adults and children, and the cultural repertoires or discourses within which we come to see ourselves as certain kinds of persons. Such forms of discipline have as their object the production of self-disciplined individuals who adhere to explicit and implicit rules of conduct and norms of conscience as if they were their own. In this book we refer to such normative practices as moral regulation.

Historians in the West have documented the powerful effects of modern state schooling from the nineteenth century onwards on the organization and experience of childhood, childrearing, and parenthood. Notions of childhood as a distinctive and foundational phase in a person's life are historically recent, and they are inconceivable without reference to modern schooling. It is only in recent history that the formal school became a site where adults made competing claims on children's time and space, while attempting to shape the minds and bodies, as well as the "character" and conduct, of young people. It was here that social and moral norms of modern childhood were fashioned, and it was from here they spread. But these norms did not spread by themselves; they were taken up and lived by children, parents, and teachers, even as norms were, and continue to be, negotiated, subverted, and resisted. One objective of this book is to contribute to a historical and sociological understanding of the complex interweaving of disciplinary practices and regulations organized through, and emanating from, modern schools. We also attend to how these practices and regulations were embodied and refused in the lives of those who populated schools and other educational sites.

Historians of education have been faulted for writing the history of education from an adult point of view, a view from a particularly "official" adult world where formal documentation and official records are maintained.[1] Most histories of education recount the institutional and structural development of school administrations, educational policy, theory, and curriculum. But under the influence of labor, social, and women's history, the field of study has grown over the last twenty-five years so that historians of education today investigate deeper contexts and cultures inside schools of the past, questioning how class, gender, sexuality, race, and ethnicity shape schooling experiences and outcomes, the training and treatment of teachers at work, and the social and political role of parents and the local community in early public schooling. Yet even in the newest versions of the social history of education, many stories remain untold.

Often the stories that we remember and tell about our own schooling are not so much about what we learned, but how we learned and with whom. There are stories about teachers we loved, teachers we hated and those we feared, and others that we ridiculed and mocked. Among the children we might have gained friends for life, while others are remembered with intense dislike or fear, and of many more we may have no memory at all. There were good days and others full of tears and broken hearts, and many, many days of boredom, monotony, and endless repetition. Most striking in our memories may be moments when we "did wrong" and were punished or humiliated by teachers or other pupils. For many students those moments were a daily litany of repeated pain and frustration. How did we experience those lessons? Who imposed those often bewildering rules, regulations, and behavioral norms? How did we learn those rules as children, and how did our teachers and parents learn how to enforce them? How did we learn to refuse or subvert school discipline, even when it seemed we consented? In a broader historical framework, how did some practices, norms, and behavioral assumptions become naturalized and taken for granted? How were these normative assumptions experienced and taken up by children and adults? How can we write histories of education that begin to explore such questions?

School Discipline as Moral Regulation

Formal schools have demanded certain patterns of conduct by children, teachers, administrators, and parents. Over time a narrow range of behaviors, beliefs, and values have come to be seen as evidence of good teaching and learning. The work of mobilizing such forms of discipline has involved a huge, various, ubiquitous, and historically and culturally changing apparatus of rules, technologies, and practices. Compared with constraining and overtly controlling forms of discipline, moral regulation may require no direct physical contact and may not appear as punishment or as exercise of authority and power. This is because moral regulation entails the disciplining of personal identities and the shaping of conduct and conscience through self-appropriation of morals and beliefs about what is right and wrong, possible and impossible, normal and pathological.

The significance and power of moral regulation hinge on its social organization as a web of self-imposed forms of conduct and self-monitoring practices. One key question that analyses of moral regulation in education seek to answer is how such monitoring is worked out by those who inhabit schools and other educational sites. The papers in this book examine how moral regulation has been organized in schools, and in the broader educational spheres of family and community, in the past and up to the present. Several of the papers discuss how pupils, teachers, and parents have experienced and often resisted, subverted, and transformed moral regulation and school discipline. Indeed, some of the authors suggest that although moral regulatory practices are pervasive and powerful, one of the persistent stories of moral regulation is its failure. Wherever there is moral regulation there is resistance; wherever social forms are imposed there is human capacity to subvert and exceed their constraints.

Investigations of moral regulation entail more than the tracing of histories of particular disciplinary regimes. Also significant is an understanding of the broad ethos and concrete practices of representation that are specific to capitalism and modern forms of regulation and rule. Such a focus provides a perspective that helps to historicize the construction of, and relations between, the social and the individual. It is in this broad sense that Philip Corrigan and Derek Sayer conceive of moral regulation as a "project of normalizing, rendering natural, taken for granted, in a word, 'obvious' what are in fact ontological and epistemological premises for a particular and historical form of social order."[2] This opens up the possibility of seeing relations between the social and the individual as historically contingent and contested rather than determined, predictable, and necessary.

For Corrigan, moral regulatory practices are integral to historical processes of state formation, especially to those hierarchical relations through which people are invited to see themselves as members of political communities, as simultaneously free individuals in, and as subordinate subjects to, regimes of government and rule.[3] State schooling in capitalist societies forms an important set of sites where such invitations are differently offered, and where "freedoms" are made available in ways that claim generality and equality, while producing and reproducing relations of power and difference. Within schools the connections between moral regulation and nation-building, state formation and the construction of citizenship can be made visible, but what investigations of moral regulation bring into view is that these connections are neither linear nor uniform; rather they are uneven and contradictory in their forms and effects, and are frequently contested by those whom they name and target.

Some authors argue that investigations of moral regulation ought to go beyond the state, and that many important examples of moral regulation have only tangential relations to the state.[4] While we do not find it useful here to take sides in debates about whether relations between the state and moral regulation are necessary or contingent, modern schools are interesting in this regard, as they in many ways straddle the historically constructed divisions between state and civil society, between public and private. We would suggest that some forms and practices of moral regulation through schooling relate to specific state "intentions" or "projects," while also encompassing a series of disciplinary practices, mechanisms, conditions, and effects that can be traced only indirectly to any particular political will or function of state rule. The work of schools is both shaped by state laws, curriculum policies, employment practices, funding, architecture, and so on, and it is maintained by students, teachers, and parents in their everyday routines and interactions.

The concept of moral regulation provides a lens with which to view the complex social worlds of schools of the past and the present, and to ask questions about how subjectivities are formed within them. While attending to how conduct, fear, desire, and pleasure are shaped through schooling, moral regulation also suggests alternative ways for thinking about the educational features of power relations more broadly—that is, for thinking about how social and political forms educate.[5] In relation to schooling histories, it allows us to see that hierarchical and different experiences and outcomes of schooling can be explained neither simply by way of consent nor by reference to externally driven systems of logic or rationality. At the same time, accounts of moral regulation do not abandon reference to socially organized relations of power around axes such as class, race, gender, sexuality, and, particularly for schooling, age.[6]

Through detailed studies of historically situated practices, the papers in this volume challenge social control theories of education which posit that schools are simply designed for intentional purposes by a powerful elite, and that the people who populate schools are compliant or complicit victims or mere cogs in an all-powerful wheel. Nevertheless, studies of moral regulation draw attention to the simultaneous construction of social order and particular forms of individuality, thus refuting voluntarist explanations of schooling experiences, outcomes, and change. In this regard we can see the affinity, as well as some distinctions, between studies in moral regulation and Michel Foucault's work on modern forms of power.

Foucault's investigations into the operation and effects of decentralized and disciplinary power in Western European societies from the eighteenth century onwards have informed the work of many historians of education who are rethinking the discourses, practices, and effects of modern compulsory state schooling.[7] His argument that modern forms of power are enacted through a network of technologies of surveillance and observation, and by way of hierarchical ordering and normalizing judgments, is of particular relevance to studies of discipline and moral regulation. According to Foucault, power and knowledge are intimately connected and mutually constituted in and through such technologies, which aim simultaneously to know, regulate, and constitute the "population" and the "individual."[8] Foucault proposed that, rather than being the generative source of social change and cultural meaning, the modern subject—the autonomous, free, rational individual—is constituted as an "effect" of historically specific disciplinary regimes and power relations.[9] He argued that

This form of power applies itself to immediate everyday life which categorizes the individual, marks him [sic] by his own individuality, attaches him to his own identity, imposes a law of truth on him which he must recognize and which others have to recognize in him. It is a form of power which makes individuals subjects. There are two meanings of the word "subject": subject to someone else by control and dependence; and ties to his own identity by a conscience or self-knowledge.[10]

Foucault's research on how the individual subject is produced through the disciplinary powers and knowledge regimes of prisons, psychiatry, and sexual regulation, for example, suggests useful lines of investigating how particular kinds of subjectivity are produced as effects of modern schooling. By drawing attention to the constitutive dimensions of power, his work challenged more conventional notions of power as simply confining, constraining, and external, or as a matter of individual and collective possession.

Foucault offered strategies for looking at the discursive and disciplinary pedagogical practices through which we are differently constituted as subjects, and through which we come to know ourselves as unique individuals. He provided a way of exploring the daily routines of surveillance, management, and categorization through which schools work to produce specific forms of subjectivity in pupils, teachers, and parents. His account of the examination has inspired education historians to reread how practices in which students "perform" their knowledge and skills produce "teachers" and "pupils/students" as their subjects.[11] Detailed organization of space and time, promotion of specific forms of bodily appearance and posture, and explicit and implicit rules of teachers' and pupils' conduct and interactions provide other examples.[12]

Foucault's allusion to the double meaning of the word *subject* in the above quotation is analogous to our earlier discussion of moral regulation as both socially organized rules and norms and as practices of self-regulation. His frequent claim that "wherever there is power, there is resistance" comes close to our position that moral regulation is never omnipotent, and that disciplinary regimes always fall short of their targets. Education is experienced differently by different individuals, not by some accident or fault of design, but because differentiation and individuation constitute a condition structured into the very organization of modern schools and school systems. And, as anyone who has spent more than a few minutes in a classroom will know, human beings who populate those spaces refuse, subvert, invent, negotiate, and resist the terms of their subjectification in pedagogical practices and discourses.

We take these insights on how power operates in modern societies through dispersed practices of regulation, and how the organization of modern power comes to be imbued with morality in the broadest sense, in order to ask how formal schooling aims to shape the everyday conduct, sentiments, and values, as well as the knowledge and skills of children and adults who come in contact with them. While children are primary targets of these disciplinary practices, adults are also caught up in regimes of discipline and moral regulation, albeit in different and often conflicting ways. As some of the papers in this volume show, women who teach, for example, may be agents of disciplinary power in relation to children who populate their classrooms. At the same time women teachers are subjected to, and variously take up, gendered forms of moral regulation and discipline that position them as subordinate employees in the sexual division of labor in state schooling bureaucracies, as persons whose authority as teachers is frequently contested in sexualized terms, and as beings whose femininity is seen either as preparing them "naturally" for teaching or as undermining their capacity for rationality.

Feminist writers have attempted to address the "feminization" of school discipline and moral regulation by examining the historical construction of early "child-centered" and progressive pedagogy. They have both questioned the "good intentions" of child-centered pedagogy and highlighted the tensions between pedagogical authority and feminine powerlessness that became embodied in the role of child-centered women teachers. Carolyn Steedman has traced the complex historical trajectory of the female teacher as a "mother made conscious" whom progressive educational theorists and administrators expected to carry the emotional and physical weight of running a caring, child-centered classroom. Valerie Walkerdine has explored the more recent discourse and practice of child development theory and "progressive" pedagogy in England. She shows how naturalist assumptions about the "developing child," the mother, and the teacher are embedded in these theories and how they produce "normalizing effects" in classroom practices.[13]

Given the complexities and nuances of the subject, histories of discipline, moral regulation, and the cultural repertoires of schooling do not lie waiting, ready to be "found." Rather it is a matter of asking different questions of the sources historians already work with, including diaries, letters, memoirs, and interviews, and of reconstructing the life of past schoolrooms through them. We need to rely on our historical interpretation of contradictions, inconsistencies, and silences in the sources, in order to make meaning out of the apparently meaningless, to construct narratives of dialogues between children and adults of the past, and to inquire into the continuing productivity of moral regulatory practices.

The Chapters
The idea for this book came out of conversations between the editors during the 1992 Canadian History of Education Association conference in Lethbridge, Alberta. Although the three of us work in different countries, we were struck by the similarities of many of our historical questions about the experiences of students, parents, and teachers under disciplinary regimes of the modern school in Denmark, Canada, and the United States. We also shared a dissatisfaction with the ways in which those experiences had been investigated and interpreted by historians. We identified a common set of themes in our current research, revolving around questions of how school discipline was and is organized in ways that seem to "seep into" the very being of those who populate(d) schools; and how schools call(ed) for continuous and visible demonstration of moral "virtue" and "character" in the conduct of pupils, teachers, and parents. We also shared an interest in the disciplin-

ary effects of practices and arrangements that did not appear, in the first instance, to be "about" discipline.

Ning de Coninck-Smith stumbled over a series of cases in which Danish parents and teachers clashed over physical punishment. She began to see the history of schooling at the turn of this century as a story of constant fights over children's bodies, time, and space. Recently she has investigated educational and scientific ideas of the nineteenth century to discover how the status of children's play has changed within educational theory. In both contexts she was reminded of the central role of self-discipline in the schooling of children. Kate Rousmaniere, in her oral history interviews of retired New York City women teachers, was struck by how many teachers still felt personal guilt and remorse at having lost their self-control with students many decades before, even if they could recall only one or two such moments. What was it that made women teachers carry the sense of personal responsibility for their lost tempers throughout their lifetimes? Kari Dehli was researching how class and gender relations were constructed and articulated through home and school associations in Toronto, Canada, at the turn of the century when she began to question the ways in which Anglo-Saxon, middle-class women fashioned positions for themselves as political and professional subjects in local boards of education and the emerging welfare state. In particular, she wondered how these women participated in constructing notions of the "good" and "intelligent" mother, and how such notions were inserted into practices that regulated and differentiated the work and lives of teachers, mothers, and children.

Beginning with the notion that schools do not just teach subjects, but also shape the subjectivities of those who come into regular contact with them, we invited contributions that would explore how the interior and exterior organization of authority relations of schooling have changed over time. The papers discuss the histories of disciplinary practices of students, teachers, and parents, and how dominant discourses about education have developed normative practices and methods for regulating ways of being and knowing in and beyond schools. The authors take care to historicize, differentiate, and contextualize terms that are often taken for granted in educational histories, such as *teacher, student, child,* and *parent.* Far from being simply descriptive, these familiar terms suggest and delineate specific relations of authority and dependence, assume notions of competence, skill, and knowledge, and imply moral judgments about proper behavior, conduct and beliefs. And, as some of the papers show, there has been considerable struggle about the meanings and effects of such commonsense terms.

The authors draw together and question the historical construction and contestation of forms of power and forms of discipline in, through, and of schooling. They also attend to "why" questions by asking who benefits, who gets hurt, who wins, and who loses in regimes of school order. These are not linear narratives of unidimensional and unproblematic "good" and "bad"; rather, they describe power that is both centralized and dispersed, both diffused everywhere and exercised from some social locations more than from others, with far more painful effects on some subjects than on others. The papers attend to practices and discourses of schooling, communities, and families, and they speak to strategies of rule and of resistance; they address forms of education structured through relations of hierarchy and domination and talk of powerful disciplinary regimes and of innovative refusals and subversive accommodations.

The authors open up different strategies for looking at, thinking about, and interpreting schooling histories. They suggest that attending to the moral ethos and cultural forms of schooling, as well as the ways in which those forms were lived, negotiated, creatively appropriated, and resisted, offer useful ways of rethinking the historical formation of schools and their subjects. Inquiry into moral regulation provides a way of interpreting the production, performance, and effects of power and resistance that are integral to the histories of schooling. Thus, the collection is both about discipline and moral regulation as a topic within the field of educational history, and it suggests ways of looking at and interpreting educational historiography differently.

While some of the authors consider the discourses and practices of organizations, policy-makers, parents, and popular media, others address what we might call the "inside" of schools: the experiences of children and adults in the day-to-day life within their boundaries. They ask how children and adults experienced, expressed, or performed the construction of identities or subjectivities in and through schooling, and how they responded to, reacted to, and often resisted those constructions. They cross the doorstep of the school with the purpose of studying school practices and experiences; they focus on daily experiences and meanings of the ordinary teacher, student, and parent; they discuss how, and if, the normative and normalizing practices of school discipline functioned and how they were embodied in new forms of conduct; and they ask how people were not only disciplined but also self-disciplined and how they experienced this. Some of the chapters provide detailed social histories of the interior organization of schooling and discuss changes in disciplinary relationships and behaviors within schools over time. They deal with school cultures, teachers' work, and power relations within individual schoolhouses, classrooms, and communities. The focus on relations within schools encompasses studies of teachers, students, and parents, as well as the physical and political organization of schooling.

Bruce Curtis's paper traces the changing role of corporal punishment in European pedagogical theory from the mid-sixteenth to the early nineteenth century, as formal education was extended to working-class children. While never entirely removed from the arsenal of school government, physical violence was marginalized in favor of psychic and emotional means of securing order and obedience. Curtis argues that these shifts can best be understood in relation to the more general project of bourgeois hegemony—that is, the attempt of this class to achieve political, cultural, and moral leadership. While Curtis traces historical shifts in educational theory over time, Christina Florin and Ulla Johansson compare the disciplinary regimes of three Swedish schools between 1850 and 1900. They show how class and gender interacted in the construction of specific forms of regulation and modes of exercising authority by teachers over pupils, forms and modes that sought to assert the hegemony of the Swedish bourgeois class, and of bourgeois men in particular.

One of the key features of school discipline in formal, state schools is their capacity to compel the vast majority of children to attend, and to punish those who are "irregularly" present or consistently absent without proper authorization. But, as Ning de Coninck-Smith shows in her chapter, the school's authority to control children's time has not always been met with compliance. She tells the story of how the school authorities in a town near Copenhagen were pressured to abolish their virtual prisons for "truant" children and institute more humane forms of pupil discipline as a result of popular protest and organizing.

The next four chapters focus on the moral regulation of teachers and on the ways in which ideologies shaped not only teachers' working conditions but also their very social and individual identities. Harry Smaller's paper on nineteenth-century Ontario argues that while many of the disciplinary practices of schools were targeted on children, it was equally important that teachers adhered to codes of conduct and morality. Teachers were not only subject to these codes during school hours, but during their "free" time as well, and even into retirement. The figure and positioning of women teachers as particular embodiments of the moral in schools are the topics of the papers by Kate Rousmaniere, Hanne Rimmen Nielsen, and Marjorie Theobald. On the one hand, the maternal, nurturing, and loving teacher came to symbolize the good and the moral in nineteenth- and early twentieth-century progressive educational ideologies. As Kate Rousmaniere shows in her study of nineteenth-century American women teachers' first experiences in the classroom, this moral pressure created an impossible ideal for women teachers to strive for, but to never attain. Hanne Rimmen Nielsen's study of dismissed women teachers in early twentieth-century rural Denmark describes what happened to women teachers who were accused of not following that normative role and identity. Marjorie Theobald demonstrates how the early Australian school system gave women teachers a unique chance for advancement; yet, at the same time, these possibilities were diminished with the gradual bureaucratization and centralization of the school system and the interwoven normative expectations of women teachers' behavior and identity. Through a close reading of records from commissions of inquiry, Theobald also shows how one woman teacher fashioned a complex political agency of sorts from the contradictory subject-positions made available to her within discourses of morality, gender, sexuality, and danger.

Drawing on her research on colonial Bengal, Himani Bannerji shows how notions of child-centered and progressive pedagogies were mobilized by middle-class women at the turn of the nineteenth century in their arguments for more comprehensive education for girls and women and in their own childrearing practices. Centering on the changing notions of motherhood, her account of middle-class women's writing on women's education is situated in relation to a class-internal struggle on the ground of gender and patriarchy and to a broader class and nationalist politic. Kari Dehli's paper also analyzes middle-class women's participation in public debates about education and schooling. She describes the organizing activities of a group of Toronto women who fashioned an educational politics for women soon after they had gained the right to vote in local school board elections. She shows how notions of the "intelligent" and the "good" were mobilized as central metaphors in the political discourse of these white, Anglo-Saxon, and middle-class women as they sought to justify their right to educational citizenship, while at the same time distinguishing themselves from "other" women.

The penultimate chapter of the book takes us up to the present. In it Philip Corrigan provides a contemporary and very recent history of the British Tory government's attempts to reintroduce a very explicit moral content and moralizing discourse into that country's schools. He shows the extent and details of these efforts, at the level of policy, and he also demonstrates the contradictions and hypocrisies inherent in them. By attending to a contemporary moment in educational policy-making and schooling practice, Corrigan also reminds us that it would be a grave mistake to presume that moral regulation somehow "belongs" to the past.

Taken together, the authors unsettle several assumptions commonly taken for granted about schooling, by questioning and unmasking as partial and divisive the apparently self-evident and easy definitions of "good" and "moral" school practice. We hope that, taken as a whole, this collection will contribute to the construction of different, oppositional, and alternative ways of speaking in and about education.

Endnotes

1.   Linda A. Pollock, *Forgotten Children: Parent-Child Relations from 1500 to 1900* (London: Cambridge University Press, 1983); Barbara Finkelstein, "Incorporating Children into the History of Education," *Journal of Educational Thought*, Vol.18, No. 1, April 1984, pp. 21–41; Finkelstein, "Redoing Urban Educational History," in Ronald K. Goodenow and William E. Marsden, eds., *The City and Education in Four Nations* (Cambridge: Cambridge University Press, 1992); Finkelstein, "In Fear of Childhood: Relationships between Parents and Teachers in Popular Pri-

mary Schools in the Nineteenth Century," *History of Childhood Quarterly,* Vol. 3, Winter 1976, pp. 321–335; J. H. Plumb, "Children, the Victims of Time," in *In the Light of History* (London: Penguin Press, 1972); Kathleen Alaimo, "Childhood and Adolescence in Modern European History," *Journal of Social History,* Vol. 24, No. 3, Spring 1991, pp. 591–602; Ludmilla Jordanova, "Children in History," in Geoffrey Scarre, ed., *Children, Parents, and Politics* (Cambridge: Cambridge University Press, 1989); Valerie Polakow, *The Erosion of Childhood* (Chicago: University of Chicago Press, 1982); and Carlo Ginzburg, "Clues: Roots of an Evidential Paradigm," in Carlo Ginzburg, *Clues, Myths, and the Historical Method* (Baltimore: Johns Hopkins University Press, 1989).

2. Philip Corrigan and Derek Sayer, *The Great Arch: English State Formation as Cultural Revolution* (Oxford: Basil Blackwell, 1985), p. 4. As Mitchell Dean has argued, the aim of historical and sociological investigations of moral regulation is not to ask how "'Society' necessarily stamps itself on the personality." Instead, such inquiry is concerned with "the means by which 'constructed' identities come to be formed, re-formed and taken to be natural and normal." Mitchell Dean, "'A Social Structure of Many Souls': Moral Regulation, Government, and Self-formation," *Canadian Journal of Sociology,* Vol. 19, No. 2, 1994, p. 146.

3. Philip Corrigan, "On Moral Regulation: Some Preliminary Remarks," in *Social Forms/Human Capacities* (London: Routledge, 1990), pp. 102–129. See also Corrigan, "Dichotomy is Contradiction," *Sociological Review,* Vol. 4, 1975; "State Formation and Classroom Practice: Once Again on Moral Regulation," in Geoffrey Milburn, Ivor F. Goodson, and Robert J. Clark, eds., *Re-interpreting Curriculum Research: Images and Arguments* (Lewes, Sussex: Falmer Press; and London, Ont.: Althouse Press, 1989); and the introductory essay in Philip Corrigan, ed., *Capitalism, State Formation, and Marxist Theory: Historical Investigations,* (London: Quartet, 1980).

4. Mariana Valverde and Lorna Weir, "The Struggle of the Immoral: Preliminary Remarks on Moral Regulation," *Resources for Feminist Research,* Vol. 18, No. 3, 1988, pp. 31–34; Mariana Valverde, *In the Age of Light, Soap and Water: Moral Reform in English Canada, 1885–1925* (Toronto: McClelland and Stewart, 1991); Mitchell Dean, *Critical and Effective Histories: Foucault's Methods and Historical Sociology* (London and New York: Routledge 1994).

5. See Corrigan, "State Formation and Classroom Practice," "On Moral Regulation"; Valverde and Weir, "The Struggle of the Immoral."

6. Corrigan, "State Formation and Classroom Practice."

7. See, for example, Stephen J. Ball, ed., *Foucault and Education: Disciplines and Knowledge* (London: Routledge, 1990); Fiona M. S. Paterson, "Schooling the Family," *Sociology,* Vol. 22, No. 1, February 1988, pp. 65–86; and David Hogan, "The Market Revolution and Disciplinary Power: Joseph Lancaster and the Psychology of the Early Classroom System," *History of Education Quarterly,* Vol. 29, No. 3, Fall 1989, pp. 381–417.

8. Michel Foucault, *Discipline and Punish: The Birth of the Prison* (New York: Vintage, 1979); *The History of Sexuality,* Vol. 1 (New York: Vintage, 1980); *Power/Knowledge: Selected Interviews and Other Writings, 1972–1977,* Colin Gordon, ed. (New York: Pantheon Books, 1980).

9. Michel Foucault, *The History of Sexuality.*

10. Michel Foucault, "The Subject and Power," in Hubert L. Dreyfus and Paul Rabinow, eds., *Michel Foucault: Beyond Structuralism and Hermeneutics* (Chicago: University of Chicago Press, 1983), pp. 208–226.

11. See, for example, Keith Hoskin, "The Examination, Disciplinary Power and Rational Schooling." *History of Education,* Vol. 8, No. 2, 1979, pp. 135–146; and Daphne Meadmore, "The Production of Individuality through Examination." *British Journal of Sociology of Education,* Vol. 14, No. 1, 1993, pp. 59–73.

12. Ball, *Foucault and Education.*

13. Carolyn Steedman, "'The Mother Made Conscious': The Historical Development

of a Primary School Pedagogy." *History Workshop,* Vol. 20, Autumn 1985, pp. 149–163; Steedman, "Prisonhouses." *Feminist Review,* Summer 1985, pp. 7–21; Valerie Walkerdine, "'It's Only Natural': Beyond Child-Centred Pedagogy," in Ann Marie Wolpe and James Donald, eds., *Is There Anyone Here from Education?* (London: Pluto Press, 1983); Walkerdine, "Developmental Psychology and the Child-Centred Pedagogy: The Insertion of Piaget into Early Childhood Education," in Julian Henriques et al., eds., *Changing the Subject: Psychology, Social Regulation and Subjectivity* (London: Methuen, 1984); and Walkerdine, *Schoolgirl Fictions* (London: Verso, 1990), see esp. chaps. 1, 3, and 5.

Chapter Two
"My Ladie *Birchely* must needes rule"
Punishment and the Materialization of Moral Character from Mulcaster to Lancaster

Bruce Curtis

The extension of education to working-class populations in late-eighteenth and early nineteenth-century Europe was accompanied both by the generalization of established pedagogical practices and by the development of novel ones.[1] Collective instruction replaced individual instruction, and new devices and instruments were applied to students. Particular attention was paid by educational reformers to the effective schoolroom governance of large numbers.

As in other political domains, educational governance came to be characterized by a theoretical and practical concern with forming an active subjectivity and a willing acceptance of subordination on the part of those governed.[2] One dimension of this project was a marginalization and limitation of the role of physical violence in processes of governance, and an increasing reliance upon moral and emotional discipline.

This shift in the nature of governance is related to the undermining of patriarchal authority over servants, apprentices, and journeymen in the household by industrial capitalist relations of production. The direct influence of ruling classes, exerted through immediate personal contact and control of key ideological and cultural institutions, became increasingly difficult to sustain, given the distance between social classes opened by industrial capitalist development. In this context, influential bourgeois intellectuals sought to anchor rule in the autonomous selves of the ruled. This project called for programs of direct moral discipline in new social institutions, and the creation of new means of surveillance and inspection. The politics of subjectification involved a movement away from spectacularly violent punishments.[3] Governance came to aim at the formation of characters and consciences which could be relied upon to be freely obedient, and to renounce the punishment of the flesh as ineffective and "inhuman."

This essay traces the role of physical punishment in (especially English) pedagogical theory from the 1580s to the early 1800s. Conditions of rule in the schoolroom directly parallel more general conditions of governance in society.[4]

Michel Foucault's work has located the movement from torture to rehabilitation in penal matters primarily in the second half of the eighteenth century. The institutional chronology is similar in the domain of education: here, however, experimental work and intellectual argument from a much earlier period aimed to marginalize physical violence and to substitute "humanizing" modes of governance. Some of these political–technical innovations were later adapted to mass schooling.

I suggest that the key transformations at work in the period investigated here lie in the attempts by educators, after Rousseau especially, to "hide the hand" of educational power, and in changes in the subjects of education, from ruling-class boys to working-class children of both sexes. The beating of students, earlier seen as a necessary element in the capacity of teachers to rule in the schoolroom, came to occupy a place at the margins of legitimacy.

Sixteenth- and Seventeenth-Century Theories of School Government

Richard Mulcaster, a tutor to the young Princess Elizabeth and the teacher of a grammar school for the company of merchant tailors in London, discussed questions of correction and punishment at length in his *Training Up of Children* (1581). In what was already a standard pedagogical proposition, Mulcaster argued that the best way to make children learn is to encourage them to do so voluntarily, and without fear of punishment.[5]

Nonetheless, for Mulcaster, physical punishment and correction in school government were inevitable. As with most educational writers, Mulcaster took the conditions of governance in the schoolroom to be the parallel of those of the dominant form of political rule.[6] "The *rod* may no more be spared in schooles," he claimed, "then the *sworde* may in the Princes hand," and moreover, "my ladie *birchely* will be a gest at home, or else parentes shall not have their willes." He claimed that, since masters of large schools and parents at home could have their way only with the use of corporal punishment, it would be improper to avoid administering it to those who deserved it.[7] Correction through corporal punishment was exemplary and valuable both for the person corrected, whose faults were thereby prevented, and for those witnessing punishment, and Mulcaster scoffed at the idea that this example might produce any untoward fear or terror in the minds of those witnessing it.[8]

Yet, since correction which did not secure repentance would harden the student, caution was needed to deliver punishment in a circumspect manner and to ensure that offenses did not pass undetected. Beating consumed time at school, but this time was usefully spent only if correction in fact took place, a recurrent theme in later discussions of the subject.[9]

Given the necessity of applying physical punishment when governing large schools and when faced with deserving "wittes," Mulcaster outlined steps which teachers should take to ensure their punishment practices would be supported by parents and the community in general. To avoid "school inconveniences," teachers should print and publicly display a list of "schoole *ordinaunces.*" Both students and parents should be acquainted with these rules and regulations, which would cover the manner of teaching, advancement through classes, times of admission to the school, hours of attendance, and holidays. In particular, these rules and regulations would specify what and how much corporal punishment would attach to various offenses.[10]

Before punishing any student with the rod, the teacher should ensure that the fault in question be "confessed, if it may be, without force, and the boye convited by verdit of his fellowes, and that very evidently." Without public confession and without the support of the rest of the scholars for the teacher, children would convince credulous parents that they had been mistreated. Teachers were urged to avoid punishing for faults at lessons or "misses" and to be careful in extreme cases to hold "conference with the parent" and to secure "evident proofe before punishment."[11]

Mulcaster discussed at length the necessity of securing the support and cooperation of parents and neighbors if the teacher was to "plant pleasure" in his experience of schoolkeeping. Teachers were counseled to meet with all those interested in the welfare of children, and parents should be ready to take the advice of their well-meaning neighbors. Mulcaster was keenly aware of the discouragement teachers might face from the opposition of parents to their schooling practices, but stressed that "their friendly and faithfull communicating workes perpetuall obedience in the childe." Parents were urged to consult with the schoolmaster on all matters of dispute, and schoolmasters themselves were urged to meet with other teachers to share knowledge and information.

If education was to be successful in the large sense, and if punishment and correction were to be effective, it was necessary in Mulcaster's view that children be subject to the same behavioral demands in the community at large. This was a matter that involved the character of political order and the safety of the state. Certainty in the conduct of school, household, and church was "a point which all writers that deal with the *oeconomie* of householdes, and pollicie of states do so much respect." This was so because "the fine blossomes of well trained families, do assure us of the swetest flowres in training up of states, for that the buddes of private discipline be the beauties of pollicie."[12]

The combination of cooperation of the whole community in educational matters and certainty and constancy in methods and courses of study would produce consent to the structure of political order. This consent would be firmly based upon the free compliance of the educated to a set of internalized political standards.[13] This, of course, was both the political problem faced, and the solution to it advocated, by nineteenth-century writers concerned with the discipline of working-class populations. In the latter century the solution was called "training" or "habituation," but it remained the practice of a regular discipline which would become *constitutive* of the educated subject.

Mulcaster was addressing the question of the education of ruling-class boys. What distinguished this and many other contemporary accounts from those of the nineteenth century was the support the former offered for exemplary and public physical punishment. When the "community" which was to agree on necessary punishments was homogenous in its class character and secure in its educational destiny, visibly violent conditions of educational governance were less likely to become a matter of conflict than they were in the nineteenth century, when educational means were used to establish the dominance of one class over another.

Perhaps in keeping with their general concern for a pedagogy based on the child's pleasure in sensory perception, the seventeenth-century English followers of John Amos Comenius, the influential Protestant educator, paid little attention to the question of corporal punishment. Comenius himself argued that corporal punishment was not fitting for intellectual errors. "When a musician's instrument emits a discordant note, he does not strike it with his fist, or with a club, nor does he bang it against the wall: but continues to apply his skill to it, till he brings it into tune."[14] Comenius did support the use of corporal punishment for moral offenses and insisted that it be meted out at once, rather than in cold blood.[15] Yet those influenced most by Comenius attempted to avoid the necessity of corporal punishment by designing an intrinsically pleasurable pedagogical situation. This is the case in John Dury's *Reformed School,* published by Samuel Hartlib (ca. 1650) and designed to promote the formation of an "association in Christ" for the reformed education of children. In the "pettie schoole" for those aged from eight to fourteen, things were to be arranged so that

nothing may be made tedious and grievous to the Children: but all the toilsomeness of their business the Governour and Ushers are to take upon themselves; that by diligence and industry, all things may be so prepared, methodized and ordered for their apprehension; that all their work may unto them be as a delightfull recreation by the variety and easiness thereof.[16]

In addition, the masters and ushers of the school were to exercise a careful and constant observation over the behavior of the students and, indeed, this vigilance was said to be "the Master-peece of the whole Art of education," for it would reveal the true nature of children to their masters.[17]

Dury recommended the introduction of scrutiny and examination that would extend to all aspects of the child's activity and that would enlist the efforts of the children themselves. Dury wrote that, in addition to "Monitors, Spyes are to be appointed to oversee them," and "that the lying and deceitfull spirit may be hunted out from amongst them; a special reward is to be proposed unto every one that shall, upon due admonition of his neighbour before witnesses, discover to the Usher any matter of falshood practice by any." Dury was prepared to allow corporal punishment, but again in "moral" matters only and then after all other means had failed. "In Case of grosse failing," he wrote, "after due admonitions, some exemplary punishments of shame and smart may be used, that all may feare."[18]

The course of instruction in the "reformed school" was broad and varied, with an emphasis upon language instruction in the vernacular and the three Rs at the elementary level, rising to "oeconomicks," "logick, poesie & rhetorick" and other subjects for those over fourteen years of age. The interest engendered by living language was to be sustained by a schoolroom itself designed to aid in the process of government. Each school was to possess a room equipped with a gallery large enough to accommodate all the students. In the individual rooms, there was to be a "high seat for the Usher; that he may overlook all his Scholars, with twentie distinct places, so ordered for the Scholars to sit or stand in; that their faces may be all towards him: and each in his place may have his own desk. . . ," clear anticipations of early nineteenth-century practices.[19]

While we may well question the extent to which student solidarity would have acceded to Dury's plans for "spyes," in principle his "reformed school" sought to minimize the application of physical violence through the design of pleasurable pedagogical relations and structures. Scrutiny and observation—ideally self-scrutiny and self-observation—would be effective correctives.

A similar set of plans is to be found in Charles Hoole's *New Discovery of the Old Art of Teaching Schoole,* which also first appeared under the Commonwealth (1659). Hoole examined at length the general problem of the maintenance of the authority of the teacher in the school. Teachers were again counseled to avoid excessive punishments, and to teach in such a way that they gained the support of students and parents. School work was to be encouraged by creating competition among the students through the "taking of places," and "the Master should be verry sparing to whip any one for his book, except he be sullenly negligent." Even in such a case as that, Hoole claimed that the master should prefer shaming to the beating of students, especially those who were "slow witted and of tender spirit."[20]

A number of practices and tactics were suggested by Hoole in place of physical violence. Monitors from among the older students should be appointed in large schools; at the end of each school day they would "give a bill to the Master of their names that are absent and theirs that have committed any disorder."[21] The teacher would collect all of this information about student misdemeanors and absences and preserve it in a book or "Bill." Vigilance by monitors would allow for the maintenance of order in school "with seldome and moderate correction; a thing to be desired by every Schoole—master," and Hoole stressed the importance of the "awe" inspired in students by the knowledge that a record of their offenses was kept. The book and the Bill as material representations of good moral character were effective, of course, only to the extent that they appealed to a created moral sense and conscience. About the latter, Hoole had little to say.

However, he did emphasize that the authority of the teacher over his scholars was the first condition of a successful education. Authority was "the true mother of all due order" and was something that "the Master must be careful in every thing to maintain." If he did not do so, "he may command what he pleaseth, but withall, he must give the Scholars the liberty to do what they list." Governance of others demanded self-governance by the teacher. The teacher who lost control of his passions should leave the school and walk away until he was calm.

Perhaps the best way to create and sustain authority according to Hoole was by kindness combined with a relentless scrutiny. This knowledge/power was to be tempered with forbearance. It was sometimes better "to forbeare blowes . . . then to punish him so for a fault, as to make him to hate you."[22]

Yet if physical punishment were necessary, Hoole was concerned that it be regulated carefully. He specified the instrument to be used, the number of blows to be delivered, and their target. "The Ferula," he hoped, "might be utterly banished out of Schooles" and replaced by "a good sharp birchen rod, and free from knots; (for willow wands are insufferable, and fitter for a Bedlam then a School) as it will break no bones, nor endanger any limbs." Even toward those students "that seem to extort a rod from the Master . . . and . . . will enforce him to fight," Hoole enjoined "such clemency in his hand, as not to exceed three lashes; in the laying on of which, he may contribute more or less weight, with respect to the demerits of the fault." Finally, Hoole warned that the teacher who did beat a student must be certain to predominate.[23]

Obadiah Walker, Locke's neglected predecessor, whose *Of Education* (1673) enjoyed contemporary success, again insisted upon the political necessity of education. If education were not given to "Subjects," "what a confusion would it be?"

without obedience, without breaking their own humors and passions, every one following his own lusts, without regarding any other, without discretion, civility, even without humanity itself. 'Tis good Education of Youth, that makes virtuous men and obedient Subjects; that fills the Court *with* wise Counsellers, *and the* Common-wealth *with* good Patriots.[24]

Walker, who attempted to provide a book of etiquette for gentlemen and a "psychology of the soul" as well as a handbook for educators, emphasized the virtue of governing in the schoolroom without physical violence where possible.[25] He urged teachers to govern through "love," to "beget" in the student "an affection towards you (for love begets love) and then the great difficulty of your work is past."[26] Walker stressed the "reconciling of praescience and liberty" by the teacher. The teacher should make instruction pleasant to the student, and should combine injunctions with explanations. This was contrary to what Walker claimed usually took place in most English "great Schools," where students typically acted out of fear of punishment. But Walker also opposed those who argued that "Children of Persons of quality" should not be beaten at all. These people claimed that a child not reformed through "chiding, will be also obstinate against beating." Walker insisted that beating was necessary for all children, as a last resort of the teacher.[27]

But, again, the teacher should be economical in the exercise of the instruments of schoolroom governance. He was warned against *"unseasonable reprehensions,"* for example when the offender was "in passion, *or* in publick, *or* your self in passion."[28] The teacher should also avoid constant chiding or nagging, which "breeds insensibility and carelessness, and authorizeth his fault by your own."[29] Walker clearly perceived that fear of punishment could not lead to an internalized political discipline. "What is done willingly is best done," he pointed out, and "what we do for fear of punishment we really detest, and, were we left to our selves would not do it." He insisted that the best form of education was exercise and habituation, but this was only partly a conventional argument against the temptations of idleness, that "great spring and origine of lust," for Walker anticipated later arguments in his insistence that practice and repetition are the keystones of character formation.[30] "Yet by accustoming to do it, though for fear, the bugbear, that caused our hatred, is driven away, and by litle and litel we acquire an habit of, and by degrees a love to, it."[31]

John Locke's *Some Thoughts Concerning Education* (1693), intended as a handbook of domestic education for the English bourgeoisie, carried this emphasis upon habituation and exercise as agents of education further and enriched the tactical analysis of the governance of students and children. Unlike his predecessors, Locke began with a lengthy analysis of physical education and the habituation of the body. Here the (male) individual stands forth in his entirety as a product of education—as Locke put it, "The difference to be found in the Manners and Abilities of Men, is owing more to their *Education* than to any thing else."[32] Education begins by forming the body and shaping its manner of functioning, and Locke's emphasis is continually upon the activation of the forces of the educated. Locke advocated dress reform to allow upper-class children greater freedom of movement and to expose them more directly to their physical environment. He urged the careful organization of the child's diet, the strengthening of its body, and the regulation of its functions. Five pages, for example, are devoted to a consideration of the best method of the child's "going to stool."[33] But already for Locke this strong and healthy body is important mainly as a support for the character and as the source of points of entry for educational governance. The key problem for Locke's educational politics is the internalization of government by the educated, the transformation of rule into self-control. As he put it,

Every Man must some Time or other be trusted to himself, and his Con-

duct; and he that is a good, vertuous, and able Man, must be made so within; and therefore, what he is to receive from Education, what is to sway and influence his Life, must be something put into him betimes, Habits woven into the very Principles of his Nature; and not a counterfeit Carriage, and dissembled Out-side, put on by Fear, only to avoid the Present Anger of a Father, who perhaps may dis-inherit him.[34]

For Locke, at least as far as men in the ruling class were concerned, the successful operation of the bourgeois state demanded self-government; obedience based only on fear of punishment was ineffectual. When faced with fear of punishment, "the Child submits, and dissembles Obedience." But in the absence of fear "he gives the greater scope to his natural Inclination, which by this way is not at all altered, but on the contrary, heightened and increased in him."[35] For this reason, the use of physical violence and fear was to be severely limited in Locke's pedagogy.

In its place, parents and tutors should attempt to govern the child through its emotions, particularly through its desire for approval and its fear of disapproval. These things were to be cultivated in the child from the outset, and were more effective than "Threats or Blows, which lose their force when once grown common."[36] At the same time, educators should avoid the cultivation of improper desires and appetites. The child could be governed emotionally through flattery and bribery, or through rewards and punishments of the body, but these were dangerous tactics. Rewarding the body merely encouraged the development of "those Appetites, which 'tis our business to subdue and master."[37] Governance would succeed most where the child was successfully taught to "preserve his Credit": to become sensitive to the good opinion of those around him, and particularly of his parents.

This sensitivity could not be developed by corporal punishment, the disciplining of the flesh. It "only patches up for the present" the fault of the child "and skins it over, but reaches not to the Bottom of the Sore."[38] Constant physical punishment would only produce "a low spirited, moap'd Creature, who . . . will probably prove as uncomfortable a thing to his Friends, as he will be, all his life, an useless thing to himself and others."[39] Parents should attempt to orient the child entirely to a desire for approval. "If by these Means you can come once to shame them out of their Faults . . . and make them in love with the Pleasure of being well thought on, you may turn them as you please, and they will be in love with all the Ways of Vertue."[40]

Locke's remarkable theoretical movement away from the flesh to the conscience and his insistence upon the general educability of the subject is deepened by his critique of education by precepts and his insistence upon habituation and exercise. Locke criticized prevailing educational methods for their overemphasis upon the memory and upon rules. Children were often incapable of understanding the "*Rules* and Precepts" with which their minds were charged, and hence these they would "constantly as soon forget as given. . . . Children are *not* to be *taught by Rules,*" Locke insisted.[41] In sharp contrast to many of his near contemporaries, he also opposed the posting in the schoolroom of lists of rules and offenses, for these were themselves educative, showing the child offenses of which it might know nothing and encouraging a calculating attitude to obedience.[42] Thus, Locke evidenced a clear perception of the general productivity of the learning situation itself.

Locke proposed that education be made a pleasant, varied, and stimulating activity. The child was to learn by "exercise," by the performance of tasks and activities designed to create desirable habits and tendencies. Locke urged the construction of educational toys, and the unification of play and instruction that would make pleasure an educational adjunct.[43] Education would activate the energies of the child, direct these judiciously through an admixture of severity and liberty, and lead to the internalization of good moral character—itself verified by scrutinizing the child.[44]

The centrality of a conception of the child as an abstraction—made concrete through particular practices—in Locke's educational propositions must be stressed. This completely socialized individual (who, it must be remembered, is male and bourgeois) has the potential to become an active political subject, and it is for that reason that education must implant itself in the individual and successfully colonize his will. The expanding political economic opportunities for the rising bourgeoisie shape Locke's educational conceptions and his view of violence. But the problem of educational violence is also shaped by the contradictory necessity of reconciling economic violence with social pacificity, of permitting relations of dominance and subordination in the sphere of production and exchange, while preventing their spillover into armed struggles.

For Locke, the emotional, physical, and moral disciplining of the child is possible because education takes place in a context of physical violence to which the educator may have ultimate recourse. Violence was to be applied to the *"Fault"* of "Obstinacy or Rebellion," and while Locke here too argued that "the shame of the Whipping and not the Pain, should be the greatest part of the Punishment," he insisted that submission be secured, once the course of punishment began.[45]

Ideally, such punishment should be delivered by a tutor or servant in the parent's presence, so that the child would not attribute the blows to the parent (who in consequence would become a more abstract authority) and also so that "passion" would not govern the application of punishment. Likewise parents should not punish immediately after an offense "lest Passion mingle with it."[46] Still, Locke stressed again, if punishment were applied, it must continue until the child submitted.

The Chastisement should be a little more Severe and a little more Severe, and the Whipping (mingled with Admonitions between) so continued, till the Impressions of it on the Mind were found legible in the Face, Voice and Submission of the Child.[47]

Hiding the Hand of Punishment

As we have seen, the child for Locke had become a cipher in a double sense: a vacant space to be filled by educational practices of discipline and habituation; the celebrated *tabula rasa* on which is inscribed social character; and something which must be read, verified, and scrutinized by the educator. Jean-Jacques Rousseau took Locke's propositions a radical step forward by attempting to make the conscious design of the pedagogical process disappear from the view of the child.

Émile (1762) was an extremely influential treatise, especially in its emphasis upon "natural punishment." Rousseau wrote for a largely bourgeois audience and was concerned primarily with the domestic education of boys. "The poor man has no need of education," he noted, for "the education of his own station in life is forced upon him, and he can have no other." The education of girls was sharply limited to lessons in domestic subordination.[48] Rousseau also accepted that education must begin with the discipline of the body, for here the material supports of moral forces were to be found. Education for Rousseau was primarily *habituation*—training through exercise—and he accepted the critique of a preceptorial education.[49]

"True happiness," Rousseau wrote in a famous passage, "consists in decreasing the difference between our powers and our desires."[50] An education which would produce a happy and useful child should take pains to limit the imagination—the source of the disproportion between the powers and the desires—and to strengthen the powers as much as possible. This should be done by ensuring that the child's unreasonable desires were brooked by "natural" obstacles, and in this Rousseau took issue with Locke's argument that children were essentially rational creatures.[51] Children were to be allowed the "natural liberty" needed to follow their own desires, so long as these did not involve the development of a dependence on others. The student desiring to run should not be forced to sit still; the student who needed help to perform activities beyond its power should not be encouraged.

Again, Rousseau argued that the educator should use "force with children and reasoning with men; this is the natural order."[52] Children were to be put in their place and kept there until this came to seem normal to them. The material conditions of education (which itself was always individual and domestic) were to be simple in Rousseau's plan. The student was to be allowed to treat its environment in the way it wished, so long as it also bore the consequences for doing so. If the student broke a vase, for instance, the teacher was not to scold or beat it; the loss of the vase would serve as a natural limitation on the liberty of the child. Rousseau also emphasized that moral education should begin with the enumeration of the child's rights, and not its duties, of which it could have little understanding or in which it could have little interest. The first idea the child needed was "not that of liberty, but of property."[53]

When the child was advanced somewhat in the world of moral instruction, the educator faced the problem of dealing with vice, deceit, and falsehood. Here punishment became necessary, and Rousseau again insisted that the educator organize this punishment in such a way that it appeared a natural consequence of the moral default. The child guilty of lying would be disbelieved in the future; the child determined to anger or provoke its teacher should be frustrated.[54]

While writers before Rousseau had addressed the structure of the educational situation with a view to increasing its productivity—for instance through the creation of visible seating arrangements, systems of behavioral accounting, and through the manipulation of play—Rousseau's *Émile* involved a central disjuncture in the theory of educational governance. Rousseau attempted to hide the hand of the educator, to construct an educational situation in which, to the educated at least, circumstances themselves would appear to dictate the path of development. Émile would move through the world, finding his capacities for some things strengthened, his imagination limited, his willfulness brooked, his sense of property and propriety stimulated—all by the material circumstances of his existence. Émile would become the ideal member of society for Rousseau through the practical experience of civil society itself, and it is Émile's capacity for pleasure within definite social forms and activities that energizes him. This anticipation of the educational-state-as-condition had an enormous contemporary appeal.[55]

The parallel between Rousseau's educational project as moral economy and Adam Smith's political economic project in *The Wealth of Nations* (1776) must be stressed. Both identify an automatic or "natural" order of social relationships while at the same time agitating for the institutionalization of the structural supports upon which these relationships in fact depend. Just as bourgeois economic life demands a particular kind of implicit state activity (frequently misapprehended as "non-interventionist"), a bourgeois education will itself be set in a framework of implicit political relations. Both of these works transformed the domains in which they appeared.

Collective Instruction

The insistence of Locke and Rousseau on the organization of the pedagogical situation as the means to the internalization of moral character by the student was made in the context of a domestic education for upper-class boys. The governance of students in groups presented a different set of problems, and schoolmasters in the late eighteenth century supported the judicious use of physical punishment. Only in the first decades of the nineteenth century did the hidden hand grasp collective instruction.

George Chapman, a former master of the Dumfries grammar school and the master of a large private academy near Banff, considered the problems of school governance in *A Treatise on Education*, which appeared in 1784. The Scottish schools were already accessible—if briefly—to sections of the developing working class, and Chapman attended to the problems of managing boys of different social classes. This involved a defense of collective education itself.

Chapman argued against those who claimed that "public" education made boys slavish and would "prepare them for absolute subjection to their political government".[56] On the contrary, a judicious teacher could provide the best kind of political socialization in school. Students would learn to obey commands with pleasure because they would be convinced of their reasonableness. Boys would enjoy being governed rationally, and such governance would be healthful for a boy as well, "for the briskness of his spirits, flowing from the happiness of his condition, will strengthen his constitution, enliven his genius, and sweeten his temper." This would make boys good citizens, for they would see the necessity of judicious government and be shocked by "crude or arbitrary exertions of power."[57] Chapman also argued that public education allowed the teacher to draw upon "sympathy" and "emulation," forms of collective energy that had a beneficial impact upon character.[58]

Education for working-class boys was not to be extensive. These students should be employed in learning to read and to write, and perhaps in learning psalmody as well. Care was to be taken to prevent them from acquiring habits of idleness, "so hurtful to the morals of individuals, and so destructive to the state."[59] Chapman urged that to

reconcile the lowest class of mankind to the fatigues of constant labour, and the otherwise mortifying thoughts of a servile employment, pains should be taken to convince them, when young, that subordination is

*necessary in society; that they ought to submit to their masters or superi-
ors in every thing that is lawful.*[60]

For students from other classes, Chapman was especially concerned to make what he called "a well-regulated liberty" into "an
innocent and successful engine of education."[61] Governing in the
schoolroom either by "menaces and compulsive methods," or by
"promises and flattery," was inadequate. Boys would pretend to be
convinced while they were terrified or hopeful, but all the time they
would be "secretly disgusted at our tyranny." They would "learn to
dissemble, and to impose upon us, that they may avoid the punishment which they dread, or obtain the reward which they expect."[62]

The key to successful educational governance in Chapman's view
lay in the establishment of reasonableness and affection between
teachers and students. While teachers might allow themselves a certain severity with a new school, the success of education depended
upon their ability to inspire students with respect and affection.
Teachers were themselves to be exemplars of good moral character,
and governance was most effective where students were concerned
not to displease teachers. "A reasonable liberty" allowed to students
would remove the temptation to disobedience, and a judicious discipline would prevent them from developing a desire for an impossible degree of liberty.[63] Pleasure in education was to be gained from
the study of natural objects.[64] Yet even the best schoolmaster might
find himself forced to punish students physically.[65]

This position was also adopted by Chapman's contemporary
Vicesimus Knox. Knox accepted that corporal punishment was at
times inevitable and was divinely sanctioned, but it was also to be
avoided under ordinary circumstances. Before applying the rod, and
even on "the more hardened culprits," parents might have children
"confined from play on a holiday . . . debarred from a meal . . . sent
to their chamber before their companions; their pocket allowance
may be retrenched; or an additional task may be assigned."[66] But
these punishments wore out quickly, and when they did, corporal
punishment should be applied, as it should for the "immoral actions" which were known to "abound in schools." Still, care should
be taken by teachers to ensure that the physical pain was accompanied by shame and disgrace.[67]

From the Flesh to the Conscience

In the last decade of the eighteenth century and the first decades of the nineteenth, attempts were made to translate the propositions of domestic education developed by upper- and middle-class writers into systems of instruction for the industrial working class and the urban poor. These sections of society could no longer receive an adequate self-education in poverty and subordination. Education for the working class drew upon the principles of the factory division of labor. It also included projects and plans to materialize moral character in a new and elaborate semiology that did not include corporal punishment.

Joseph Lancaster, an English Quaker schoolmaster, published an influential plan for the organization of the instruction of large numbers of pauper children in 1805 entitled *Improvements in Education, as It Respects the Industrious Classes.* This work was intended as a manual for the establishment of pauper schools that would provide instruction both systematic and productive.[68]

Lancaster attempted, in the pauper schoolroom, to situate moral discipline in the self-activity of the learner. "The predominant feature in the youthful disposition," he observed, "is an almost irresistible propensity to action." If this activity could be "properly controlled by suitable employment," it could become "a valuable auxiliary" to the schoolmaster. "This liveliness" was never to be "repressed," but always "directed to useful ends."[69] To achieve this, Lancaster urged that students be grouped in classes under the supervision of student monitors. Competition was to increase energy. "Every boy is placed next to one who can do as well or better than himself; his business is to excel him, in which case he takes precedence of him."[70] "Taking places" was a common educational practice when Lancaster was writing, but he was innovative in devising a set of material representations of good moral character, which themselves became objects of accumulation. Students wore numbers on their clothes, and those failing to answer questions correctly were forced to exchange their numbers for lower ones. Printed tickets were distributed, "lettered variously, as, 'Merit',—'Merit in Reading', —'Merit in Spelling',—'Merit in Writing,' . . ." and the leading scholars in each class also wore pictures on their chests printed on pasteboard.[71] Tickets and pictures were forfeited with the loss of a place and, on the other hand, merit tickets were distributed that could be accumulated and exchanged for prizes. A special monitor existed in the school whose function was to keep track of the accumulation of merit tickets. "When boys have obtained their tickets for writing the stipulated number of times, they are permitted to choose any prize of the value appropriated to the number on their tickets." A variety of prizes existed, including "toys, bats, balls, kites, &c.," but Lancaster was pleased to note that "the books with prints or pictures are more in request among the children and generally more useful than any other prizes whatever."[72]

Lancaster also implemented a number of devices and practices designed to increase the productivity of pedagogical labor while making it visible and verifiable. Instruction was collective, and instruments were intended to demonstrate to the eye of the monitor and master that students were in fact engaged in pedagogical activity. For instance, in the spelling classes, all the students were provided with slates and pencils and wrote words dictated to them by the master or monitor. This procedure was more productive than the method of teaching spelling in most common schools.

Now these twenty boys, if they were at a common schol, would each have a book; and, one at a time, would read or spell to their teacher, while the other nineteen were looking at their books, or about them, as they pleased; or, if their eyes were rivetted on their books, by terror and coercion, can we be sure that the attention of their minds is engaged, as appearance seems to speak it is?[73]

This last query exercised schoolmasters and educational writers both before and after Lancaster: how could one ensure that pedagogical practice in fact enveloped the subjectivity of the student? how could one make the "heart" accessible to the ends of pedagogy? how could one ensure one was not merely producing people skilled at dissembling? Lancaster argued that through collective instruction of the sort he advocated in the area of spelling (as elsewhere), "the twentieth boy may read to the teacher, while the other nineteen are spelling words on the slate instead of sitting idle." All students were engaged in learning at once, and the method of writing on the slate meant that "every boy's attention to his lesson may be seen on his slate."[74]

Student behavior was made visible, legible, just as a new semiology of good moral character was put in place. Students were seated
in long parallel rows during periods of collective exercises for the
whole school, with monitors at the end of each row and the master
overseeing the whole from a raised platform. The monitors were
equipped with demerit tickets (containing messages such as "'I have
seen this boy idle',—'I have seen this boy talking'") that students
were compelled to return to the master at the end of the day. The
roll was called by having each student stand against a number inscribed on the walls of the schoolroom. Absences were immediately
visible, and the "monitor of absentees" kept a list of the addresses
and occupations of all parents, who were at once informed. Monitors themselves were subject to reports to the master by their students, and the monitors' "whole performances are so visible, that
they dare not neglect them."[75]

The material representation of moral character was extended
in Lancaster's punishment practices. Weights of from four to six
pounds were hung from the necks of miscreants, and misbehaving
students were at times shackled together and forced to march about
the schoolroom until tired. Their hands might be tied behind their
backs or attached to their shackled ankles, and students were paraded about the room with labels describing their offenses attached
to their clothing.

In the case of truants being reported; when they are brought to school,
either by their friends, or by a number of boys sent on purpose to bring
them, the monitor of absentees ties a large card round his neck, lettered
in capital letters, TRUANT; and he is then tied to a post.[76]

"Incorrigible" students were tied up in blankets and left alone in the
schoolroom overnight. "When a boy comes to school with dirty face
or hands," wrote Lancaster, "and it seems to be more the effect of
habit than of accident, a girl is appointed to wash his face in the
sight of the whole school."[77] Students were sometimes paraded about
the schoolroom with a member of the opposite sex leading them
and proclaiming their fault.

Occasionally boys are put in a sack, or in a basket, suspended to the roof of the school, in the sight of all the pupils, who frequently smile at the birds in the cage. *This punishment is one of the most terrible that can be inflicted on boys of sense and abilities. Above all it is dreaded by the monitors; the name of it is sufficient, and therefore it is but seldom resorted to on their account.*[78]

These punishments were described as alternatives to "others more severe," and Lancaster emphasized that the successful operation of a school demanded the existence of a broad range of punishments, since any given punishment lost its force if repeatedly applied.[79]

Lancaster's pedagogical practices attracted an enormous middle-class support, and were enthusiastically embraced by the Benthamite radicals. Although such devices as the "birds in the cage" were rejected by Lancaster's supporters, his system was generalized by the British and Foreign School Society, and it enjoyed a considerable popularity among middle-class reformers in Ireland, the United States, and Upper Canada until the 1830s at least.[80] Of course, the system was unpopular with the working-class populations it was intended to remake, and from the 1830s it fell increasingly into disrepute. Rote learning, it was discovered, could not produce rational, intelligent, and loyal political subjects.

Yet Lancaster's proposals are remarkable in that corporal punishment no longer appears as a means of moral discipline. From a necessary good in the sixteenth century, to a necessary evil in the eighteenth, the beating of students had, in theory, disappeared by the early nineteenth century—or, at least, the possibility of an education in which beating would not be necessary was commonly admitted.

The limitations of Lancaster's innovations are clear, especially in its first versions. The flesh was still the conduit of punishment, and punishment remained spectacular. Yet punishment was already meant to reach inward to the subjectivity of the student. Its efficacy no longer resided solely in the message the spectators of it would derive. Weights hung on the neck, for instance, address that "predominant feature in the youthful disposition," which is activity. They restrict and restrain that inner force. They are carried by the flesh, but they are not dissipated by its soggy mass; they reach the character. Shame and humiliation were measured and graded and administered in more or less precise amounts.

Yet, in a way that I believe is continuous with Rousseau's hidden hand, Lancaster attempted to engineer a situation saturated with moral learning. The student cannot but learn in this situation, and this learning is itself relatively indifferent to the persona of the teacher. The mechanical arrangements of the learning situation are intrinsically instructive.

Conclusion

The distance traveled in reality from Mulcaster to Lancaster should not be exaggerated. Monitorial schools in England and elsewhere and state schools generally throughout the nineteenth century were unable actually to govern students without recourse to physical violence.[81] The beating of students remained routine. Another serious wave of attacks on the use of physical violence in school governance began with the publication of Pillans's *Principles of Elementary Teaching* in 1828 and continued throughout the 1830s and 1840s.

Nonetheless, in theory, if only belatedly in practice, school governance came increasingly to rely upon emotional instruments. The state school's monopoly over the means of educational violence receded and became part of an implicit structure of rule, always present when necessary, but not always necessarily present.

In my view, the history of punishment in school government is to read as an element in the process of class hegemony and domination. Current attacks on the application of any sort of punishment at school are better seen as tactics in a social politics of domination and subordination than as unambiguous indications of ethical advance.

Endnotes

1. Initial research for this article was conducted while I was supported by the Social Sciences and Humanities Research Council of Canada. An early version of it was presented to the Canadian History of Education Association, Halifax, 1986. My thanks for the translation to Michèle Martin.
2. Michel Foucault, "The Subject and Power," in Hubert L. Dreyfus and Paul Rabinow, eds., *Michel Foucault: Beyond Structuralism and Hermeneutics* (Chicago: University of Chicago Press, 1983) pp. 208–226.
3. Michel Foucault, "Nietzsche, Genealogy and History," in Michel Foucault, *Language, Counter-Memory, Practice* (Ithaca, NY: Cornell University Press, 1977).
4. It is interesting to compare the debate over the elimination of corporal punishment in the English military with the position I take here. Despite Strachan's attempt to detail the role of reform of the army in the nineteenth-century revolution in government, neither Dinwiddy nor Steiner makes other than passing

mention of the possibility that campaigns against corporal punishment in the army might have wider political foundations. It is also remarkable that neither of these writers makes any mention of Foucault's key essay on "Governmentality," in which an important argument about the homologous character of governmental forms is elaborated. See Hew Strachan, "The Early Victorian Army and the Nineteenth-Century Revolution in Government," *English Historical Review,* Vol. 95, 1980, pp. 782–809; J. R. Dinwiddy, "The Nineteenth-Century Campaign against Flogging in the Army," *English Historical Review,* Vol. 97, 1982, pp. 308–331; E. E. Steiner, "Separating the Soldier from the Citizen: Ideology and Criticism of Corporal Punishment in the British Armies, 1790–1815," *Social History,* Vol. 8, 1983, pp. 19–35; and Michel Foucault, "Governmentality," in Graham Burchell et al., eds., *The Foucault Effect: Studies in Governmentality* (Chicago: University of Chicago Press, 1991), pp. 87–104.

5.   Richard Mulcaster, *Positions, Wherein Those Primitive Circumstances Be Examined, Which Are Necessarie for the Training Up of Children, Either for Skill in Their Books, or Health in Their Bodie* (New York: De Capo Press, 1971 [1581]), p. 28.

6.   Philip Corrigan, Bruce Curtis, and Robert Lanning, "The Political Space of Schooling," in Terry Wotherspoon, ed., *The Political Economy of Canadian Schooling* (Toronto: Methuen, 1987), pp. 1–43.

7.   Mulcaster, *Positions, Wherein . . . ,* pp. 277–283. ·

8.   Ibid., p. 283.

9.   Ibid., p. 279.

10. Ibid., pp. 276–278.

11. Ibid., pp. 276–283.

12. Ibid., p. 294.

13. Ibid., p. 293.

14. In John William Adamson, *Pioneers of Modern Education in the Seventeenth Century* (New York: Teachers' College Press, 1971), p. 76.

15. Ibid., p. 76.

16. John Dury, *The Reformed School and the Reformed Library Keeper* (Menston, England: Scholar Press, 1972 [1651]), p. 24.

17. Ibid., p. 33.

18. Ibid., pp. 36–37.

19. Ibid., p. 76.

20. Charles Hoole, *A New Discovery of the Old Art of Teaching Schoole* (London: London University Press, 1913 [1659]), p. 36.

21. Ibid., p. 38.

22. Ibid., pp. 276–277.

23. Ibid., pp. 277–278.

24. Obadiah Walker, *Of Education* (Menston, England: Scholar Press, 1970 [1673]), p. 12.

25. He urged his readers, for example, to do "nothing that may offend anothers *sense* or *imagination.* To strike or pinch a man, is a clowns salutation. Nor carion, or excrement is to be shewed to your companion, for you know not how squeamish he is. Approach not your mouth so near in discoursing, as to offend or bedew any one with your breath, for all mens breaths are offensive." Ibid., p. 215; cf. Norbey Elias, *The Civilizing Process* (New York: Pantheon, 1978).

26. Walker, *Of Education,* p. 38.

27. Ibid., p. 39.

28. Ibid., p. 40.

29. Ibid.

30. Ibid., p. 58.

31. Ibid., p. 41.

32. John Locke, *Some Thoughts Concerning Education* (Menston, England: Scholar Press, 1970 [1693]), p. 33. However, as Corrigan and Sayer show, "men" in this context means men of the governing classes. Those who sold their labor power were of quite a different order, and one that had yet to be recognized as having a

political will. Philip Corrigan and Derek Sayer, *The Great Arch: English State Formation as Cultural Revolution* (Oxford: Basil Blackwell, 1985); C. B. Macpherson, *The Political Theory of Possessive Individualism* (Oxford: Oxford University Press, 1962).

33. Locke, *Some Thoughts*, pp. 25–30.
34. Ibid., pp. 43–44.
35. Ibid., p. 50.
36. Ibid., p. 55.
37. Ibid.
38. Ibid., p. 60.
39. Ibid., p. 50.
40. Ibid., p. 58.
41. Ibid., pp. 63, 66.
42. Ibid., p. 98.
43. Ibid., p. 178.
44. E.g., ibid., pp. 142–145.
45. Ibid., pp. 83–85.
46. Ibid., p. 94.
47. Ibid., p. 100. Cf. Foucault, "Nietzsche, Genealogy and History," p. 148, "The body is the inscribed surface of events." Teachers in mid-nineteenth-century Canada attempting to follow this logic often beat students bloody. See Bruce Curtis, *Building the Educational State: Canada West, 1836–1871*. (Sussex: Falmer Press; London, Ontario: Althouse Press, 1988), chap. 8.
48. Jean-Jacques Rousseau, *Émile, or of Education* (London: Dent, 1974 [1762]), p. 20.
49. Ibid., pp. 20–30.
50. Ibid., p. 44.
51. Ibid., p. 53.
52. Ibid., p. 55.
53. Ibid., p. 62.
54. Ibid., pp. 65; 86–87.
55. For example, Richard Lovell Edgeworth's young mind was greatly impressed by *Émile*. Edgeworth's *Practical Education* (1815) embodied some of the propositions of *Émile* and was itself very influential for educational reform in the nineteenth century. Edgeworth was an influential member of the first Irish Education Commission as well. One of his sons was reared according to Rousseau's plan, but with mixed results: "He was generous, brave, good-natured, and what is commonly called good-tempered; but he was scarcely to be controlled. It was difficult for him to urge him to anything which did not suit his fancy, and more difficult to restrain him from what he wished to follow." When in Paris in 1770, Edgeworth took the boy to visit Rousseau, and after a short walk alone with him, Rousseau declared him quick, but inclined to xenophobia. R. L. Edgeworth, *Memoirs of Richard Lovell Edgeworth* (Shannon: Irish University Press, 1969 [1820]), I, pp. 178–179; 258–259; 274; 353. For the educational-state-as-condition, see Curtis, *Building the Educational State*.
56. George Chapman, *A Treatise on Education* (London: Cadell, 1784), p. 48.
57. Ibid., pp. 48–49.
58. Ibid., pp. 46–47; David Hamilton, "Adam Smith and the Moral Economy of the Classroom System," *Journal of Curriculum Studies*, Vol. 12, 1981, pp. 281–291.
59. Chapman, *A Treatise on Education*, pp. 71–72.
60. Ibid., pp. 73–74.
61. Ibid., p. 145.
62. Ibid., pp. 145–146.
63. Ibid., pp. 159–160.
64. Ibid., pp. 159–160; cf. J. H. Pestalozzi, *How Gertrude Educates Her Children* (New York, 1915).
65. Chapman, *A Treatise on Education*, pp. 224–225; 225n.

66. Vicesimus Knox, *Liberal Education, or a Practical Treatise on the Methods of Acquiring Useful and Polite Learning* (London: Charles Dilly, 1795), II, pp. 31–32.
67. Ibid., p. 32.
68. Hamilton, "Adam Smith"; Carl Kaestle, *Joseph Lancaster and Monitorial Education* (New York: Teachers' College Press, 1973).
69. Joseph Lancaster, *Improvements in Education, as It Respects the Industrious Classes* (London: Darton and Harvey, 1805), p. 31.
70. Ibid., p. 89.
71. Ibid., pp. 89–90.
72. Ibid., pp. 91–93.
73. Ibid., p. 50.
74. Ibid., p. 52.
75. Ibid., p. 61.
76. Ibid., pp. 113–114.
77. Ibid.
78. Ibid., p. 102.
79. Ibid., p. 105–106.
80. Kaestle, *Joseph Lancaster*; Bruce Curtis, "The Myth of Curricular Republicanism: The State and the Curriculum in Canada West, 1820–1850," *Histoire Sociale/Social History,* Vols. 16, 32, 1983, pp. 305–329.
81. Curtis, *Building the Educational State,* chap. 8.

Chapter Three
Three Cultures, Three Stories

Discipline in Grammar Schools, Private Girls' Schools, and Elementary Schools in Sweden, 1850–1900

Christina Florin and Ulla Johansson

If it were possible to go back in time to nineteenth-century Sweden and enter the classrooms of a typical grammar, elementary, and private girls' school, one would see many similarities between the three rooms.[1] The teachers stand at their elevated desks, teachers who all seem to demand their pupils' full attention and who have a more or less public function to supply knowledge, morals, and values. The pupils sit at identical desks with their hands virtuously resting on the desktops and with their desks arranged in identical neat rows. The pupils all look very well-behaved and disciplined, which is probably not just the result of the photographer's presence. If we could give life to the moment frozen by the camera, the bell would perhaps ring and the teachers would let go of their grip of the situation. The children would rush out with a hullabaloo into the schoolyard where they would start playing noisy games.

In spite of their similarities, these three images represent different school forms belonging to completely different traditions.[2] Grammar schools were derived from medieval cathedral schools, whereas elementary schools and girls' schools were nineteenth-century phenomena. Grammar schools were financed with public funds granted by the Riksdag. Elementary schools were financed with local taxes and state subsidies, whereas girls' schools depended on private donations and fees paid by the parents.[3] Only boys went to grammar schools,[4] only girls to girls' schools, whereas both boys and girls crowded into elementary schools. The pupils also came from different social classes. Elementary school was a school for the "working" people's children. The sons and daughters of the middle classes went to grammar schools and girls' schools.[5] The latter two types of school were also very exclusive. At the end of the century, 3–5 percent of

Swedish young men went to grammar school, and the proportion of girls in girls' schools was even smaller (about 2–3 percent). In 1886 there were 95 grammar schools and 124 private girls' schools in the towns.[6] At the end of the century elementary school, which in theory had been introduced in 1842, incorporated almost all Swedish children.[7] Most elementary schools were located in the countryside, as 90 percent of the population of Sweden lived there or in very small towns. However, with the breakthrough of industrial capitalism, at the end of the century these old patterns began to loosen up.[8]

These three different schools formed a status hierarchy that was also reflected in the teachers' positions. At the top was the grammar school teacher—always a man—with a long academic education. He was a civil servant who had taken his oath in the presence of the representatives of the king.[9] One step below we find the girls' school teacher, with a four-year education from the royal college for women teachers. At the bottom we find the elementary school teachers, both men and women, with a four-year lower secondary education.[10] The teachers were also recruited from different social strata. The grammar school teacher and the girls' school teacher usually came from the upper middle classes and the male elementary school teacher from the peasantry. His female colleague was, typically, the daughter of a civil servant.[11]

The pupils in the three rooms were also part of a state bureaucracy with partly different patterns for administration and control. Each elementary school was under the control of a local school board, a decision-making and executive authority with the vicar as chairman. The state control over these local authorities was executed mainly by school inspectors. Girls' schools were, to begin with, under private management of local boards recruited from the notables of the town. The state subsidies introduced in the 1880s resulted in stricter state control toward the end of the century. The grammar schools were administered directly through the state educational bureaucracy. In the mid-1800s the bishop was the most important link in the control chain, but at the end of the century the bureaucracy had been secularized, which led to extended responsibilities and authority for the headmaster. This was ratified in 1905 through the establishment of the National Board of Grammar Schools. Thus, state control was a prominent feature of the Swedish educational system.[12]

The state bureaucracy and control constituted the framework for an internal disciplining process with teachers and pupils as actors. To what extent did this process have similar structural features? To what extent was it characterized by differences in social recruitment, in gender composition, in the teachers' social and educational background, and in the goals and curricula of the schools? And how was moral regulation in grammar schools and girls' schools part of bourgeois class and gender formation? Were there different and conflicting definitions of masculinity and femininity? What was the impact of the disciplinary process in elementary school for the construction of a bourgeois hegemony? This article focuses on such questions. Our analysis includes Max Weber's notion of authority, and we discuss if this must not be modulated when we trace the exercise of authority in relation to class and gender.[13] Michel Foucault's notion of power will also be analyzed in a feminist perspective.[14]

We have used different types of sources: records from staff meetings and local school boards, regulations and rules, memoirs and diaries. We have conducted systematic studies of grammar school and elementary school including case studies of a few schools.[15] Since our data for girls' schools are of a more impressionistic nature our results are, in this respect, to a large extent based on the findings of other researchers.[16]

A Classroom Struggle for Time and Space

To begin with we can observe a significant similarity between the three school forms. The teachers in grammar school, elementary school, and girls' school all had the public mission to teach the pupils to subordinate themselves to grownups, to obey the impersonal rules for everyday life in school, and, ultimately, to accept the prevailing order of society. However, the teachers did not have the same means at their disposal. The grammar school teacher was supported by detailed government regulations for pupil behavior. He had a head teacher, fellow teachers, and the bishop himself at his back—as a civil servant he could lean on the whole state authority. The authority of the elementary school teacher was also ultimately based on the government elementary school regulations prescribing that the children had to go to school to learn certain things,[17] but he did not get the same massive state backing as the grammar school teacher. He could instead mobilize the resources of the local community for his educational work. His legitimacy was bestowed on him by the local school board headed by the vicar, and he could lean on the local regulations established by the school board. He could also use the representatives of the repressive state apparatus. Pupils who tried to escape the disciplining process by refusing to go to school could be separated from their parents and kept in institutions for "vicious" children.[18]

If we use Max Weber's terminology, we could say that the position of the grammar school teacher and, to some extent, that of the elementary school teacher, rested on a bureaucratic authority anchored to impersonal rules prescribed by law.[19] But in this respect the girls' school teacher was worse off. Since teaching in girls' schools was not a public affair, it was not regulated in state decrees. The girls' school teacher depended on the fact that the parents chose to put their daughters into her particular school. Her authority was therefore based on a kind of informal personal contract with the girls' parents, who voluntarily gave up their authority over their daughters while they were at school. In the disciplining process she had to mobilize a charismatic authority in order to get the girls to subordinate themselves to the order and rules of the school.

Thus, there were variations in the teachers' formal authority, but they were all backed up by the routines that always in some form regulate life in institutions.[20] These routines, the foremost foundation of discipline, were embedded in the institutional milieu and they had some joint features: time and space were the dimensions around which school's symbolic organization and everyday life were structured. The disciplining process was therefore a struggle for the control over time and space—a struggle where the teachers, with all the authority they could muster, were left alone to confront a large number of more or less unruly girls and boys. In this chapter we will take a closer look at this struggle in the three school forms. We will begin with grammar school.

The boy in grammar school had to adjust himself to many timetables. A rough frame was provided by the division of the year into terms and by the regulation that "the pupil shall infallibly present himself at grammar school at the beginning of the term on the stipulated day and hour."[21] His daily life was governed by the schedule requiring that he appear at the lessons at the appointed time. The rest of his time was also defined by formal schedules: schedules for written examinations, schedules for homework, preparation for tests he had originally failed, and reading as a punishment for disobedience.[22] In some schools corporal punishment was even scheduled at a special "beating-hour." Since these schedules also defined the use of time, we can speak of time disciplining in a twofold sense.

Everyday life in elementary school was, to begin with, not scheduled according to the same detailed timetables as in grammar school.[23] The division into terms was, for a long time, regulated by the agricultural rhythm and was adjusted to the weather. According to the local regulations of 1850 for the elementary schools in the parish of Skön, the beginning of spring term could be postponed for two weeks owing to "heavy snowfall or extreme cold." On the first day of the autumn term in 1867 only two children, in addition to the teacher's own three children, turned up at school. The reason for this, according to the local school board, was that the children had to help their parents with potato harvesting, which was regarded as a valid reason to postpone the start of the term for a couple of weeks.[24]

The class teacher system of elementary school also allowed for a greater amount of flexibility than the specialist teacher system of grammar school. The elementary school teacher was quite free to decide on the schedule for various activities, whereas the grammar school teacher could hardly change the daily routine. His work had to be coordinated with that of his colleagues, since different classes changed both subjects and teachers at the same time. The specialist teacher system thus allowed for smaller deviations in this respect, a fact that was observed as early as in 1817:

It will be easier to check upon each teacher's precision to appear in the classroom at the appointed time and to remain there during the prescribed time with the specialist teacher system than when he is hardly seen by anybody else than his pupils during the whole day.[25]

Gradually, with growing state control and standardization, a process in which time was an important instrument, detailed regulations were issued for the length of the terms and the school day at the same time that the teaching became more time-regulated. The 1878 normal plan, providing a number of models for the organization of the school day, was an important contribution to this standardization. The fact that the state grants came to depend on the extent to which the timetables were kept was, of course, an effective method to force the elementary schools to conform to the supremacy of time: owing to the threat of withdrawn state grants, the vicar of Skön was not very pleased with teachers whose daily teaching time was ten minutes too short.[26] However, most teachers welcomed the stricter rules for the use of time, since these rules, in practice, facilitated their work.[27] This indicates that they were aware of the fact that time was an important ally in the disciplining process.

Was there a similar time disciplining process in girls' schools? It is likely that they also gradually adapted themselves to time regulations. The very first girls' schools lacked fixed syllabuses, which probably meant that there were no detailed schedules for the school work. The girls' school system expanded during the second half of the nineteenth century, and, owing to the shortage of teachers, many teachers were recruited from grammar school. These teachers were likely to transmit the routines of grammar school, the basis of which was the schedule, to girls' schools. A similar function was fulfilled by the state college for women teachers and the training school (the state normal school for girls) established in connection with the college. Normal school became the model for many girls' schools that gradually adapted themselves to a bureaucratic structure with time as the organizing principle of school work. The following example from a girls' school in Stockholm shows that nobody—not even a male Ph.D.—could ignore this principle. The school's headmistress came to attend Dr. Lundberg's lesson, but he had not yet arrived:

He was five minutes, ten minutes, fifteen minutes late. Our respect for the headmistress made us sit quiet as mice. She became more and more nervous and when he finally entered she stood there pointing at her watch. We followed the course of events excitedly. "I'm sorry I'm late— but I simply couldn't make it in time!"—"Don't let it happen again," she said. Poor Dr. L.! We all sympathized with him.[28]

In all these school forms we find traces of a time disciplining

process modeled on grammar school. There was also a spatial disciplining process according to which the teachers, with various means,
tried to establish spatial control in the concrete sense of the word,
which was not always an easy task.[29] The teacher stood alone in
front of a number of often unruly pupils who literally filled the room.
He could, in the last resort, send the pupils out of the classroom.
This was done when pupils were regarded as a menace to the teacher's
authority and to the order in the classroom, but it was a double-
edged instrument. It is true that the order could perhaps be restored,
but there were sinners for whom the treatment was more of a reward
than a punishment.

In order to control the room a future grammar school teacher
was given the following good advice:

*Don't walk around in the classroom, choose a spot from where all the
pupils can see you and you can see them—including their hands.— But
don't act as if you were nailed to this spot. Each pupil must know that
any moment you can and will, if necessary, be there at his side.*[30]

Thus, the idea of the panopticon, invented by Jeremy Bentham and
mentioned by Michel Foucault, was represented in the Swedish grammar school pedagogy.[31] Some grammar schools were constructed so
that there was a special place from which the headmaster could keep
a strict watch over the entry into the assembly hall where the whole
school gathered for roll-call at the beginning of each term, morning
prayers, and commencement days. Each pupil had his own place in
the assembly hall:

*Everything was done in good order and according to a minutely planned
schedule. In the assembly hall we were placed according to rank and
position, the smallest boys at the very front. We marched into the hall in
four long rows side by side, two through the aisle and one through each
side entrance to our fixed places. It was a nice and impressive spectacle to
watch 700 schoolboys quietly and confidently take their places and, later,
leave in the same quiet and confident manner to start the day's work.*[32]

The assembly hall became a symbol of social order that was emphasized by the platform where the headmaster, the teachers, and some-

times also the bishop presided. From this elevated spot the head-master read the decrees of the Grammar School Act to the gathered boys at the beginning of each autumn term. But the space also played a symbolic role in the disciplining process. The division into school classes indicated the basic positions around which a spatial hierar-chy was formed. Each stage had its own rights and duties. The pu-pils in the highest classes no longer had to put up their hands and stand up when they answered a question; they were addressed by their surnames, and the simple school cap was replaced by a velvet cap with a number of gold stripes corresponding to the form they were in. The higher rank was also accompanied by other privileges; for example in Skara, the pupils in the highest classes in grammar school were allowed to walk back and forth on the pavements of the town, often to the chagrin of the rest of the inhabitants.[33]

The class was also divided into hierarchies. The boys in gram-mar school were placed according to rank and position, and they were seated in order of knowledge according to the principle of the best pupil at the very front and the worst in the class at the very back. This spatial tyranny also applied to the school calendar, but the "whipping-class" was even more tyrannical. This was a form of disciplinary punishment which meant that the pupil was placed at the very back of the classroom and announced to be subject to im-mediate corporal punishment in case of additional misdemeanors.

The spatial disciplining also manifested itself in other ways. The introduction of the subject classroom was a breakthrough for the principle of *Each thing in its own place*. Separate rooms for separate subjects drew an even sharper line between different natural phe-nomena. There was also a spatial disciplining in a mental sense, so that knowledge was arranged, systematized, and spread, it was hoped, into the right place in the pupils' heads. The classification in biology of thousands of plants in Carl Linne's sexual system, the enumera-tion in history of sovereigns, years, battles, and peaces, the endless rules of Latin with just as many endless exceptions—that is how the room was structured, making one "so afraid to break all these forms and rules that you never got outside the fence."[34]

A similar mental spatial disciplining also took place in girls' school and in elementary school. In this respect the male grammar school teachers who taught in girls' schools did not make a distinction between the girls in girls' school and the boys in grammar school. A state commission of the 1880s also criticized girls' schools for having taken over too much of grammar school pedagogy, with its focus on cramming.[35] Similar criticism was also leveled against elementary school with its cramming of the catechism, but the class teacher system and the lack of separate rooms for separate subjects led to less marked boundaries between different subjects in elementary school.

Nor did the hierarchies developed around the school class in grammar school have their direct counterpart in elementary school, which for a long time remained undifferentiated according to age and in which the teacher worked with pupils of all ages. The introduction of primary school, whose purpose was to supply the first reading instruction, became the first step in an organizational differentiation, but the transition from primary to elementary school was not connected with new privileges and rights for the pupils.[36] Nor did the division into two primary school classes and four elementary school classes introduced by the 1878 normal plan lead to the same status hierarchies as in grammar school. Moreover, the pupil population in the rural parts of Sweden did not allow one teacher to teach only one class. The same teacher had to teach two or more classes at the same time, which meant that the pupils were not arranged into class-bound hierarchies in the same way as in grammar school. In this respect there were greater resemblances between girls' school and grammar school—at least in some places. Status could be indicated by means of the school cap both in girls' school and in grammar school: "For those who had been promoted to a higher class it was for many years important to mark their school caps with the number of the new class and the correct number of silver stripes."[37] The girls in the higher classes in the girls' school in Jönköping had, like the older boys in Skara, the right to walk on the pavement in front of the school building.[38] The following rule applied in case of bad weather at the Hilda Berg girls' school in Gothenburg: "On rainy days the younger girls could go out for a breath of the air in the assembly-hall, the older girls stayed in their classrooms by an open window. We younger girls looked forward to this privilege."[39]

The spatial hierarchies established on the basis of the seating arrangements according to classroom performance in grammar school materialized a bourgeois meritocratic ideology. This meritocracy had male overtones and was not applied in girls' school, where there were no exams and where the ideology of individual performance was toned down. It is true that the girls' performance was examined and assessed, but, for example, in Jönköping the school authorities tried to keep the results of these judgments secret. The pupils were forbidden to open the envelope with their marks on the school premises.[40]

The Bell-Lancaster system applied in the early undifferentiated elementary school was characterized by knowledge hierarchies. The pupils were divided into different circles according to level of performance, and the more advanced pupils became monitors of these circles.

This position was much coveted, not only for the honour of it but also for its privileges. This resulted in a veritable system of bribery. Owing to very rough treatment by the monitor, the pupils tried to make him or her more favourable towards themselves by means of various gifts, but if these gifts were not forthcoming, the rod would not be spared.[41]

This Bell-Lancaster method, imported from England, enabled the teacher to handle and control a large number of people at the same time. It had a clearly disciplining function: it resembled a mass military service with multiplication tables, phonetic method reading, and so on. However, this method became the object of increasing criticism and was finally abolished. All visible knowledge hierarchies in elementary school disappeared with this method, with one exception—the phenomenon of "standing in the corner." This phenomenon was, in one respect, the equivalent of the whipping-class in grammar school. Standing in the corner at the back of the classroom could be a disciplinary punishment. But pupils who had not done their homework or who could not answer the teacher's questions were also subject to this punishment.[42] This order was perhaps sufficient in elementary school—you either had sufficient knowledge or not. Thus, you could content yourself with a very rough classification.

So far we have dealt with the disciplining process primarily from the point of view of the schools and the teachers. But, as we have already indicated, there was also a classroom struggle for time and space between the teachers and the pupils. There are many examples of grammar school pupils who tried to manipulate the time frames of the school by means of late arrivals and truancy. In the pupils' own folklore there were silent protests against the time drill. A teacher in Skara used to be called the "Second-hand" since the church bell always rang when he took the first step out on the schoolyard. There was a touch of the ridiculous about him and he was regarded as a dull perfectionist, whereas the pupils were more sympathetic toward teachers who were not always on time. They sometimes fetched teachers who had overslept instead of reporting it to the headmaster.[43]

Truancy and late arrivals were rare phenomena in girls' schools, but in elementary school they could escalate to the refusal to attend school—and even with the parents' consent. The teachers and the elementary school inspectors' reports of low attendance could often be explained by the parents' need for their children for household work. This truancy was, consequently, sanctioned by the parents, but the children could also take liberties on their own. The following quotation describes the situation in northern Sweden in the 1880s:

The former teacher had not dared to let the children take a break too often because they would wander off into the village and come back when they liked, or only when the headteacher went to fetch them. The teacher had chosen to bribe the pupils with cookies and candy to make them return of their own free will, so if they did not get anything they did not return.[44]

In their struggle for space the pupils actually had an advantage over the teacher since they, literally, filled up the classroom. The following quotation shows that the teachers' techniques of controlling the room could easily be overcome:

Once we agreed that we should try to get hold of some mice in boxes. When the reading lesson had just started one or several boxes were opened. Three mice ran out on the floor. There was a hullabaloo in the class. Everybody got up and chased the mice.[45]

This drama was carried out in a grammar school, but it was not easy
to maintain the spatial discipline in elementary school, either. Many
teachers went to school in a state of anxiety:

I was both afraid and excited when I went to school on Monday morn-
ing. The first thing I had to do was to pick up the caps. Then I gave them
a lecture which, however, had the effect that they rushed out of the class-
room like savages when the bell rang.—I didn't know what to do, how
to get the better of these savages. I went to my room and prayed to God
for help.[46]

We have not found any evidence of such riots in girls' schools. Even
if the teacher left the classroom in the pupils' hands things would go
very smoothly, and even insignificant misdemeanors would be blown
out of all proportion. Let us illustrate this with an example from
Åmål: A class that was left alone when the teacher was ill was told to
read the textbook on their own. Giggling, two girls started to push a
pencil-box over the table. The door opened and the form mistress
entered the room. She gave them a proper punishment lecture, and
order was restored after the sinners had repented their crime and
humbly asked for forgiveness.[47] This episode forms a sharp contrast
to what could happen in an elementary school class when the pupils
in an elementary school were left alone:

The best days for many boys were when the teacher was invited to 11
o'clock coffee at a neighbour's. He appointed a chief monitor who was
supposed to maintain order. But that was the wrong man in the wrong
place. He made diligent use of the cane in his attempts to make the
others respect him and to take the wind out of the clamorous crowd. The
boys started fighting each other; books, pointers and other missiles danced
through the air which resounded of proper Indian war-whoops.[48]

We have observed certain differences between time and spatial
discipline in these three school forms. How can these differences be
explained? Were they related to class and gender patterns?

Grammar school was a school for middle-class children, and
grammar school culture agreed very well with a bourgeois culture. It
is true that the term *bourgeois culture* is not an unambiguous con-

cept, but most researchers agree that there was a core of bourgeois virtues. It included a methodical and rational way of life, and it was based on the ideology of individual performance, self-discipline, and respect for education—and many of these things formed part of the everyday life of grammar school. The minutely prepared schedules promoted a rational way of life, with time as a limited resource. The spatial disciplining with the guiding maxim *Each thing in its own place* was also an acclimatization to a methodical way of life. The ideology of individual performance was deeply rooted in grammar school, where the pupil's road was bordered with endless tests and exams. The seating arrangements according to level of knowledge was another manifestation of the same idea.

Grammar school was an instrument in fostering bourgeois boys into men, but the same methods were sometimes also used for the girls. This does not agree very well with the official middle-class ideology in which the goal-directed rationality of male public life formed a sharp contrast to the warm care and spontaneity of the female family sphere. According to the bourgeois way of looking at things, girls' school was supposed to prepare girls for the home, but, in reality, girls' school was not immune to the ethos of grammar school. How can these contradictions be explained?

In our opinion, the strict discipline in girls' school was an un-desired result of the fact that grammar school was the norm for the organization of daily life in girls' schools. This norm was transferred by all male extra teachers recruited from grammar schools. The strict discipline can also be explained by the fact that girls' schools con-formed to a male bureaucratic structure because of the state grants and, thus, came to be characterized by male ideals and male think-ing.[49] But even if this was a contrast to the bourgeois ideology of femininity, it was functional in relation to the social reality outside school, where a growing number of women could now be found in public service.

Gradually, the men and women of influence of that time real-ized that a new gender order was taking shape. This is how we would like to explain the debate that started at the end of the nineteenth century on the aim and direction of girls' schools. A state commis-sion established disapprovingly that girls' schools had become too much like grammar school and that it was time to restore order. In other words, the masculinization of girls' schools must be broken. This was the beginning of a feminization of the curriculum that also went hand in hand with a feminization of the teaching staff: from now on the teaching staff was dominated by women—and it was not just any women. A growing number of them were educated at the Royal College for Women Teachers, a guarantee of "genuine" femininity.[50] Thus we can conclude that the grammar schools and the private girls' schools can be seen as an instrument in the formation of the bourgeoisie as a hegemonic class but that this project of class formation was gendered. It was a matter of bourgeois masculinity in grammar school, and changing contested forms of bourgeois femininity in private girls' schools.

The middle classes thus used grammar schools and girls' schools to foster their own children, whereas they used elementary schools to discipline the children of the people. And it seems as if they were not quite so successful with the children in elementary school. One explanation of this is that the same routines could not be applied in elementary school, which had to do with many provisional arrangements for quite a long time. Time frames and spatial hierarchies could not be maintained because of part-time reading, ambulatory schools, and schools in which several classes were taught by one teacher at the same time. The maintenance of such a large-scale time and spatial order would have required greater resources than the Swedish agrarian economy could mobilize at the time. But it should be pointed out that the intention of the state authorities was to construct spatial hierarchies by means of a differentiation of the pupils into different classes.[51]

There was also the difficulty of controlling mass education. One way of tackling these difficulties was to create posts for government elementary school inspectors whose job it would be to supervise the work and recommend improvements.[52] Some of them kept special watch over discipline—for example, Inspector C. J. Meijerberg's reign of terror in Stockholm's elementary schools. It was his mission to create a model elementary school, which, in his opinion, was synonymous with keeping pupils, parents, and teachers in good discipline.[53]

We have already pointed out that there were many examples of violent resistance to school, which manifested itself in truancy, defiance, and all kinds of pranks. But in the memoirs of former elementary school pupils it is always boys who make trouble, and the reader asks, in vain, what the girls did during these riots. It is clear that they did not take an active part in these disturbances. This means that opposition had more to do with sex than class, since grammar school boys also rioted. Troublesome girls were very rare in girls' schools, and, significantly enough, such a girl was regarded as having transgressed the gender boundaries. Ulla Bjerne gives us the following description of her pranks:

Occasionally I'm seized with remorse, but mostly it's for fear that I shall be caught doing mischief. Our form mistress tries to make us believe that God keeps some kind of record of everything we do. But I don't believe it. He must have more important things on his mind than the sins of a schoolgirl.—Among the townspeople, where the coffee-drinking hags sensually chew my monstrous person, I discover that some men take up an amused and indulgent attitude.—When they meet me they smile and say: Hallo, Boy![54]

It seems that schoolgirls at the turn of the century were obedient and easily disciplined. Their protests against school were, in most cases, discreet and harmless. Girls did not disturb the order of time and space either in girls' school or in elementary school.

The Disciplining of the Body

The time and spatial disciplining discussed above was partly connected with the construction of mental structures, but there was also a physical side to it. It was a matter of sitting still and controlling your body: "Our English teacher always said: 'Sit properly!' Without my knowledge my legs always manage to get out of the narrow desk. But, surely, it's not my legs that are learning English!"[55] Formation in line outside the classrooms, well-organized entries into assembly halls, hands on desktops, rules of how to move in narrow corridors and classrooms—this was all part of a hidden curriculum code of which the aim was to control the body in the literal sense of the word. But there was also an open pedagogy for the disciplining of the body: the pupils should learn to control their sexuality, they were taught cleanliness and hygiene, and, last but not least, corporal punishment was frequently used. Questions of class and gender also appear in this context.

Grammar school and elementary school teachers could, by lawful means, administer corporal punishment to their pupils, but it was supposed to be done under orderly circumstances, especially in grammar school. However, the memories of school life in those days show that many teachers made frequent use of their fists. Pinching, boxing pupils' ears, corporal punishment in the presence of others, and other forms of violence in school have engraved themselves on the pupils' memories and arouse pain many years later:

Many teachers weren't content until they had whipped somebody with the cane. Even worse than the cane was some teachers' habit of smacking our faces or grabbing us by the hair and shaking our heads until we almost lost consciousness.[56]

The memoirs of former elementary school pupils bear witness to the same sort of violence. In this respect the female teachers were no better than their male colleagues, even if they may have used somewhat gentler methods: "We had a rather strict lady in elementary school. If you did any mischief she took a special grip of your hair. She lifted you by the hair and then she pushed you aside, so this was something you tried to avoid."[57]

The aim of corporal punishment was, very tangibly, to inculcate the boundaries between the permissible and the impermissible. However, at the end of the century this physical abuse was questioned. Instead, it was claimed that the teachers should appeal to the pupils' "inner police" and to their sense of duty.[58] Such techniques were very much in accordance with the forms of discipline practiced in girls' schools as in the following example from the Åhlin girls' school in Stockholm:

I never looked upon the influence exerted by school as a form of constraint. It tried to promote obedience, duty, diligence and precision.—The headmistress of the school was the incorporation of the strong goal-directed fulfilment of duty. It radiated from her to the female teachers around her and to most of the pupils.[59]

Girls in elementary school apparently were not very often subject to corporal punishment. This can partly be explained by the fact that they did not defy order in the same way as the boys, but there was also a gender-cultural code condemning physical violence against women. According to this code it was the boys' bodies that should be hardened, not only through corporal punishment but also through scheduled physical training. Military drills and weapon exercises were introduced in the 1860s with the aim of promoting young people's physical education to "a powerful, strong and tough species."[60] This was not just an empty phrase. To the boys' great delight there was a lot of drilling in the Swedish grammar schools. Physical training, which was introduced at this time, was based on the ideas of Per Henrik Ling. Military and mechanical drill was a means to assimilate the individual bodies to a collective order.

The regulations of weapon exercises and physical training were applied in both elementary and grammar school but, in reality, they had greater impact on grammar school. It is true that boys in some elementary schools were also ordered to play military games, but such elements were abolished from elementary school as early as the 1880s. However, physical training still included military elements, such as marching and the formation in lines and columns.[61] Ling's form of physical training was, of course, based on a male physical ideal, but, in practice, it was also used for girls in elementary school. They could at the very most be exempt from "indecent exercises" like tough fitness training.[62]

In practice, physical education in elementary school was quite inadequate. At the turn of the century, 94 percent of all schools lacked special rooms for physical training, which therefore had to be conducted either in the classroom or in the schoolyard, probably weakening the disciplining effect. Nor did physical training have a very strong position in girls' schools, where it was also conducted according to Ling's methods: according to a state inspector there was no reason why girls should not perform the same exercises as boys. And, of course, he did not approve of the fact that "the exercises are carried out in everyday clothes and, generally, on high sharp heels as is the custom of today."[63] It was not until well into the new century that another and gentler methodology was being used, a methodology more in correspondence with feminine ideals:

"Physical training still followed the universally prevailing Ling system but the exercises were often exchanged for . . . games and folk-dancing in the sunny playground. . . . In time rhythmic floor exercises also gained ground."[64]

A sound mind in a sound body—that was the ideal of grammar school. But the question was whether the mind was cultivated at the expense of the body. The debate depicted the schoolboy as a pale, stooping, and short-sighted crammer, and the health of the grammar school boy was discussed in many government reports. Several studies showed that the Swedish grammar school boy was in a poor state of health. Forty-five percent of the pupils were reported to suffer from serious physical diseases,[65] and the girls in girls' schools were even worse off: 61 percent of the girls suffered from some kind of disease, and it was even feared that the schoolwork would have an injurious effect on the girls' reproductive organs.[66] The cure was less homework, better and ergonomically designed desks, better lighting, and so forth. The concept of school hygiene was introduced and it became an important issue to design the school environment in accordance with it.

However, government representatives were not very worried about the health of the elementary school children. No state committees were set up in order to study their physical status, but professional groups like elementary school teachers and district medical officers became engaged in the issue. They drew attention to the poor sanitary conditions. Unhealthy air, privies of low standard, and cold and damp premises were carriers of all kinds of diseases. The cure, once again, was health education and hygiene.[67]

In elementary school there was also a tradition of cleanliness education. According to the first school regulation of Skön, the children should come to school "properly dressed according to their means but always with a clean face and clean hands." In some schools the day began with a proper inspection of the pupils' cleanliness, and it was no good coming with dirty hands or with tangled, disheveled hair.[68]

The bodily disciplining also included the controlling of one's sexual instincts. One method was simply to prevent contact between the sexes, and both grammar and girls' schools were based on the principle of separating the sexes. In elementary school, a mixed school, boys and girls were also often kept apart. In town schools the pupils were divided into boys' and girls' classes, and some schools even had separate entrances for girls and boys. In mixed classes boys were seated in one half and the girls in the other half of the classroom. The idea was to protect young people from contact with the opposite sex, to keep them away from potential desires. Girls in girls' schools were subject to very strict control. At the Kjellberg girls' school in Gothenburg (nicknamed the "convent"), it was considered improper that grammar school and girls' school should have vacations at the same time because of the risk of flirtation. It was almost dangerous to a girl's reputation for her to be seen together with a boy in the street.[69]

But this principle of sexual segregation was probably a double-edged sword. Judging from all the love poems flourishing in grammar school magazines, boys had many fantasies of the fair sex. The Västerås patriotic student association debated issues like "Is school-boy love real love or not?"[70] In the female world of the girls' schools, younger male teachers aroused tender feelings in the girls:

The science teachers were often young and aroused, to a greater or lesser degree, the usual schoolgirl crush. No teacher managed to raise the temperature as much as Dr. Stuxberg. He was extremely good-looking, he had a charming Gotland dialect and his teaching was a revelation to us.[71]

The elementary and grammar school teachers were also warned about the dangers of masturbation. In Stockholm in the 1860s public attention was drawn to this phenomenon, "an insidious vice" that was prevalent among the pupils of the town. "The hands on the desk" was one of many recommended preventive measures. Another cure was fresh air and tough physical training.

The coarse disciplining of physical training was designed for boys' bodies. The purpose of the school subject called textile craft was to train the fine motor ability of the girls. Another purpose of this subject was to impress ideals like order, precision, diligence, and cleanliness on the pupils. The memories of textile craft education in elementary school girls in Skön tell us how they, over and over again, had to unravel imperfect knittings and struggle with their needlework until it was perfect. This taught them the lesson that carelessness will not do.[72] The same lesson was taught in domestic science: keep things clean and tidy, wash your hands, put the household utensils back where they belong, wipe up if you spill something, use neat aprons and caps—these are some examples of rules that the girls in Skön had to take down at the beginning of the term of domestic science, and the same message was also communicated in girls' school.[73] It can be regarded as a moral lesson, as disciplining the mind, but it also had an evident physical dimension—it was actually a question of the eradication of bad physical habits and of the disciplining of the body.

Substitutes for Parents

The teachers in these three school forms were all supposed to adopt some kind of parental role. However, the creation of this role was characterized by the different class and gender situations in these schools. The grammar school teacher was supported by the grammar school statutes, which gave him a patriarchal image. He was to be a substitute for the father—both symbolically and in the literal sense of the word. Many pupils were boarders, and it was the duty of the teachers to visit them in their lodgings. The teacher's social background harmonized with that of his pupils, and, the school form being voluntary, parents were not forced to leave their children in the teacher's charge. In spite of the fact that there was a very strict discipline in grammar school and that very rigorous corporal punishment was not unusual, the parents generally accepted the authority of the teachers and the school. The mother of a pupil in Västerås, for example, did not hesitate to apply to the headmaster for help with her son, who mixed with girls of doubtful reputation.

It seems that the girls' school teachers got the same backing from the girls' homes, even from non-middle-class parents. At the turn of the century a girls' school class in Gothenburg was given the essay topic "My Room," an impossible subject for a working-class girl:

How was I supposed to write anything about this? I lived with my mother and my two brothers and my two sisters in a two-room flat. Everyone I knew lived in small flats and had many children. I could not imagine a room of one's own.

When the girl came home from school that day she told her mother that she was not going to write an essay on such a silly topic. Her mother replied: "You're going to write the essay and that's that!"[74]

This kind of respect for school could also be found in elementary school, even if many parents were not prepared to give in to the teacher's authority in this school form. Elementary school was, for a long time, beset by difficult problems of legitimacy, and many parents questioned its right to guide their children. This is how one teacher described his battles with the parents:

Many parents can be quite unreasonable. As soon as a child has been reprimanded or received a beating they immediately complain to the teacher. And then I get a scolding. The hardships I have to experience before I get the parents to understand the meaning of law and order are beyond description.[75]

The teachers tried to mobilize different forms of authority against rebellious pupils and willful parents. We have already pointed out that in his profession the grammar school teacher was supported by the state. Some headmasters and teachers were also the incarnation of bureaucratic authority:

The headmaster . . . was like a Roman proconsul, a born ruler. . . . He seldom smiled and when he did there was something alarming in his smile. He was impressive without the least effort. He radiated silent power—and the image of the conscientious civil servant, the incarnation of the State's concept.[76]

This headmaster thus combined a bureaucratic and charismatic authority. His profession was based on tradition, and he also had a patriarchal image. However, these Weberian ideal types of authority are gendered. Weber has not considered different forms of women's authority strategies. The girls' school teacher who could not rely on government statutes and regulations had to play on her personality. She can be said to have represented a matriarchal authority with elements of both strictness and warmth. The following quotation describes five sisters who were in charge of a famous girls' school in Stockholm:

The Åhlin sisters all parted their hair in the middle and combed it down over their ears with plaits at the back of their heads. They were dressed either in black or in dark grey, in plain dresses with collars of the same material falling down over the sleeves. They wore textile shoes and their footsteps were so soft that we couldn't hear them. . . .Aunt Carin was awe-inspiring and she was in charge of the whole establishment. We loved Aunt Julia. . . .Aunt Mina was very eccentric, but she had a sense of humour, and she was kind.[77]

Their disciplining techniques resembled those of a mother trying to arouse the sense of guilt in her children, and they were probably as effective as those of a punishing father. A girls' school teacher's mild admonitory speech had a different and more profound socialization effect than a veritable sermon. It was difficult for the girls to defend themselves against such an invisible pedagogy, since these methods promoted their empathy and sensitivity to other people's reactions. This can be an explanation of the fact that there were hardly any disciplinary problems in girls' schools.[78]

A bureaucratic authority was not a guarantee of order in the classroom. A successful teacher had to possess personality and charisma. This was evident from the fact that some grammar school teachers were subjected to disrespectful pranks even if they were supported by the prevalent system of sanctions. It was the same with the elementary school teachers. In the recollections of school life we meet teachers who, very gently, got their pupils' respect, while others were at the mercy of the class from the moment they entered the classroom.

Three Cultures—Three Stories

The words "power" and "discipline" often imply that the upper classes use force against the lower classes. We tend to forget that those in power have to control themselves and their children. A bourgeois father with ambitions for his son had to be prepared to, literally speaking, sacrifice his son's soul—power had its price. This is one explanation for the apparently paradoxical fact that discipline in grammar school was both tough and rough. The time and spatial drills taught the pupils a bourgeois life pattern. The aim of corporal punishment and bullying was, on one hand, to make the pupils submit themselves to a given order and, on the other, to prepare them for a future powerful position with the right to control others. This was a vital difference between grammar school and elementary school. In grammar school the disciplining was a cathartic process with the power and the glory as the final goals. There was a distinct age progression in grammar school. Discipline gradually became more relaxed and the pupils were granted certain privileges according to their age. According to the system based on bullying, the pupils got a higher rank: from persons who used to be punished to persons with the right to punish. Those who survived this ordeal felt that they deserved their privileges. Grammar school can therefore be regarded as an instrument in the formation of the bourgeoisie into a hegemonic class.

The disciplining process in elementary school did not incorporate this kind of progression. The pupils left school at an earlier age and, thus, were not given any age privileges. Nor have we found any evidence of regulated bullying. There was certainly violence between the pupils, but this violence was not ritualistic or systematized as in grammar school. This lack of progressive privileges harmonized with the fact that these pupils were not expected to make a career.

Thus, the disciplining process had different consequences for different social classes. But there was also a gender-specific socialization—grammar school formed part of the bourgeois male project. Grammar school was intended to turn the boys into men, both physically and mentally, and to develop the bourgeois man's intellectual ability. Physical training and war exercises aimed at strengthening their physical powers. The father-son relation between teachers and pupils was intended to strengthen the boys' male identity. The teacher was both the loving and the punishing father. The grammar-school boy had to live with the double message of love and violence as the ingredients of a male identity. The time and spatial disciplining in private girls' schools resembled that of grammar school. The girls were also supposed to be trained for a middle-class way of life and to be punctual, to keep the house tidy, and to serve as models to their sons. However, corporal punishment was not used. The teachers appealed to the girls' conscience, sympathy, and solidarity with the teachers.[79] This probably meant that the girls acquired an emotional capital that could give them power over the other members of their families. No social power positions at a higher level were, however, based on this capital.[80] It was, on the other hand, an asset for the intermediate positions in the division of labor awaiting many girls' school pupils—the post and telegraph offices, the schools, and nursing are examples of vocations created for women. For these vocations a girls' school education came in handy, because what could be better for an employer than the docility and pleasant manner of a girls' school pupil?

It should be observed that the teaching profession in elementary school was also feminized.[81] The women teachers may also have used more gentle disciplining techniques and treated boys and girls differently. If so, girls in elementary school also received a certain amount of emotional capital adopted to their future life. Thus, notions of gender differences were manifested in the organizational structure of the education system, in the labor market, and in the disciplining process of school.

Thus, grammar school and girls' school represented two different aspects of the formation of the bourgeoisie: one connected with public life and the other with the intimate sphere of the home.[82] The story of the elementary school differs from that of the other two, which is not surprising given the social background of the pupils, its duration, its ineffective organization, and its position as a compulsory school for an often reluctant population. Even if elementary school also aimed at transmitting bourgeois values and training the pupils for a bourgeois way of life, it was not so effective as the other two school forms. Time and spatial discipline did not have the same impact on life in elementary school. Many parents questioned the legitimacy of the school and the teachers. The short schooling prevented the message from being internalized in the same way as in the other two school forms. This was not a very big problem as long as the pupils were not expected to take up positions as autonomous political and economic subjects in their adult life. The extension of the franchise meant, however, that the demand for civic qualifications in ordinary people increased. After World War I such changes were reflected in extended compulsory school attendance, a curriculum with civic overtones, and in a stronger standardization of the work in elementary school.

On the other hand, one can say that the state elementary schools became very "successful" indeed, both in relation to disobedient pupils and reluctant parents, whose criticism and subversion of the school's authority came to be regarded as both illegal and deviant. This meant that a regular and proper schooling actually became the norm and that, based on this norm, the parents' criticism and the pupils' sometimes legitimate protests against the drills in school became classified as anomalies. Their resistance may also have ensured that working-class and rural children remained within their social class.[83] Thus, elementary school also played an important role in the establishment of a bourgeois hegemony.

However, these three school forms also contributed to the national project of promoting and emphasizing patriotism. The national feelings were supported by the instruction in Swedish history, by typical Swedish school songs, by textbook editions of famous Swedish authors, by the celebration of national festival days, and so on. Such activities in the everyday life of the schools formed the basis for a joint national identity at the same time as the educational system became engaged in the state service.

Education as state formation was part of the bourgeois project, but it was not only a matter of class relations and class power; it was also a matter of gender relations and masculine forms of power. The educational system thus played a crucial role in the establishment of these gender relations and in the consolidation of masculine power. School prepared boys and girls for different tasks in the national state, and the national symbols meant different things to girls and boys. The home became an overall metaphor for the native country, the nation, and the state. Such pictures characterized the teaching in various subjects.[84] This meant that citizenship and national identity were gendered.

We have already pointed out that various forms of partly invisible disciplining techniques operated in these three school forms. According to Foucault, such techniques contribute to the social construction of the human subject. But, unlike Foucault, we have focused on how different gender orders are constituted and contested in school and how, consequently, the social construction of the individual is affected by class and gender. Modern forms of power require and produce different and differentiated types of human subjects. That is one reason why there are so many stories embedded in the history of school discipline and moral regulation.

Endnotes

1. We would like to thank Kari Dehli and Ning de Coninck-Smith for their constructive and inspiring comments on this essay.

2. Cf. Bengt Sandin, *Hemmet, gatan, fabriken eller skolan. Folkundervisning och barnuppfostran i svenska städer 1600–1850* (Lund: Arkiv,1986); Lars Petterson, *Frihet, jämlikhet, egendom och Bentham. Utvecklingslinjer i svensk folkundervisning mellan feodalism och kapitalism 1809–1860* (Stockholm: Almqvist and Wicksell International, 1992); Tomas Englund, *Curriculum as a Political Problem. Changing Educational Conceptions, with Special Reference to Citizenship Education* (Lund: Studentlitteratur, 1986); Gunnar Richardson, *Kulturkamp och klasskamp. Ideologiska och sociala motsättningar i svensk skol- och kulturpolitik under 1880–talet* (Göteborg: Akademiförlaget, 1963); Olof Wennås, *Striden om latinväldet. Idéer och intressen i svensk skolpolitik under 1800-talet* (Stockholm: Almqvist and Wicksell,1966); Gunhild Kyle, *Svensk flickskola under 1800-talet* (Göteborg: Göteborgs University 1972).

3. Grammar schools had been financed by the state, under the authority of the church, ever since the Reformation in the sixteenth century. In the course of the nineteenth century there was a large increase in state subsidies to elementary schools and, at the end of the century, the state paid the bulk of expenses. After 1875 private girls' schools could also get state subsidies of very limited extent.

4. In this respect the Swedish secondary school system was different from North American secondary schools. Cf. Robert D. Gidney and Wyn Millar, *Inventing Secondary Education. The Rise of the High School in Nineteenth-century Ontario* (London, Ont.: McGill-Queen's University Press, 1990); David Tyack and Elisabeth Hansot, *Learning Together. A History of Coeducation in American Public Schools* (New York: Russel Sage, 1992); John L. Rury, *Education and Women's Work. Female Schooling and the Division of Labor in Urban America, 1870–1930.* (Albany: State University of New York Press, 1991).

5. In the middle classes we include the following four heterogeneous social classes: big businessmen, university graduates or civil servants, white-collar workers, and small businessmen. We will sometimes use "bourgeois classes" as a synonym for the middle classes. Cf. Ulla Johansson and Christina Florin, "'Where the Glorious Laurels Grow . . . .' Swedish Grammar Schools as a Means of Social Mobility and Social Reproduction," *History of Education*, Vol. 22, No. 2, 1993, pp. 147–162.

6. Kyle, *Svensk flickskola*, p. 56.

7. At the end of the nineteenth century only about 3 percent were entirely without education, and the great majority of the Swedish children thus went to elementary school. Cf. Margitta Schelin, *Den officiella skolstatistiken i Sverige åren 1847–1881* (Umeå: Umeå University, 1978).

8. This is usually dated back to the 1870s. Then there was a very rapid development and, as early as at the turn of the century, capitalism entered into its second phase, organized capitalism. Cf. Rolf Torstendahl, "Technology in the Development in the Society 1850–1980. Four Phases of Industrial Capitalism in Western Europe," in *History and Technology*, Vol. 1, 1984, pp.157-174.

9. Christina Florin and Ulla Johansson, *"Där de härliga lagrarna gro . . ."*, in *Kultur, klass och kön i det svenska läroverket 1850–1914* (Stockholm: Tiden, 1993), pp. 144–180.

10. Christina Florin, "Social Closure as a Professional Strategy: Male and Female Teachers from Co-operation to Conflict in Sweden, 1860–1906," *History of Education*, Vol. 20, No. 1, 1991, pp. 17–26.

11. Florin and Johansson, *"Där de härliga . . ."*, pp. 171–175; Silvano B. Lópes, *Högre utbildning för kvinnor. En studie av Kungliga Högre lärarinneseminariet.* Unpublished essay (Umeå: Umeå University, Department of History, 1993);

Folkundervisningskommitténs betänkande I:3. Bilagor. Historik och statliga utredningar (Stockholm: Norstedt, 1911).

12. Ulla Johansson, "Historien om likvärdighet i svensk skola," In *Likvärdighet i Svensk Skola* (Stockholm: Skolverket, 1994).

13. Max Weber, *Ekonomi och samhälle I. Förståendesociologins grunder* (Lund: Argos, 1983), pp. 146ff.

14. Louise McNay, *Foucault and Feminism. Power, Gender and the Self.* Cambridge: Polity Press, 1992); Jana Sawicki, *Disciplining Foucault: Feminism, Power, and the Body* (New York: Routledge, 1991).

15. We have carried out a case study of a grammar school in Västerås, a medium-sized town in central Sweden. Cf. Florin and Johansson, *"Där de härliga . . .".* We have also used our previous research on elementary school. Cf. Ulla Johansson, *Att skolas för hemmet. Trädgårdsskötsel, slöjd, huslig ekonomi och nykterhetsundervisning i den svenska folkskolan med exempel från Sköns församling* (Umeå: Umeå University, 1987); Christina Florin, *Kampen om katedern. Feminiserings-och professionaliseringsprocessen inom den svenska folkskolans lärarkår 1860–1906* (Stockholm och Umeå: Almqvist and Wicksell International, 1987).

16. There are, unfortunately, many and big gaps in our knowledge of girls' schools, particularly of the teaching and everyday school life. The information we have been able to collect is often contradictory and difficult to interpret. Our conclusions are, consequently, very tentative.

17. However, compulsary school attendance was not introduced until 1882, when according to a revised elementary school act all children were compelled to attend school from the age of seven to twelve.

18. Cf. Maria Sundkvist, *De vanartade barnen. Mötet mellan barn, föräldrar och Norrköpings barnavårdsnämnd 1903–1925* (Linköping: Linköping University, 1994).

19. Weber, *Ekonomi,* pp. 146ff. However, in reality the authority of these teachers was a combination of bureaucratic, charismatic, and traditional elements.

20. Here we have been inspired by Michel Foucault. Cf. Michel Foucault, *Discipline and Punishment. The Birth of the Prison.* 2nd ed. (New York: Penguin Books, 1982), pp. 135-230.

21. *Svensk Författningssamling. Kongl Majits nådiga stadga för rikets läroverk,* No. 53, 1878.

22. The Town Archives of Västerås, Rudbeckianska skolans arkiv, records of staff meetings, 1859–1900.

23. Bengt Sandin has documented the struggles and conflicts surrounding the disciplining process in elementary school during an earlier period. See Bengt Sandin, "Education, Popular Culture, and the Surveillance of the Population in Stockholm between 1600 and the 1840s." *Continuity and Change,* No. 3, 1988, pp. 357–390. A similar study has been carried out by Bruce Curtis in Canada. See Bruce Curtis, *Building the Educational State: Canada West, 1836–1871.* London, Ont.: Althouse Press, pp. 140-216.

24. Johansson, *Att skolas för hemmet,* p. 30.

25. *Förslag till en törbättrad Skol-Ordning, jemte Betänkande och Bilagor, i underdåmghes upprattadt at den i nåder tilltörordnade Uppfostrings-Comité* (Stockholm, 1817), p. xv.

26. Johansson, *Att skolas för hemmet,* p. 31.

27. This is evident from all the reports from the general Swedish elementary school teacher meetings held regularly during the latter part of the nineteenth century. Cf. Florin, *Kampen om Katedern,* pp. 239ff.

28. B. Rud Hall, ed., *Minnen från privatläroverk* (Stockholm: Föreningen för svensk undervisningshistoria), p. 130.

29. For the relation between school order and school buildings, see Malcolm Vick, "Building Schools, Building Society: Accommodating Schools in Mid-Nineteenth-

Century Australia." *Historical Studies in Education*, Vol. 5, No. 2, 1993, pp. 231–250.

30. Einar Sahlin, "Ett didaktiskt kanon för profkandidater och yngre lärare," *Pedagogisk Tidskrift*, 1893, p. 97.
31. Foucault, *Discipline and Punishment*, pp. 195–228.
32. Carl Svedelius, *Norra real 1876–1926* (Stockholm: P. A. Norstedt and Söner, 1927), p. 85.
33. Abraham Ahlén, *Mina ungdomsminnen från Skara* (Stockholm: P. Palmqvist, 1911), p. 35. Skara is a small cathedral city in central Sweden.
34. Herman Ekelund, "Från Braheskolan i Jönköping," in *När jag gick i skolan. Skol- och ungdomsminnen från 1800-talets senare hälft berättade av 34 svenska män och kvinnor.* (Uppsala: J. A. Lindblads förlag, 1934), p. 24.
35. *Undersökning af Sveriges högre flickskolor. Underdånigt utlåtande afgifvet den 19 januari 1888 af utsedde komiterade* (Stockholm: Norstedts, 1888).
36. At least not any official privileges. On the other hand, as the pupils grew older they probably took greater liberties in relation to their younger schoolmates.
37. Elisabeth Dahr, *Flickskolor i Jönköping* (Uppsala: Föreningen för svensk undervisningshistoria, 1975), p. 94.
38. Ibid., p. 93.
39. Ragnhild Bågenholm, *Min barndom i Majorna* (Göteborg: Ewald Elanders bokförlag, 1955), p. 131.
40. Dahr, *Flickskolor*, p. 93.
41. B. Rud Hall, ed., *Hågkomster från folkskola och folkundervisning* (Uppsala: Föreningen för svensk undervisningshistoria, 1933), p. 55.
42. Cf., e.g., ibid., p. 42. Barbara Finkelstein also concludes that elementary school teachers in America rarely made distinctions between misbehavior and poor academic performance. See Barbara Finkelstein, *Governing the Young. Teacher Behavior in Popular Primary Schools in Nineteenth-century United States* (New York: Falmer Press, 1989), pp. 95–114.
43. Ulla Johansson and Christina Florin, "Order in the (Middle) Class," *Historical Studies in Education/Revue d'histoire de l'éducation*, Vol. 6, No. 1, 1993, p. 28. B. Rud Hall, ed., *Minnen från folkskola och folkundervisning, VIII* (Uppsala: Föreningen för svensk undervisningshistoria, 1945), p. 16.
44. Fritz Netzler, *Helsingborgsminnen från min ungdom* (Munkedal: Carl Zakariasson, 1985), p. 270.
45. Hall, *Minnen, VIII*, p. 17.
46. Ibid., p. 143.
47. B. Rud Hall, ed., *Minnen från folkskola och folkundervisning, VIII* (Uppsala: Föreningen för svensk undervisningshistoria, 1946) p. 17.
48. B. Rud Hall, ed., *Minnen från folkskola och folkundervisning, V* (Uppsala: Föreningen för svensk undervisningshistoria, 1942), p.194.
49. The government grants were, of course, in the hands of men, and that is why the grant stipulations were male.
50. Silvano B. Lopéz, *The Royal Teacher Training College for Women. The Construction of a Women's Élite.* Unpublished essay. (Umeå: Umeå University, 1994).
51. The national curriculum of 1878 recommended such forms of schooling even if the local authorities were allowed to adjust their organization to local conditions. See also David Hamilton's analysis of the emergence of class teaching in *Towards a Theory of Schooling* (London: Falmer Press, 1989).
52. The same function was fulfilled by the state school inspectors in Canada. Cf. Bruce Curtis, *True Government by Choice Men? Inspection, Education, and State Formation in Canada West* (Toronto: University of Toronto Press, 1992).
53. Florin, *Kampen om Katedern*, pp. 60–63.
54. Ulla Bjerne, *Livet väntar dej* (Stockholm: Bonniers, 1955), pp. 108, 112.
55. Ibid., p. 100.

56. Eugen Hemberg, *En nittioårings minnen. Vandringar i kulturens och naturens tempel* (Malmö: Bokförlaget Scania, 1936), p. 27.

57. From an interview with a former male elementary school pupil in the parish of Skön.

58. This indicates that more refined techniques, as described by Foucault (1982), were emerging. Thus, this shift in discipline was not unique to Sweden. Cf. also David Hogan, "Modes of Discipline: Affective Individualism and Pedagogical Reform in New England, 1820–1850," *American Journal of Education*, Vol. 99, No. 1, November 1990, pp. 1–56; Ulla Johansson, "Ordning i klassen! Disciplin och straff i 1800-talets lärda skola," in Stig G. Nordström et al., eds., *Utbildningshistoria 1990* (Stockholm: Föreningen för svensk utbildningshistoria, 1990).

59. Ellen Hagen, Ljudlösa steg i Åhlinska flickskolan," in *När jag gick i skolan*, p. 225.

60. *Svensk Författningssamling. Kongl Majits Nådiga cirkulär" lill Domkapitlen angående underwisningen i gymnastik och militär-övningar wid elementarlärowerken, folk-skolelärar seminarierna och folkskolorna*. No. 3, 1863.

61. Claes Annerstedt, *Idrottslärarna och idrottsämnet. Utveckling, mål, kompetens— ett didaktiskt perspektiv*. (Göteborg: Göteborgs University, 1991), pp. 125ff.

62. Ibid., p. 127.

63. The National Archive: Ecklesiastikdepartementet, departementsschefsakter, läroverksbyrån 1878–1887, skrivelse den 11 nov 1882.

64. Dahr, *Flickskolor*, pp. 44–45; cf. also Annerstedt, *Idrottslärarna*, p. 129.

65. *Läroverkskomiténs underdåniga utlåtande och förslag angående organisationen af rikets allmänna läroverk afgifvet den 25 augusti 1884* (1884), del II.

66. *Undersökning av Sveriges högre flickskolor* (1888), pp. 157–239.

67. Curt Wallis, *Om folkskolans hälsovårdsförhållanden och medlen att förbätten desamma* (Stockholm: Fritze, 1896); Carl Dahlborg et al., *Betänkande avgivet utav kommitterade, som utsetts av Svenska Provinsialläkar föreningen för utredning av skolhygieniska spörsmål rörande folk- och småskolor å landsbygden* (Stockholm: Ivar Hæggstöms tryckeri, 1914).

68. Johansson, *Att skolas för hemmet*, pp. 240ff.

69. Märta Edquist, "Sanningen om 'klostret,'" in *När jag gick i skolan*, p. 276.

70. Florin and Johansson, "Dar de härliga . . . ", pp. 48ff.

71. Gurli Linder, *På den tiden. Några bilder från 1870-talets Stockholm* (Stockholm: Albert Bonniers Förlag, 1924), p. 229.

72. Johansson, *Att skolas för hemmet*, pp.106ff.

73. Ibid., pp. 117–166.

74. Bågenholm, *Min barndom*, pp. 122ff.

75. Hall, *Minnen från folkskola, V*, p. 31.

76. Göran Åberg, *Högre allmänna läroverket i Jönköping 1878–1968* (Uppsala: Föreningen för svensk undervisningshistoria, 1991), p. 27.

77. Hall, *Minnen från privatläroverk*, p. 128.

78. This conclusion is consistent with Basil Bernstein's theory of the visible and the invisible pedagogy. The visible pedagogy with a strict teacher is more likely to cause overt resistance than the invisible pedagogy appealing to feelings of sorrow and gratitude. See Basil Bernstein, *Class, Codes and Control*. Vol. 3, *Towards a Theory of Educational Transmission* (London: Routledge and Kegan Paul, 1975), pp. 116–140.

79. Cf. James C. Albisetti, *Schooling German Girls and Women. Secondary and Higher Education in the Nineteenth Century* (Princeton: Princeton University Press, 1988).

80. The Norwegian sociologist Hildur Ve's notion of responsible rationality refers to a similar tendancy for women to take human needs into consideration more so than those who usually act according to the principle of limited technical rationality. Hildur Ve, "Women's Experience—Women's rationality," in Inga Elgqvist-Salzman, ed. *Education and the Construction of Gender* (Umeå: Umeå University, kvinnovetenskapligt forum, 1991).

81. Florin, *Kampen om Katedern.* See also Alison Prentice and Marjorie R. Theobald, eds., *Women Who Taught. Perspectives on the History of Women and Teaching* (Toronto: University of Toronto Press, 1991); James C. Albisetti, "The Feminization of Teaching in the Nineteenth Century: A Comparative Perspective," *History of Education,* Vol. 22, No. 3, 1993, pp. 253–263.

82. Cf. Leonore Davidoff and Catherine Hall, who have shown that the formation of the English middle class was strongly genderered. Lenore Davidoff and Catherine Hall, *Family Fortunes. Men and Women of the English Middle Class, 1780–1850* (London: Hutchinson,1988).

83. Cf. Paul Willis, *Learning to Labour. How Working Class Kids Get Working Class Jobs* (Aldershot: Gower, 1977).

84. Inger Andersson, "Formal Education in Reading and Writing and the Formation of a Swedish National Identity," and Christina Florin and Ulla Johansson, "The Trinity of State, Church, and School in Nineteenth-Century Sweden," in Ryszard Kucha and Ulla Johansson, eds. *Polish and Swedish Schools in the Nineteenth and Twentieth Centuries* (Lublin: Marie Curie-Skoldowska University Press, 1995).

Chapter Four
A History of School Detention, or "The Little Confinement"
A Contribution to the History of Truancy in Denmark from 1875 to ca. 1914

Ning de Coninck-Smith

In the Copenhagen Municipal Archives I came across a pensioner's memoir from 1968, written by a man who had been born in 1898.[1] The author had begun his schooling at an old public school in Frederiksberg, a municipality neighboring Copenhagen. The year after—probably in 1906—he and his classmates were transferred to the town's newest school, the school on Pigeon Street [Duevejen Skole]. One of the things he wrote about the new school and the time he spent there (until 1912–13) was the following:

Our gym teacher told us that the new school was so modern that they had a machine with a built-in caning rod, so that the teachers only had to put children in at one end, and we would come out the other with our punishments complete, without the teachers having to exert themselves; that sounded like something I might make up myself, but this sadist really told it to us, and you can well imagine with what misgivings we little seven-year-old boys moved into the new school. Well, the new school was modern, all right, in one respect—namely, in that it had a prison, yes, you've read that right, a prison with bars on the window up in the caretaker's quarters. One of my own classmates did time in there, you know; I think it was for those kids whose parents didn't want to do anything to make sure that their children were going to school, for especially serious hooky. When I was twelve years old they put this boy up there, who lived off the same stairwell I did, by the way, . . . but who was younger than me, he was, shall we say, a little strange, and he had a nervous breakdown from being stuck up there, and that got the attention of the children's advocate Peter Sabroe, and the affair was splashed all over the papers, and so the thing was abolished.[2]

It was the combination of the word *modern* with the conditions the author described that struck my eye. I associated the word *modern* with teaching reforms, the abolition of caning, and the strong arm of love, but here was a story about the exact opposite, a story whose simple moral could be that changing schooling's physical conditions does not automatically change pedagogical practice. But this was also a story that lay somewhat outside the area one generally reads about in personal histories on the subject of school, or in the authorized accounts of the history of education.

Of course it is quite possible that the author was using the concept of modern sarcastically. After all, he was a seventy-one-year-old, stuck in the middle of the welfare state of Denmark in the 60s with the youth rebellion right around the corner, and probably thinking: "It's nothing now but the rat-race and dog-eat-dog; something is rotten in the state of Denmark." Gone were the good old days, when charity and family togetherness provided a counterpoint to "the daily grind," as he wrote at the end. Nonetheless, the author's use of the word *modern* set me to wondering about when such children's prisons had been "modern." Were they something new in the history of schooling, as this recollection suggested, or did they date to older times? Why were they instituted? What was, or had been, the pedagogical philosophy behind their establishment? And—not least—how much were they used?

It was not simply an unusually good memory that caused this story to imprint itself so firmly in my mind; when I read about it again five years later, I felt my original impression being confirmed. On the contrary, it touched on some theoretical and methodological ideas I had at the time—and have elaborated on—concerning the ways in which the history of schooling should be understood and written about. For one thing, the affair might have been taken straight out of Michel Foucault's books on the great confinement and modern society's techniques for maintaining order and disciplining the population.[3] It was both fascinating and provocative that Foucault's theories applied to Danish conditions. But did they really apply?

For another thing, this story contained a glimpse of the everyday life of the school, with its sociocultural conflicts and oppositions, both between small and big, and reciprocally among groups. This is an aspect of the history of schooling that historians of the subject often

can illuminate only from the standpoint of the school. It is more difficult to discover how it appeared from the other side of the teacher's
desk, from the points of view of pupils or parents, except in situations
of open conflict, such as that with which this story seemed to be concerned. Or to put it as Carlo Ginzburg and others have done: no one
would dream of alleging that such a story is representative in the traditional sense of that word, but it does represent a certain knowledge
that cannot be found in other places.[4]

As if these two reasons were not sufficient for beginning a
scientific project in the spirit of Foucault, the story became even
more interesting in light of the fact that the city of Copenhagen,
starting in 1879, had a system similar to the one in Frederiksberg—
namely a detention home on Vesterfaelled Street for children who
"have been guilty of truancy and misconduct." The question
became whether the little confinement inside the great one was a
generally utilized pedagogical tool of the time, directed at those whom
we would characterize today merely as pupils who do not fit in.

Back to Frederiksberg

In 1876 the Frederiksberg Town Council asked the Ministry of Ecclesiastical Affairs and Public Instruction for permission to set up a
room off the school caretaker's quarters, with windows, tile oven,
bed, and so forth, for the "temporary placement of neglected children." This phrase referred to a child who was "guilty of truancy or
other misconduct." The children that the school committee had in
mind were those "who, in addition to being absent from school,
leave home, beg or filch food by day, and sleep on steps, in doors, or
elsewhere outside the home by night." The goal of the little confinement was of course to punish the children concerned. But to a large
degree the detention was also an attempt to prevent "the pernicious
results, which wicked examples have on the discipline and moral
bearing which ought to inform the school's work."

The school committee had lost faith in both corporal punishment and the example set at home, "since perhaps there are precisely
those unhappy circumstances in the home that have engendered the
inclination to take up the life of a vagabond," and until then had
placed the children either in the poorhouse or in a reform school.
The consequences had been worse than expected, presumably

because the parents had opposed the placements.[5] Now the township wanted a place where it could put the children without first asking the parents. The school committee's idea was that only if the stay in the detention cell lasted longer than twenty-four hours had the parents to give their consent. They were, however, supposed to be informed when the confinement began. It was imagined that the maximum confinement might last a week.

The children would receive food and other care at the expense of the school committee, and during the time in which they are not attending school, they would be kept at constant work picking oakum. The punishment thus derives from the fact that the child is deprived of his freedom, and additionally, loafing and disobedience will immediately result in corporal punishment.

Practical problems could arise if two or more children were supposed to be confined at the same time, or if it was a case of children of opposite sexes. The school commission was of the opinion that these problems could be solved by hiring someone who could reside together with the children, and by fitting out yet another room, so that the sexes could be kept separately.

The ministry was well disposed to the idea of the detention cell, but after having checked with the Ministry of Justice it decided it could not allow the children to be placed without the parents' consent from the beginning of the confinement. Despite this curtailment of the original purpose, the detention cell was set up, and until 1913 all new schools in Frederiksberg were equipped with just such a room in conjunction with the school caretaker's quarters. The school committee in Frederiksberg assumed "that parents would appreciate this assistance being offered them in the upbringing of difficult children."[6]

According to the *Ordbog over det Danske Sprog* [Dictionary of the Danish Language], the word *internat* [detention home, detention room] made its first appearance in 1876, when the Ministry of Ecclesiastical Affairs and Public Instruction responded positively to the application from the Frederiksberg parish council. The idea's historical forerunners are most probably the children's cages used at German philanthropies of the Enlightenment to confine misbehaving pupils. These cages later developed into house arrest in the bourgeois families that had enough space for the children to be given their own rooms.[7] It is not as likely that the prison cell was taken as the direct model, since imprisonment of children in the 1870s had become a questionable subject. But the similarity is striking.

The Fight over Children's Bodies, Space, and Time

Mass schooling started in Denmark at the end of the eighteenth century, and a royal decree from 1814 is normally considered the constitution of the Danish elementary school system. The decree stated that parents were responsible for their children's education and that this had to take place between age seven and the year of confirmation, normally fourteen or fifteen. Schools in the countryside were very different from the schools of the city. In the countryside children's labor remained more important than school far into the twentieth century. In the city a crucial change took place during the last three decades of the nineteenth century. School hours increased by 30–50 percent depending on the age and sex of the child, and the school authorities became less permissive when children were absent: parents were fined much more harshly than before. This fight over children's time, bodies, and space first occurred in the big towns, which in a Danish context means Copenhagen and its neighboring municipalities. And this is precisely where our story begins and ends, thirty-seven years later.

The establishment of the detention cell in Frederiksberg was a final element in a campaign to reduce absences from school. In 1864 the number of days absent, after absence for reasons of sickness have been discounted, amounted to 13 percent of the total school days in the town's school system. Ten years later this figure was down to 3 percent, and it sank still further in the next few years. According to the preserved documents, there were almost as many girls as boys who were truant, but the so-called chronic truants, whose parents had to pay a fine more than four times during a year, were boys. In the 1875–76 school year, four boys were absent from school for nineteen to twenty-four days. The majority of unexcused absences involved children who were absent from one to six days.[8] The general decrease in absences was a result not of harsher fines—which otherwise were the most frequently used means in the Danish school systems for enforcing respect for the school and its work—but of the fact that the school system had consciously endeavored to make schooling more attractive. School meals, vacation trips in the summer, prizes for diligence, and an all-day school for children of parents with greater professional ambitions were introduced, while at the same time, the surveillance of absences was intensified, starting in 1872. That year the town hired its first caretaker for the school. In addition to looking after the cleanliness of the building, he was supposed to try every morning and afternoon to find the children who had not come to school.[9]

We know very little about how and how often the detention cells were used before they became a publicly debated issue in 1913. In 1901, the school superintendent in Frederiksberg reported that the cells for the previous fifteen years had been used an average of seventy-four days annually, and that the highest number of days in one year had been 160. At this time, the municipality had seven schools. Thus, at around the turn of the century, every cell was in use at least ten days a year. Apparently, confinement was a less widespread form of punishment in the school system in Frederiksberg in the years leading up to the First World War. In 1913 it was reported that the cells had been used twenty-seven days in the 1911–12 school year. In 1912–13, five pupils had been confined for twenty-eight days, which means that five children had been put under lock and key for an average of at least five days. In an 1893 report to the Ministry of Ecclesiastical Affairs and Public Instruction, school superintendent Joakim Larsen described quite concisely how a confined boy was treated:

During incarceration, the child must remain day and night [in the cell] and receive his food at the school's expense. The punishment consists, then, in the fact that the child is deprived of his freedom, in addition to which disobedience and laziness immediately result in corporal punishment. The principal monitors the effect of the punishment and endeavors to influence the confined child. By this method, a halt in incipient degeneracy is sometimes achieved.[10]

Before we turn to a discussion of why, around 1913, the cell was considered so old fashioned that it was abolished by the school system in Frederiksberg, we will take a detour out of the town, and look at the City of Copenhagen's detention home on Vesterfaelled Street.

Character Formation—A New Educational Vision

In 1879 the Copenhagen school authorities opened their detention home on Vesterfaelled Street, three years after the city reached the decision to create one. Those three years had been taken up with the construction of an appropriate building in Vesterfaelled Street on the outskirts of the city. The plan had originally been for the detention home to house both boys and girls, but in actuality only boys were placed there. Apparently there were not as many problems with girls in the school system. The detention home functioned as a municipal institution until 1933, but its character changed along the way. Until 1905 it was, on the whole, run along the lines of the original aims, which were identical with the aims of the detention cells in Frederiksberg. Through the deprivation of freedom and the application of strict discipline, the goal was to punish those "boys, who had been managing to avoid both" of those things, as the city council's report put it in 1877. After child welfare departments were instituted in 1905, the detention home gradually became one of many institutions, but it continued to have a strong connection with the school system of Copenhagen.[11] The detention cells at Frederiksberg and the detention home in Copenhagen shared three fundamental traits.

First, the authorities in both communities wanted to find new ways to evade the parents' constitutional rights regarding their children, ways which were supposed to lead to the salvation of the individual child, and simultaneously save all the other children from the moral contagion of which the truant pupil was a carrier. Such considerations were decisive in the decision to locate the new houses of correction close to the children's neighborhoods. In this way it was hoped that the parents would more willingly give their consent. All previous institutions had been placed far out in the country.

Second, there was a common conception that truancy was the worst crime children could commit against their school—and against themselves. Therefore the punishment should "correspond to a kind of reform school or regular prison," as the superintendent of the

Frederiksberg schools is reported to have expressed himself in 1913 when the cells were criticized.[12] Third, faith in detention was an expression of a pedagogical thinking that had the formation of character as its goal and upbringing as its means. The formation of character was the pedagogical catchphrase of the second half of the 1800s. Industrialization, urbanization, liberalism, and the rise of bourgeois democracy helped to transform Danish society at a faster pace than at any previous time in Danish history. As a result of these social changes, the traditional elementary pedagogy, with its emphasis on rote learning of elementary secular and religious knowledge that had been passed down through generations, became obsolete. With a society in rapid transformation, where social networks and structures of authority—especially in the towns—were far looser than in the feudal village society, the willingness to work and to make one's own way was thought to be located primarily in the individual. The goal of the formation of character was precisely to inculcate the school's and the society's norms and values in the child. The only question was, How?

With the royal decree of 1814, caning was installed as the only way of physically punishing the children, and only as a last resort. Instead, the personality of the teacher and the teacher's relations with the children were seen as essential for the maintenance of order and discipline in the school. The ideal school should be like any middle-class home, where children flocked around their loving parents, and where the risk of losing the love und respect of the educator kept children at bay. From the end of the eighteenth century, emotions and consciousness were given a still larger place within education, and consequently psychological punishment became of growing importance. The creation of the detention home and cells were in accordance with these new educational visions; isolated in the home or in the cell, the boy would have the best chance in the world to change his mind, behavior, and attitude toward the school.

The maintenance of discipline in school occupied many column inches in the pedagogical periodicals of the time. Precisely in 1879—the year in which the City of Copenhagen's detention home in Vesterfaelled Street took in its first boys—one could listen at a school meeting on Pentecost to a lecture on "School Discipline." In the lecture the speaker attempted to modernize the concept of discipline, so that it would encompass more than mere outward obedience. His definition ran thus:

"Discipline" means whatever is done in order to engender obedience, in order to hold others to their responsibilities. Discipline in school, like all good discipline, must take aim not only at external obedience, but also at the internal, the heart's obedience, and it seeks to hold the child to his responsibilities, as much to further his development as for the sake of instruction. By school discipline, therefore, I am not thinking exclusively about what one generally calls discipline: that children should go quietly to and from their seats, and so on, which everyone knows well enough has its own importance. But discipline takes aim essentially at the outer things, at the form; it is sometimes only a kind of polishing, an outer varnish, and that is not nearly enough; our discipline should also represent a positive influence on the children's temperaments, on their goodheartedness and character; we should set our sights on a kind of discipline that is not merely for school, but for life. *We should indeed "watch over the youth entrusted to us," we should work to fortify the children in the pursuit of truth, in being open and honest in all their dealings, and we must fight against lies, falsehood and cunning. We should accustom them to voluntary obedience, to bowing their wills before that of another, which is justified in holding sway over them to the extent that it is right and good; and willfulness, defiance, disrespect, quarrelsomeness and suchlike must be eliminated. And we should hold them to diligence and good order, to alertness, endurance, punctuality and the rest, whereas laziness, negligence, carelessness and similar bad habits must be weeded out. Now when I, in connection with this task, use the phrase "school discipline"— analogous to house discipline and church discipline—I willingly concede that the word has a serious, somewhat forbidding and old fashioned sound; but since it also concerns a serious school issue of long standing, I don't hesitate to use it.*[13]

The quotation shows the attitude that lay behind the establishment of school detention in both Frederiksberg and Copenhagen, and it bears witness to the fact that the new forms of education had the same goals as the old—namely, to force the child to obey, to have faith in authority, and to respect the school's mission. But since the appropriateness of caning had now come into question, the procedure for achieving these goals had partly changed.

Routines at the Detention Home

Between 1879 and 1905, fifteen hundred schoolboys in Copenhagen ranging in age from ten to fourteen went through the detention home because they had skipped school, wandered around in the streets, or committed petty larceny. Some were there for a short time, others for several months, and a few for several years. Most of them were sent home when they had served out their sentences, and something over half had later brushes with the authorities. But for the school system, the detention home's decisive effect lay not in the concrete results one could point to, but in its indirect effect on other schoolboys:

The Detention Home performed, in any case, the great service to the school of quickly removing the bad elements, and perhaps when all is said and done, the indirect benefit that it conferred in this way is of greater significance than everything else, although this is naturally not liable to direct proof or quantification. It can also be noted that the mere threat of sending a boy to the Detention Home has often shown itself to be an effective tool, with regard both to the pupils and to the slack parents, who, with this eventuality staring them in the face, have made an effort to avert the dereliction of their responsibilities.[14]

There is no doubt that it was a serious thing to be sent to the detention home. The building in and of itself radiated severity, and it was arranged so that the boys were under constant surveillance. The boys received elementary instruction, but most of their time was spent working. The work consisted of cleaning, cooking, gardening in the summer, and the production of various cottage industry articles in the workroom in the attic in the winter. Through this industry, the boys were supposed to learn a work ethic as well as the enjoyment of work. Constant employment was also seen as the best protection against trouble. The school authorities in Copenhagen placed great emphasis on the spirit that was supposed to reign in the institution. If one compares the qualifications of the three first directors, one can see how family life gradually became the model for the relationship between the director and the pupils. The first director was praised for the fact that he could handle and control his boys. With his two successors it became steadily more important that they could get help from their wives, so that the director-couple could be a second parent-couple for the boys. Mother played a growing role as model for the teacher in elementary school, while the patriarch still served as the model for the educator at the boys' reform schools. The only women in the detention home apart from the director's wife worked in the kitchen.

As Foucault has pointed out, the confinement had another aim than discipline, upbringing, and surveillance. Specifically, confinement allows the collection of a certain kind of knowledge, which on one hand can be used as a basis for formulating new educational techniques, and on the other hand creates a scientific basis for the normalization process that is discipline's actual aim. Thus it was also at the detention home that directors from the 1880s and 1890s tested their psychological knowledge from the world of adult criminals on the budding criminals from the Copenhagen school system.

As already mentioned, the detention home and the detention cells in Frederiksberg were an expression of a new type of institution and a new pedagogy, which considered the formation of character and self-discipline as the foremost goal of the upbringing of children. The ideal of cleanliness also formed a part of this, both because of health concerns and as a tool in the instilling of order and self-discipline.

The detention home, in which the boys were kept around the clock, presented good possibilities for implementing the new ideals of cleanliness. The new boys' first encounter with the institution was a bath, which was subsequently repeated frequently. Before meals, hands had to be washed, hair combed, and so on. The cultivation of cleanliness could be hard. No one was allowed to sleep with socks on, the dormitory was supposed to have a temperature of from fifty-four to fifty-seven degrees, and cold rubdowns were employed to prevent both masturbation and bed-wetting. The boys' physiques were supposed to be hardened, but for many they first needed to be fattened up! Many of the boys who had lived for a long time on the city's streets and squares were both emaciated and exhausted when they came to the detention home. The annual reports frequently tell how many kilos the boys put on during the course of their stay, and how unhappy they were that they had to leave the school—because of the food!

The education was comprehensive—both in the moral and the physical realm. But this did not mean that caning had disappeared from the detention homes. In principle, corporal punishment could be employed only in the same measure as in the city schools—that is, with at most five lashes to the backside—and no place else. If boxing of the ears was not expressly forbidden, neither was it officially allowed. The source material from the detention home indicates nonetheless that caning occurred often, and that it was not particularly sparing—as regards neither the number of lashes nor the use of other methods of punishment.

Along with everything else, the detention home possessed a cell for solitary confinement, where the boys were put for the first two or three days of their stay. This cell was also used as a punishment in combination with caning, for example after serious attempts at escape.

The Boys, Their Parents, and the Detention Home

The boys who came to the detention home had mostly been absent from school because their parents had needed them to perform labor at home, or because they had turned their backs on school after too much caning. Some of them had led a sad and lonesome street life without any family or relatives. Some had alcoholic parents and suffered from lack of elementary care. Among them were also mentally retarded boys and boys with physical as well as mental diseases. Some of the boys strongly disliked their confinement and fought hard to get out. In the course of the detention home's first thirty years, four boys tried to commit suicide while they were being kept in solitary. One of them succeeded.

There were also many who tried to escape, especially in the first years, when the garden fence was so low that the boys could easily climb it. In the mid-1880s the building was made more secure, and the physical detention of boys at their admittance was initiated, in part to reduce the number of escape attempts, which experience had shown often occurred during the first couple of days. This apparently had the desired effect: the number of escape attempts sank dramatically in the years following: from thirty attempts in the first five years to only fifty in the next twenty-five. Sources speak only indirectly about the attitude of the boys, but as already noted, many were glad to have regular meals and a bed to sleep in. But the frequent corporal punishment, for offenses such as talking during grace or insufficient obedience, clearly shows that it was not always easy to get the boys to accept the detention home's routines and educational practices. A total of 99.9 percent of the boys came from the poorest elements of Copenhagen's population, from a completely different culture and a completely different social milieu than those of the detention home's directors and the heads of the school system. It is no wonder that this gave rise to daily conflicts.

Not unexpectedly, the parents were not met with much sympathy on the part of the detention home. According to the prevailing ideas of the time, the parents were part of the physical and social milieu that spread moral contagion to the children. This attitude was clearly expressed in a speech that one of the detention home's directors delivered to the Pedagogical Society in 1887. On the subject of the detention home's clientele and their social background, he said:

Let us think about these children, whom an ungentle fate has caused to be born in such homes, where not only are they not provided with a counterweight to wicked tendencies, but where such tendencies are in fact inflicted on them by the power of example; let us follow them from their more or less foul homes in the city's worst quarters, where they live cheek by jowl with the dregs of the proletariat, and where contagion thus easily breeds—let us follow them into the manifold temptations of street life, where confirmed as well as unconfirmed vagabonds vie in becoming their guides into the camp of the ungodly. [15]

If the director held such attitudes, it is not surprising that the parents' views of the detention home are, if possible, even more invisible than those of the boys in the preserved source material. Most of the boys were sent to the detention home by the school authorities or the police, and sometimes the acceptance of the parents is entered in the notebooks of the director. Other boys came on the request of a father or mother for economic reasons or as a punishment for misbehavior.[16] In one case the father had kept the boy imprisoned at home without success, and the detention home was used as a last resort.[17] Some parents were unhappy and did what they could to prevent their sons' entering the home, either out of love or because they needed their help with the younger siblings. A few went so far as to hide the boys, if they ran away from the school.[18]

Frederiksberg—The Summer of 1913

In the hot summer of 1913 the school system of Frederiksberg found itself in a situation that made it impossible to defend the detention cells. Since the idea had received a green light from the Ministry of Ecclesiastical Affairs and Public Instruction about forty years earlier, it had spread to other large cities, such as Ålborg and Esbjerg. The two last-named cities, however, never got further than considering the idea—probably for economic reasons.[19] Now the detention cell had to be abolished. But what was the cause of this change in attitude?

It was not every day one could read about the school prisons in Frederiksberg in the local papers. The subject maintained a low profile, until the day in June 1913 when the Social Democratic Party's newspaper, *Socialdemokraten,* devoted the entire front page to the story of twelve-year-old Edvard—son of a seamstress whose husband had abandoned her—who had been confined for ten days in an attic room at the Pigeon Street School. Most of what we can learn about the justification for this punishment is contained in the *Socialdemokraten*'s version of the story, because the principal's report to the school committee has disappeared from the town archives. On June 18, 1913, the *Socialdemokraten* wrote :

Edvard, who is described by everyone as a good boy, is somewhat sickly, and mentally retarded. Now and then he has exhibited a tendency to skip school, and the punishments that have been the consequences of this have reinforced this tendency. The other day he accidentally damaged the binding of his atlas, and fear of the consequences caused him to skip school for three days.

The paper included a detailed description of how mother and

son had thrown their arms around each other after he had served out his sentence. The principal claimed that he had only exercised his rights and carried out his duties, and that the mother had signed a document saying she agreed with the punishment. The mother claimed that she had been pressured to sign, under threat of the forcible removal of the boy, and that her brother-in-law had shown up and offered to take the boy in hand, but had been brushed off by the principal.

In the days following, the affair was given extensive coverage in the *Socialdemokraten,* and mass meetings were held both in Frederiksberg and on the Copenhagen common. At least four hundred people appeared at a meeting called by the trade unions of the quilt-, tricotage-, and linen-seamstresses. The participants in the meeting demanded that the children's prisons be abolished, and at the same time one hundred people joined a parents' association.[20] Three days later a new meeting took place on the common (heavily attended, according to the *Socialdemokraten)* and five days later a local meeting was held in Frederiksberg with two thousand participants (also according to the *Socialdemokraten).* At this point the paper revealed that two boys were confined in two other schools, and that they also had been kept there for ten days. It is likely that the attitude of the people at these meetings was in agreement with the following quotation from a front-page article in the *Socialdemokraten,* in which an attempt was made to account for why the children skipped school:

I wonder if one of the most essential causes of truancy is not the practice of punishment, which now is so widespread in the schools? Experience shows that the teacher who exhibits friendliness and understanding toward the children, who does not look on his [sic] job as a mere trade, but as a true calling, almost always will be able to manage even the most difficult children, while the teacher who is free with the cane in and out of season, in the belief that he is dealing with a bunch of hardened criminals, is himself raising up truants.[21]

Of course it is impossible to know whether this affair really mobilized as many people as the *Socialdemokraten* stated. But the year of 1913 was not just any year in the history of Danish schooling and child welfare. It was a year in which public opinion seemed to have been greatly occupied with the mistreatment of children. First of all, it was the year in which the country's most famous children's advocate and tireless opponent of caning, Peter Sabroe, died in a train accident in Jutland in July. And secondly, it was the year in which parents' associations began to spring up in the workers' quarters of Copenhagen and Frederiksberg—probably as the result of the work of Peter Sabroe and the Social Democratic Party. And according to the teachers' own professional journal, *Københavns Kommuneskole,* these parents' associations in the greater Copenhagen area could in the fall of 1913 and in the first month of 1914 always get several hundred people to come to a meeting when the question of caning was on the agenda.[22] But pressure on the school authorities at Frederiksberg also came from another, and perhaps a more unexpected, quarter—namely, from the bourgeois press. *Berlingske Aften* wrote that the practice of detention was obsolete, and that education must be a question of humane influence.[23] The following day, *Berlingske Morgen* wrote that detention homes represented an unpedagogical and antiquated mode of punishment. It is hardly surprising that neither of the two papers found any fault in the principal's conduct. Another bourgeois paper, *Københavneren,* denounced the detention cells in Frederiksberg, but praised the detention home of Copenhagen.[24] According to *Socialdemokraten,* even the minister of education found it "very strange, that the boy has not been free."[25]

The teachers' professional organizations also put a certain pressure on the school system in Frederiksberg to get rid of the detention cells. They did this more for the teachers' sake than the pupils'—they wanted to forestall an anti-teacher campaign. It was not, in fact, the teachers' fault—their job was, according to the paper of the Danish Teachers Union, *Folkeskolen,* to:

keep discipline for the sake of both the children and the work. When the school authorities failed to come up with any other method than the cells for dealing with that kind of child, what were the teachers supposed to do, other than to use this institution to address their particular difficulties, which they had no other means to overcome?[26]

The reaction of the teachers was not a mere coincidence. The year 1913 was the year in which teachers' protests against what they considered a constant smear campaign against their profession—a campaign charging that they didn't attend well enough to their work—culminated in their refusal to celebrate, the following year, the hundredth anniversary of the law of 1914. This action was a continuation of the teachers' protests against a wage law dating from 1908, in which their own association, the Danish Teachers Union, had accepted a clause giving the local authorities the right to dismiss a teacher for conduct "sufficiently unbecoming to his position as teacher that the profit of the school's operations is thereby substantially diminished." In the years following, approximately twenty-three teachers were dismissed under this paragraph, but what the teachers were most frightened of was the possibility that "parental rule" was in the offing.

At public meetings, teachers had to defend themselves against accusations of mistreating their pupils. Hardly any wanted to give up caning, but they were not in favor of using the rod on every occasion, only as a last resort. They hoped to calm parents' animosity and put a halt to the public debate about physical punishment by the abolition of detention cells and through a closer relationship with the parents, such as parent-teacher meetings—it was better to be the host than the guest, as one teacher expressed it in the professional journal *Københavns Kommuneskole*, in 1913.

Viewed against this backdrop, it is not surprising that the municipality of Frederiksberg in the course of the summer and fall of 1913 decided to abolish its detention cells. From then on, fines would be "quickly and consistently" applied, if moral suasion was not effective. If the fines did not help, either, one might resort to compulsory removal, which the Child Law of 1905 had made possible.[27] One consequence of this was that the old detention cells could now be incorporated into the caretaker's quarters, provided that the school committee approved it. It became apparent, however, that it was not always easy to get permission, since the building and fire inspectors would not allow the premises to be converted to residential space—primarily because of concerns about fire safety![28]

Explanations

There seems to be no doubt that the prevailing mood and the opposition to school detention that developed in the summer heat of
1913, on both the right and left sides of Danish politics, were the
immediate cause of the Frederiksberg School Committee's abolition
of the detention cells. Nothing suggests that the well-known Danish
children's advocate Peter Sabroe had anything directly to do with
this affair, as the pensioner's memoirs suggests. He did, however,
become involved in 1910, when he lodged a complaint against the
detention home in Copenhagen. On the basis of testimony from
the father of a former pupil, he charged that the boy in question had
received seventeen lashes for wetting his bed; he also protested against
unrestrained caning, insufficient medical attention for sick children,
and the fact that the principal had been too intimate with the children. The affair ended, not with the closing of the Copenhagen detention home, but with the principal receiving a reprimand from
the school authorities.[29]

But a question remains as to how much the schools in
Frederiksberg needed the detention cells in 1913. School records
show that the number of days the rooms were used sank dramatically after the turn of the century. That might be the explanation for
the fact that the school system did not exert itself to keep them—
but why had the need become reduced? The answer to this question
can be located in the fact that the times had changed in the course of
the detention cells' nearly forty-year history. At bottom, the history
of the detention cells is all about the changing forms of discipline
under the impact of the progress of modern society. The rooms had
once been modern, and now they were no longer seen as such.
According to Foucault, visible, external discipline has a controlling
inner purpose, which is normalization—that is to say, discipline
impresses on each individual the limits of what is normal and what
isn't. Consequently, it can be instructive to read the history of the
development of the school detention cells as an expression of changes
in the ways in which normality is formed, and how, and with what
means, the limits of normality should be drawn.

When the detention home and cells saw the light of day, the
school systems in Frederiksberg and Copenhagen found themselves
in a difficult situation. It seemed that migration into the cities would

never end, and at the same time the workers' movement was beginning to stir both in Denmark and abroad. The expansion of the city
and industrialization both frightened and enthralled the planners of
urban childhood; the social and health-related problems were enormous, but all the same, the city possessed the intellectual, economic,
and political potential to do something about the problems. One
potential resided in the construction and extension of the public
school system in such a way that school attendance could become a
natural and obvious part of all children's lives. The planners of the
1870s imagined that, especially for the working class, school could
be like another (good and bourgeois) home; through school, the
workers' children would be given time and space to be children and
would be protected against becoming adults too early. In brief, schools
were supposed to replace the (potentially) failing parents. Without
going into all the details, we can establish that the project ran into a
few concrete obstacles, the foremost among them being the children's
income-providing work, and the children's—and parents'—
opposition to the school's interference in their lives—especially outside the actual school hours. This last was due both to the school's
involvement in the children's cleanliness and health, and to the teachers' supervision of the children's wandering around in the city. In the
years when the detention home and cells opened their doors, the
criminalized picture of the street life of children had received a powerful reinforcement from criminal statistics, which in the 1890s could
reveal that criminality among boys had increased by 120 percent
from 1875 to 1885, while that for girls had remained stable. The
increase lay principally in a violent growth in the number of disturbances of law and order, whereas the number of crimes for gain, on
the contrary, had stayed the same.[30] To the urban planners there was
no doubt. Boys of the city got worse and worse—and street life was
the root of all evil. Nobody seems to have questioned how the picture had looked before 1875 or why children's disturbances of the
public order suddenly attracted the eye of the statisticians. In a lengthy
statement to the ministry in 1893, the superintendent in
Frederiksberg, Joakim Larsen, who was the father of the detention
cells, gave his version of these worries:

Life on the street, which many of the children of the humble classes lead

outside of school, with its lack of supervision, its association with im-
moral companions, and its bad examples of apprentices and factory girls,
leads not only to truancy and brawling, but often to lying, dishonesty
and immorality. The alluring displays in many shops tempt the children
to pilfer, or to buy on credit without the knowledge of their parents.[31]

Against the background of this criminalized picture of the street, the school had increased its responsibility for the children's life and behavior. When the school detention cells were established, therefore, their indirect effect on the many was at least as important as their effect on the few who were put in them one or more times.

Copenhagen and Frederiksberg chose dissimilar solutions to the problem of engendering respect for the school's task, for its norms and values, and its view of the children's lives out on the streets. If we disregard possible economic explanations and causes that might be due to differences in the relative size of the problems, the dissimilarity can be ascribed to different evaluations concerning how visible the disciplining of children should be in the everyday life of the school. In Frederiksberg the detention cell was visible to everybody, while the detention home in Copenhagen operated in the background of the regular schools' daily life, like a quiet form of discipline. The model that the authorities in Copenhagen had chosen provided better possibilities of developing the institution gradually as the pedagogical visions of reformatories changed from prisons to homes. From the very beginning, the first director wanted to distance himself from the outside world's conception of the detention home as a prison for children. The detention home had been equipped with bars over the windows, and he requested in 1880 that they be removed, for the following reason: "In addition to causing us daily inconvenience, they also rob the building of its otherwise beautiful aspect, and give it the look of a penitentiary."[32]

Irrespective of whether or not his request was accommodated, and even whether everyday life in the detention home in Copenhagen, according to today's standards, had as strong a prison image as the detention cells in Frederiksberg, the institution and its directors worked consciously to promote its image as a second home for boys from a miserable social background. The same cannot be said of the cells in Frederiksberg.

The budding field of child psychology, which first supplemented and later supplanted the biophysical theories based on observations of adult criminals, provided the scientific foundation for the change in the view of what constituted an appropriate form of childrearing in the home and the school. One of child psychology's first tangible results, which became significant in the recruiting for detention homes, was a more finely graduated classification of pupils. A result of this classification was that slow learners were put in their own remedial classes.[33] Quite often, as in 1913, it was the boys with learning difficulties—for social or psychological reasons—who ran afoul of the teachers and the school, and who were sent to the detention home.

However, it was not only in the scientific sphere that times had changed in 1913. Among the lower classes in the cities, the attitude toward school had changed since the 1870s. Purely quantitatively, a marked fall in the number of legal and illegal absences can be demonstrated; meanwhile, the number of schoolchildren engaged in income-earning work sank dramatically after 1904. The qualitative explanations for this are far more complex and, to an extent, unresearched. It is certain, however, that the Social Democrats and the workers' movement tirelessly continued to encourage parents to put schooling ahead of their children's employment, both for the sake of the children and their future, and out of consideration for family ideals. Another important circumstance is that the real wages of the working class climbed markedly during the 1890s. This probably made it possible for many families to appropriate middle-class family ideals and do without the children's—and perhaps also, to a certain extent, the mother's—income. On the other hand, we know considerably less about how much the stricter fines from the 1890s, and a series of new regulations from 1905 to 1913, which were supposed to limit the employment of schoolchildren, affected the regularity of school attendance. But both witness the fact that urban child labor was no longer socially acceptable.

Nonetheless, the times had certainly changed, and much suggests that the direct, visible disciplining of which the cells in Frederiksberg were an expression had outlived their role. They had simply become old fashioned in a modern society in which respect for school had been established and normalized in the

everyday life of children. However, this did not mean that the
social problems in school were eliminated. Rather to the contrary, for, through the clinical eye of child psychology, problems
were identified that—perhaps—had been invisible earlier, but
that hardly were amenable to solution by way of solitary confinement. (One can well ask whether that particular solution had
ever solved any problem.) The new Child Law that was passed in
1905 spelled out the state's responsibility for the care of children. The law opened the way for the forcible removal of children from their parents, something that increased the need for
round-the-clock institutions in which to place children. One consequence was that, just as the original reason for the detention
cells as places of temporary detention disappeared, new possibilities for the detention home in Copenhagen were opened.

The detention home and cells were built at a time when children were to be seen and not heard. The same has been true—on the
whole—of the history of the detention homes; we can see that they
were there, but we don't hear why. Neither at the time, nor in later
years, did the school or its historians waste many words on them.
"God, I thought it was all a cock-and-bull story," said one, and,
"Can it really be true?" said another of the persons I sought out in
order to write the history of the detention homes. But it is true, even
if it seems strange today to think that the school, in fact, had to
struggle to attain the central and assumed, almost God-given place
in childhood that it holds today. The establishment and later the
abolition of detention cells were an integral part of that struggle.

Endnotes

1.   This is an expanded version of the article "Internaternes og skolens historie. Eller
     'Den lille innesperringen,'" in Petter Aasen and Alfred O. Telhaug, eds., *Takten,
     Takten Pass på takten. Studier i den offentlige opdragelsens historie* (Oslo: Norsk
     Gyldendal, 1992), pp. 133–156. I would like to thank the clerk of the school
     administration in Frederiksberg, Jørgen Sindholt; the clerk at the archives of the
     town of Frederiksberg, Max Anderson; and the librarian of the Pigeon Street
     School (Duevejen Skole), Lise Landbo. See also Ning de Coninck-Smith, "Paa
     den mest ryggesløse Maade. Et kapitel af gadedrengenes historie. Esbjerg og
     det øvrige Danmark 1890–1914" ["In the Most Dissolute Way. A Chapter in the
     History of Street Children, Esbjerg and the Rest of Denmark, 1890–1914"], in
     Byens rum, byens liv [The Space of the City, the Life of the City], special issue of
     Den jyske Historiker, Århus, October 1991, pp. 71–90.
2.   Recollection no. 490, Copenhagen City Archives, emphasis added.

3.   Michel Foucault, *Discipline and Punish. The Birth of the Prison* (New York: Vintage Books, 1977).
4.   See Carlo Ginzburg, *The Cheese and the Worms. The Cosmos of a 16th Century Miller* (London: Routledge and Kegan Paul, 1980); Carlo Ginzburg, "Clues, Roots of an Evidential Paradigm," in *Clues, Myths and the Historical Method* (Baltimore and London: Johns Hopkins University Press, 1989) pp. 96–125.
5.   It was not until the Child Law of 1905 that the way was opened for the forcible removal of children without the parents' consent. Earlier, this had been possible only in the cases of children receiving public assistance.
6.   Quoted here from the Frederiksberg School Committee's Protocol on Discussions, 1911–19, p. 124, meeting on September 3, 1913. The communication to the ministry is printed in Joakim Larsen, *Oversigt over Udviklingen af Fredriksberg Kommunes offentlige Skolevaesen [Overview of the Development of the Public School System of the Town of Frederiksberg]*, published by the Frederiksberg School Committee, 1886, appendix 19. The ministry's response can be found in the circular of June 6, 1876. See also the Frederiksberg Town Council's transcripts of the discussions in meetings on April, 20, 1876, and October 5, 1876.
7.   Peter Gstettner, *Die Eroberung des Kindes durch die Wissenschaft. Aus der Geschichte der Disziplinierung* (Hamburg: Rowhohlt Verlag, 1981), p. 66.
8.   Report from Frederiksberg Parish School, June 1, 1876 to Frederiksberg Parish School Committee. Case file, Frederiksberg Parish School Committee, 1876 (archives of the Town of Frederiksberg, Frederiksberg Town Hall).
9.   Instruction for the caretakers of Frederiksberg parish schools, appendix 1, in Larsen, *Oversigt.*
10. Report of November 30, 1893, from Frederiksberg School Committee to the Committee of June 2,1893, concerning Removal of Children with Wicked Tendencies from the Home and School. Ministry of Ecclesiastical Affairs and Public Instruction, 2nd Office, 1893–94.
11. Ning de Coninck-Smith, "Internatet, Københavns kommunes Internat på Vesterfaelledvej 1879–1905" [The Detention Home: The City of Copenhagen's Detention Home on Vesterfaelled Street, 1879–1905], *Social Kritik*, No. 17 (November 1991), pp. 56–82.
12. *Socialdemokraten [The Social Democrat]*, June 18, 1913.
13. *Vor Ungdom [Our Youth]*, 1879, p. 211–212, emphasis added.
14. Copenhagen School Board's report to the Copenhagen City Council, December 29, 1897, printed as a supplement to the city council's printed proceedings, 58th volume, 1897–98.
15. Emil Rolsted, "Om forsømte og forvildede Børn og unge Menneskers Opdragelse med saerlig Hensyn til kjøbenhavnske Forhold" *[Of Neglected and Delinquent Children and the Upbringing of Young People, with Special Attention to Conditions in Copenhagen]*. Speech given to the Pedagogical Society, January 10, 1887, printed in *Berlingske Tidende*, No. 10 (January 13) and No. 18 (January 22), 1887.
16. Notebooks of the Director, Vols. I–XVIII, February 1882–January 1906 [Notiser bd. I–XVIII], e.g., boys No. 492, 508, and 750.
17. Notebooks of the Director, boy No. 1,157.
18. Notebooks of the Director, boys No. 576, 1,099, 1,057, 1,143, 1,248, 1,354 and 1,356. See also the Annual Report 1901 [Arsberetningen, 1901] in "Annual report from the Copenhagen Schooldirector" [Aarsberetning fra Kjøbenhavns Borger- og Almueskolevæsen].
19. Report from Ålborg School Committee, November 1993, to the Committee of June 2, 1893, concerning Removal of Children with Wicked Tendencies from Home and School 1893–94 [Kommissionen af 2.6.1893 vedr. Fjernelse af Boern med daarlige Tilboejeligheder fra Hjemmet og Skolen]; Ning de Coninck-Smith, "Paa den mest ryggesløse Maade,"Den jyske Historiker, vol. 56, October 1991, pp. 71–90.

20. *Socialdemokraten,* June 20, 1913.
21. *Socialdemokraten,* June 24, 1913.
22. See *Københavns Kommuneskole,* Nos. 44, 45, and 46, 1913, and Nos. 1, 14, 18, and 19, 1914.
23. *Berlingske Aften,* June 19, 1913.
24. *Berlingske Morgen,* June 20, 1913; *Københavneren,* June 20, 1913.
25. *Socialdemokraten,* June 20, 1913.
26. Quoted from *Folkeskolen,* 1913, p. 330. See also *Københavns Kommuneskole,* No. 26, 1913.
27. Frederiksberg Parish School Committee, case file No. 190, 1913, and letter to the school principals of December 12, 1913, in the school committee's copybook (Archives of the Town of Frederiksberg, Frederiksberg Town Hall).
28. See the Frederiksberg Parish School Committee's case files for 1913, file No. 164, letter of November 29, 1913, from the Frederiksberg Technical Board to the School Committee (Archives of the Town of Frederiksberg, Frederiksberg Town Hall).
29. The Corporation of Copenhagen [Københavns Magistrat], First Section, case file no. 579, 1910 (Copenhagen City Archives).
30. De Coninck-Smith, "Internatet, Københavns kommunes Internat på Vester-faelledvej 1879–1905."
31. Report of November 30, 1893 (cf. note 19).
32. Undated enclosure with the Director's Annual Report for 1880. In the package "Forskellige Koncepter" [Various Concepts] (Detention Home Archives in the Copenhagen City Archives).
33. The inspiration came from the so-called Mannheim system. In the city of Mannheim, Germany, beginning in the 1901–2 school year, pupils had been divided into three groups: there were eight grades for the normally gifted, four to five refresher classes with a concluding class for the less gifted, and three remedial classes for the slow learner. See *Vor Ungdom,* 1903, pp. 792–796.

Chapter Five
Regulating the Regulators
The Disciplining of Teachers in Nineteenth-Century Ontario

Harry Smaller

Much is made in the North American educational histories about the disciplining of students—both in a positive, curricular context, and, more often, in a negative context of corporal, psychological, and other forms of punishment and control. By contrast, much less mention has been made of the ways in which teachers, from the very inception of state schooling systems, have also been subjects of regulation, supervision, and control. This disciplining has emanated from a number of sources, ranging from inspectors and school trustees to parents and even students. Further, while these forms of control have existed throughout the length of individual teachers' work lives, they have also operated strongly during teacher training programs. This paper attempts to describe some of the conditions and events pertaining to the supervision and disciplining of teachers in nineteenth-century Ontario, and to examine these controls within the context of the overall raison d'etre of the schooling system.

By the third decade of the nineteenth century, residents in Ontario (like their counterparts across eastern North America) had established a wide array of educational settings for themselves and their children—schools, Sunday schools, libraries, educational associations, apprenticeships, and so on.[1] Where parent groups themselves originated schools for their children, teachers were sometimes located through newspaper advertising.[2] In some cases, contracts were signed, such as this example of an 1826 agreement in Norfolk County, stating, "We the undersigned being deeply impressed with the necessity and utility of giving our children an education . . . And being desirous and anxious of having a school taught for that desirable purpose. Therefore we mutually agree to engage C. D. Shiemerhorn to teach said school. . . ."[3]

Another common method for establishing schools involved teachers themselves taking the initiative, and canvassing their community in the hopes of enrolling enough students to make the project financially feasible. W. Kerr of the Peterborough area explained that in 1839 he was "in communication with the whole neighbourhood" and successfully signed up sufficient parents to open a school in that district.[4] Parents hired, or at least paid for, their children's teachers, and to a great extent, teachers were directly accountable to the parents of the children they taught. These social relations may not always have been simple, especially given the possibility of differences among parents, from time to time, about what constituted good teachers and good teaching. However, it is probably safe to conclude that relations between parents and teachers during these times were relatively direct. Residents everywhere put enormous amounts of time, energy, and resources into building, equipping, and staffing schoolhouses. They were clearly interested in doing as much as was financially possible to provide schooling for their children, and where the comments and opinions of teachers of that time are available today, many remark on the commitment of these early residents. Edmund Harrison, for example, a Middlesex County teacher during this time, "always found . . . people ready to respond to any suggestions [for schoolhouse improvements], and to ensure any reasonable expenditure, according to their means."[5]

Again, while conditions varied in communities across the province, a number of reports suggest that community response extended well beyond the schoolhouse itself, to supporting the teacher. "Boarding in" was a common form of accommodation for teachers new to the community—in fact, common for women and men in many trades during and since those times.[6] While members of the educational elite railed against these practices (as we will see below), in fact many teachers appreciated the opportunity to be supported by, and to interrelate with, local community members at this level— teachers like Susan Flynn in West Guillimbury in 1837, who found herself "always a welcome guest, and was invariably treated as one of the family," and Irene Ireland of Augusta Township, for whom "a good home was provided amongst [the community] and pleasant social relations existed between teacher and people."[7] Judging from these kinds of reports, this "leveling" of relations between teachers and local residents might well have had salutary effects on all concerned. As John Ireland, a teacher in the small town of Fergus during this era, commented, "Some of the families I thought were more in need of board than able to give it. . . . Very often, however, I stayed, by invitation, overtime."[8] For the community's part, having a teacher in close contact with parents helped to promote integration, and common ground on expectations for school performance. P. Jordan, who taught in the small community of Williamsburg in 1849, stated that he "always enjoyed it [boarding] as it was an excellent way of becoming familiar with the different families."[9]

Rise of the School Promoters

As contrasted to the opinions, interests, and activities of local residents during the 1820s and 1830s, education began to take on a very different meaning among the political, religious, and economic elite in the province. Focused in the dominant media of the time—newspapers, speeches, government documents—concerns were increasingly being voiced that the existing educational settings were not adequate for the needs of the colony. In the words of William Craigie of Ancaster in 1839, for example, the "present provisions for Education are extremely defective, and inadequate to the wants of the Province."[10] Teachers, in the words of one contemporary, were often "transient persons or common idlers . . . frequently [providing] vulgar, low-bred, vicious and intemperate examples" for their students.[11]

What was needed instead, according to these particular spokespeople, was a universal, state-supported common school system. While details in their speeches, articles, and reports varied (including the amount of involvement that the local population should have in running their schools), the essence was clear: all children should be enrolled in schools that used a common curriculum and were taught by government-trained, -certified, and -supervised teachers.[12]

There was no question that these concerns were being raised within a very specific socioeconomic context: the 1830s in Upper Canada was a period of deep economic recession, high unemployment, high rates of immigration from similarly poverty-stricken areas of the British Isles, and considerable social disruption over-all. It is not surprising, therefore, that these appeals by the elite for new forms of schooling emphasized not necessarily the increased acquisition of academic skills and knowledge, but certainly the formation of proper "character" among the youth of the colony. "No man possessed of property," went the exhortations of one such school promoter, "could hesitate for a moment to pay any reason-able tax for the support of education, as he would be thereby in-creasing the value of his estate, and securing himself and his pos-terity in the possession of it."[13]

In 1835 the House of Assembly of Upper Canada commissioned Dr. Charles Duncombe and two other community leaders to under-take a study in the United States of, among a number of other issues, "the system and management of Schools and Colleges, and such other matters as are connected with the interest, welfare, and prosperity of this Province."[14] Their report, tabled a year later, strongly criticized the status quo, claiming that the province's "schools want in character, they want respectability, they want permanency in their character." The alternative was clear indeed: "Whatever may have been the state of things heretofore, it is criminal to acquire knowl-edge merely for the sake of knowledge. The man must be disciplined and furnished according to the duties that lie before him."[15] What was needed to effect these moral changes, according to Duncombe, was not "the lame and the lazy" teacher who leaves students' minds "both sluggish and deformed," but rather "teachers [who are] cor-rect gentlemanly persons well prepared for their arduous responsible office, and fit models for the youth of the country to imitate."[16]

In 1841, following the bloody but unsuccessful 1837–38 rebel-lions against colonial rule in Ontario and Quebec, the first Com-mon School Act was passed. This act provided for an unprecedented £50,000 to be allocated annually for local elementary schools, di-vided between Upper and Lower Canada in proportion to school enrollments—a far cry from the £2,500 that had been designated annually from the central coffers for schooling in Upper Canada in the 1820s and 1830s. The purpose of this legislation was clear: to begin the process of establishing a centralized school system aimed at promoting the moral regulation of the youth of the province.

Unfortunately, neither this legislation, nor a major revision in

1843, were seen (by many of the elite, at least) as being at all effective in producing the desired changes to the status quo. The removal of compulsory religious instruction, for example, certainly exercised Anglican Bishop John Strachan. Only through proper religious indoctrination, he exhorted in a letter in 1844, would the schools become effective in developing proper character among the youth of the colony. After all, "scarcely any" Anglicans, who had been properly raised in religious schools, were found in the "ranks of the Rebellion" of 1837. Rather, the vast majority were "foremost in defending the Government, and restoring peace and order." Further, according to Strachan, "Their conduct was a noble illustration of the instruction which they had received, obedience to lawful authority and the strict discharge of all the domestic and social duties; the discouragement of rash innovation, and the avoidance of those who are given to change."[17]

By September of 1844 another religious leader, Egerton Ryerson, had been appointed assistant superintendent (later superintendent) of education, a position he was to occupy for the ensuing thirty-two years. Within a month of assuming office, he left for a fourteen-month tour of schools in the United States, England, Ireland, and several European nations. He clearly found most favor with school systems, such as those of France and especially Prussia, that were highly organized, routinized, and centralized. Out of this study tour came first his lengthy "Report on a System of Public Elementary Instruction for Upper Canada," and then the draft for what was to become the Common School Act of 1846.[18]

Under the provisions of this legislation, local residents in each school section were to elect annually a board of three school trustees, which would be responsible for establishing a school and hiring a teacher. In addition to these local boards, however, several higher levels of authority were also put in place: official school visitors (local religious, political, and judicial officials), district school superintendents, and a provincial General Board of Education consisting of seven members appointed by the governor. At the top of this hierarchy there was to be a single central authority—a provincial superintendent of education, with powers to recommend regulations and oversee results across the system. In the words of historian Bruce Curtis, "The School Act of 1846 completely transformed the principles of educational organization at the elementary level in Canada West. It removed in principle most of the educational autonomy enjoyed by local educational consumers and put in place a set of administrative structures in which respectable members of local elites would be charged with much of educational management. These officials were situated in largely bureaucratic authority structures."[19]

Henceforth, these "respectable members," at both the local and provincial level, were to develop and enforce a new regime of moral regulation on, and through, an increasingly centralized schooling system. Students were the ultimate focus of this project, but for this project to succeed, every classroom in the province needed an appropriate director and role model. As Ryerson pointed out in the regulations he drew up to accompany the Common School Act of 1846,

A Teacher should be a person of Christian sentiment, of calm temper, and discretion; he should be imbued with the spirit of peace, of obedience to the law, and of loyalty to his Sovereign; he should not only possess the art of communicating knowledge, but also be capable of molding the mind of youth, and of giving to the power, which education confers, a useful direction.[20]

Over the ensuing decades of the nineteenth century, teachers became the focus of increasing regulation—an array of controls that extended over much of their lives, beginning well before their first day of paid employment. As Ryerson was to remark in a circular to all school superintendents in 1846, "The law makes special mention of the moral character of School Teachers."[21]

Teacher Training

Among the early school promoters, proper teacher training was held crucial, if a centralized schooling system was to impart the proper "character" on the youth of the province. In his 1836 report, Charles Duncombe was adamant on the matter: "Schools for the education of teachers should be immediately established and supported out of a fund permanently appropriated for that purpose."[22] A decade later, School Superintendent Ryerson was, if anything, even more determined that effective and universal teacher training form a corner-stone of his new system. "There cannot be good Schools without good Teachers," he argued in his 1846 report; "nor can there be, as a general rule, good Teachers . . . unless persons are trained for the profession." In Ryerson's mind, teacher training institutions were crucial to this project. "It is now universally admitted," he stated, "that Seminaries for the training of Teachers are absolutely necessary to an efficient System of Public Instruction,—nay, as an integral part, as the vital principle of it."[23]

By 1847, Ryerson was able to open the first normal school in the province. As much as he wished to ensure that only those with the highest academic qualifications would be accepted, in order to maintain enrollments academic standards remained very low. Even eight years after it opened, for example, the principal found it neces-sary to caution Ryerson that, in spite of the mounting criticism in the press, any attempt to screen out students, even on the basis of their bad spelling, would result in a very depleted enrollment in-deed.[24] Because of this low academic level, much of the normal school curriculum was oriented toward a "cram course" in the basics. As one regional superintendent reported to Ryerson in 1850, "Some of the Normal School Students have confessed to me that they were highly displeased with their circumstances. They are allowed, or rather forced, to skim over as many subjects in one Session, as, for any practical purpose, would rationally take two or three years. . . . [Being] overpushed, they become so far disgusted with the Books they have gone over . . . it trains them to be content with superficial views of the most important subjects."[25]

As compared with the wide latitude allowed for academic profi-ciency, however, what was clearly required and enforced throughout the normal school training was a high degree of moral self-regula-tion. Every applicant was required to submit a written character reference completed by a religious official who knew the applicant personally. In addition, careful face-to-face examination of all appli-cants was undertaken, not only by normal school staff, but also by Ryerson himself. "The Masters have, ever since its establishment, had almost daily consultations with me respecting occurrences and matters connected with the operation of this Institution."[26] As late as 1865, almost twenty years after the school's founding, Ryerson mentioned at a meeting of the Ontario Teachers' Association that he had been up "since six o'clock in the morning in examining and admitting new students to the Normal School."[27] Once students were enrolled at the school, proper behavior and decorum were both inculcated and closely monitored. Regulations required that students remain for at least one full semester before being eligible for graduation—not to ensure adequate academic development necessarily, but rather, in the words of the principal of the normal school, to allow enough time for the faculty to form an adequate opinion about each candidate's "personal habits, general tone of mind, and *style*."[28] Through the first several decades of operation, innumerable infractions were officially noted by the staff of the school, and punishments, ranging up to expulsion, inflicted.

Of particular note, in light of the overall raison d'etre of the newly emerging centralized schooling system, was the attention given to enforcing regulations relating to "proper" gender relations. Students entered and exited classes through gender-separate doors and corridors, and practice-taught in separate model schools. In the words of the architect of the building, "By this arrangement, it will be seen that except when actually in the presence of the Master, the male and female students will be entirely separated."[29] Informal communication between male and female students was completely prohibited, under pain of expulsion from the college. William Irvine of Kingston, for example, was removed from the rolls in the mid-1850s for misproprieties including that of "attempting to communicate with the female portion of the class."[30] This level of regulation was not bounded by the temporal or geographic location of the Normal School itself. Outside of school hours, and away from the school site, student-teachers were in no way free from this intrusive regulation of their morals, behavior, and deportment. Those enrolling from outside Toronto, regardless of their age or marital status, were required to live in boarding homes that had been carefully selected, and were continually inspected, by normal school staff, according to very specific criteria. The official regulations stated clearly that

1. All the Pupils-in-Training are expected to lead an orderly and regular life,—to be in their respective Lodgings every night before half-past Nine O'Clock, and to attend their respective places of Worship with strict regu-

larity. Any improprieties of conduct will be brought under the special notice of the Board of Education.

2. They are required to assemble in the Normal School every morning at the appointed hour, Nine O'Clock, when the Roll will be called, and any person failing to answer to his name will be called upon to explain the cause of such irregularity, and his explanation, if not deemed satisfactory, will be submitted to the Chief Superintendent of Schools, or to the Board.[31]

The fact that one female student was suspended by normal school officials during this period for speaking to a fellow student, while on a boat returning them home for vacation, suggests that the Upper Canada schooling reformers' agenda for moral regulation during teacher preparation was stark indeed.[32]

Teacher Examination and Certification

Another dominant aspect of teachers' lives throughout the second half of the nineteenth century was the pressing matter of certification. With the passage of the Common School Act of 1846 came the first system of teacher examination and certification in the province—an extensive array of legislation and regulations, ensuring that proper officials would be able "to examine all persons . . . with respect to their moral character, learning and ability."[33] At the outset, two levels of teaching certificates were established. Appointed district superintendents were empowered to examine teachers, and issue either a "General" certificate, good for anywhere in the district until revoked, or a "Special" certificate, good only for "one year in the School specified."[34] Renewal of this latter certificate (by far the more common of the two) meant an annual trip to the district seat, in order to undergo an examination before this educational official. In order to deal with immediate local needs, any two official "school visitors," clearly defined in the legislation as including only local religious, political, and judicial officials, had the power in emergencies to issue the special certificate to a local teacher. These certificates were backed up by the proviso that no teacher could receive, in Ryerson's later words, "a farthing" of provincial grant money unless the teacher possessed one.[35]

Much has been made about the inconsistencies in the actual

implementation of this examination process across the province. Depending upon the time, place, and examiners involved, the testing process for teachers often turned out to be either petty, or onerous in the extreme. Richard Unsworth and Margaret McPhail both stated that they began teaching in 1849 without having to undergo any form of examination, while the entire 1843 examination process for W. R. Bigg, he claimed, consisted of spelling the word "summons."[36] On the other hand, many other teachers during this time were clearly put to the task, in attempting to convince state-appointed examiners that they were suitable for conducting the proper guidance (moral and otherwise) of the province's youth. For example, one teacher reported during this time that, in addition to a written examination, he was required to spend "two hours oral wrestling with Reading, Grammar, Arithmetic and Geography."[37] Nor were these examinations necessarily dealt with sympathetically by the examiners. Superintendent Thornton of Gore District (west of Toronto) explained in 1850 that he had failed one teacher, partly because "he mispronounced not fewer than five words."[38] These contradictions suggest, if nothing else, that certification of teachers during the mid-nineteenth century depended largely upon the subjective opinions of the local elite as to the "propriety" of individuals who should be allowed to teach the young people of the community.

With the passage of the Common School Act of 1850, and further revisions in 1860, certification procedures became very onerous indeed for most of the province's teachers. Only those who had been in a financial position to attend (and successfully complete) the normal school program in Toronto could rest assured that their certificates would allow them to teach whenever and wherever they could obtain a teaching position in the province.[39] By comparison, the vast majority were required to earn their certificates through annual self-study, followed by increasingly standardized examinations held each year under the supervision of "county boards" of examiners, consisting of the school superintendents and grammar school principals of each county.[40] As the second half of the nineteenth century progressed, control over the entire teacher examination process was increasingly shifted to central officials in Toronto—not only over individual teachers in the province, but also over the regional and local structures which had originally been put into place. In 1860, the provincial Council of Public Instruction was given power to issue its own certificates, as well as to set minimum standards for all levels of teaching certificates offered by local examining boards. With the next major overhaul of the School Act in 1871, local county examining boards lost all control over the content of teachers' annual examinations. Henceforth, examination papers would

all be prepared [in Toronto] under the direction of the Council of Public Instruction . . . and sent to the County Inspectors under seal, not to be broken except on the day and place of Examination of Candidates, and in their presence. The Examination will take place on the same day and at the same hour, at the place of Municipal Council Meetings in all the Counties and Cities of the Province.[41]

In addition, county boards could no longer offer first-class certificates; these would be reserved for the central Department of Education.[42] The standards for achieving second- and third-class teaching certificates were also raised significantly, with the proviso that the latter were now to be valid for only three years, and "not renewable, unless under very special circumstances."[43] Finally, from 1877 onwards, all examinations for first- and second-class teachers' certificates were sent to the Department of Education offices in Toronto for marking.

In spite of the increasing severity of the content of the examinations, however, these county board certificates allowed their holders to teach only in certain areas, or for certain fixed periods of time, after which another round of study and testing was required. Continued employment was perpetually dependent upon passing these exams each year. In addition, it is certainly clear that this continual escalation of "standards" for teachers had little to do with their actual proficiency in the classroom (other than in evaluating their worth as proper models of proper morals). In fact, it may well have proved counterproductive in this regard. One local official reported, following the 1871 changes in regulations, that teachers in his jurisdiction were forced to spend much of their waking hours cramming for these exams. As a result, their own teaching had become "irksome" and "unsatisfactory." In attempting to pass their own exams, he complained, "they have overlooked the necessity of learning how to teach others."[44]

Supervision and Inspection

Among the other regulatory aspects of the ever-enlarging nineteenth-century state school system, ongoing and effective inspection of schools and teachers also weighed heavily in the minds of the schooling promoters. Charles Duncombe, for example, stated adamantly in his 1836 report, "Competent common school teacher inspectors should be appointed to prevent the disqualified from entering into the responsible *profession* of teaching."[45] Ryerson was even more exercised about the importance of proper supervision and inspection. In his 1846 report on schooling, he made his position clear indeed.

There is no class of officers in the whole machinery of elementary instruction on whom so much depends for its efficient and successful working, as upon the local Superintendents or Inspectors. The proper selection of this class of persons is a matter of the greatest importance.[46]

According to the School Act of 1846, all levels of officials who had been given power to certify teacher—local school visitors, and township and county level school superintendents—were also mandated to oversee their work in the schoolhouses of the province. In many locales, these officials moved quickly to regiment all facets of teachers' activities—their pedagogy, the textbooks they used, and their relations in the communities. Although these new forms of control aroused animosities among many teachers (as well as among many parents, accustomed as they had been to almost complete local autonomy over the schooling of their children), these early steps marked just the beginning of a lengthy process of centralizing the control over teachers and teaching practices.[47] In 1850, regulations were changed again, now requiring school superintendents to visit schools at least four times a year, with the power to annul certificates of teachers they found wanting.

The effects of these new regulations on teachers was marked

indeed. Throughout the next decade, the office of the Department of Education in Toronto was inundated with letters from teachers and parents in communities across the province complaining about the high-handed and arbitrary ways in which they were being regulated. For example, Mrs. Merry of Esquesing Township was engaged in a lengthy struggle during this time to regain a certificate that her superintendent "unjustly withheld." As she explained to Superintendent Ryerson in a lengthy letter, his "judgement errs."[48]

With the next major change in school legislation in 1871, structures and processes for the inspection of teachers were further enhanced. Henceforth, all local school inspectors were to be employed only full-time, rather than serving as part-time officials while undertaking other occupations in the community. In Ryerson's words, they were to be "wholly devoted to the duties of their office . . . at least five days in the week."[49] While county boards still had authority over the hiring and firing of these officials, they could choose only from those candidates who had been examined by the provincial Department of Education, and whose names appeared on an official provincewide list. However, in spite of (or because of) these new regulations for selecting school inspectors, it would appear that many teachers and parents were not any more satisfied with this new array of schooling officials than they had been during the previous two decades. While Ryerson was to emphasize the ideal of these new officials assisting teachers in their work, evidence in the literature seems to suggest that routines of inspection and evaluation were much more the norm. Even the relatively conservative journal the *Ontario Teacher* was forced to report, two years after the legislative changes, that, while "the Inspectors are supposed to be capable of doing a number of things, unfortunately owing to the peculiar nature of some of the appointments to that office, by means of special certificates of eligibility, a few are deficient in the necessary attainments."[50] In fact, in an earlier issue that year, the same journal had given space to an inspector who had very specific ideas about proper classroom management, as he described a classroom scene of which he obviously approved, if not relished: "Orderly as the Royal Foot Guards, the little battalion marched to the front and toed a red line painted on the floor near the platform."[51]

By the end of the decade, another schooling journal was to publish a letter from a classroom teacher, complaining about "crotchety inspectors" who "tyrannize" teachers in "a manner that few are aware of."[52] In this light, it is perhaps no coincidence that a school inspector of this era was to report that this "efficient inspection incurred active hostility in some places." By 1878, these officials had banded together, in "unanimous . . . support of a motion that the power of [their] removal from office should be transferred [from local control] to the Education Department."[53]

Regulating Teachers in Their Local Communities

Moral regulation of teachers during the nineteenth century extended well beyond their activities and duties in the school classroom. Social relations with local parents and residents was also an area of concern for school promoters, anxious as they were to construct teachers as models of proper moral disposition among the "backward" residents of the province. This concern on the part of the schooling elite showed itself most clearly in relation to the housing arrangements for teachers. If teachers were to maintain this position as a moral beacon for the community, it was clear, at least in the eyes of their superiors, that they would have to distance themselves, physically and attitudinally, from the direct influence of local residents. Given the economic conditions of the times, however, "boarding in" with local parents was commonplace among teachers—something that clearly exercised school officials throughout the nineteenth century. Robert Murray, the first assistant superintendent of education in Ontario, protested in 1842 that teachers' "minds have become dissipated" as a result of not being able "to choose either their place or their company." Even worse were those who "chose" to live

in the lowest taverns, and consequently to associate with the lowest and most dissipated characters in the neighbourhood. By this daily intercourse with bar-room politicians and bar-room divines they insensibly become assimilated to them in their manners, views and habits, and are thus rendered utterly disqualified for conducting the education of youth.[54]

Edward Scarlett, the county superintendent for Northumberland, was to express his disdain in 1856 for that "class of cheap Teachers, who never remonstrate for a moment against the evil of 'boarding 'round' from house to house." Their sin, he emphasized, was that "they often ingratiate themselves with members of the families with whom they are boarding." As much to blame, Scarlett felt, were "their abbettors [sic] in office,—men who feel a deep sympathy for them and with all good nature, license them to go out and blight the growing intellect of the youth of our Country."[55] The schooling elite were quite correct in their assumptions that parents, residents, and even students also played a significant role in shaping the values and behavior of many teachers across the province during these times.[56]

Ironically, as active as these school promoters were in the many aspects of restructuring the province's schools, they were exceedingly unable (or unwilling) to change regulations in the one area that clearly would have allowed teachers to establish their own separate households in local communities. At no time during the nineteenth century were any formal steps taken to establish (let alone enforce) minimum levels of salaries or other material conditions of work for teachers. Rather, teachers were continually bombarded, throughout the nineteenth century, with the message that their material conditions would change only when they had shown themselves to be professionals and improved themselves through individual study and dedication.

The Regulatory Role of Teachers' Associations

Finally, it is worth examining briefly the complex role of teacher associations during the nineteenth century, especially within the overall context of state involvement in teachers' affairs. It was first during the 1840s that local teachers' associations began appearing in communities across the province of Upper Canada. There is no question that their manifestation at this time was directly related to developments in the rise of the centralized state schooling system. As more and more provincial regulations were put into place, controlling the payment of teachers' salaries on the one hand and increasing the necessity of credentialism on the other, teachers found that they had to group together in order to develop leverage with state officials to moderate these controls. No longer could individual teachers simply count on their own personal relations with their local communities to negotiate and determine their material conditions.[57] Ironically, during this time the provincial schooling elite were also active in promoting teachers' associations—but certainly not for the same purposes as those initiated and run by classroom teachers for their own material protection. Rather, schooling promoters began looking to teachers' organizations as means through which teachers could not only be regulated, but even self-regulated. Ryerson, for example, reported that he had personally observed in Prussia the "happiest effect" of teachers who came "together at proper intervals, and under judicious arrangements." Through such teachers' associations, he reported, "the most accomplished minds would give a tone to the others; roughness and peculiarities of manner would be rubbed off." As a result, "men would learn . . . the manner of keeping their position in society."[58] By 1850, he was to inform teachers, in a provincewide circular, that a proper teachers' organization was a body of "intelligence and virtue" that would be able to promote "mutual improvement" through "professional zeal and emulation." Teachers themselves would assume responsibility for the "purg[ing]," from among their own ranks, "of every inebriate, every blasphemer, every ignorant idler, who cannot teach and will not learn."[59]

Not surprisingly then, where it was absolutely clear to Ryerson that an association was being formed on such principles, especially under the direct supervision of an education official, he expressed satisfaction. "I am glad to learn that you have got the teachers in your great township to form an association for their mutual improvement," went one such response to a local school superintendent's report.[60] What, by contrast, apparently did not find favor with Ryerson were organizations such as the Eastern District Schools' Association, consisting solely of common school teachers who stated firmly that "the members of this association are fully competent to manage their own affairs." Along the margin of a series of resolutions that the group had sent to the Education Department, in the hopes that they "may be published in the *Journal of Education*," Ryerson had written instructions to his clerk: "No answer needed."[61] Ryerson had good reason for not wanting to publicize the activities of this group, for the entire decade of the 1850s was marked by considerable tension between local teachers' associations and the Department of Education. Clearly, teachers across the province were concerned, not so much about "professional zeal" and "virtue," but rather about maintaining job security and basic salaries in light of increasing state pressures against this possibility.

Given these strained relations between local teachers' associations and state officials, it is not surprising that the latter group would be anxious to develop new structures to undermine the effects of these autonomous local organizations. In January of 1861, a number of provincial education officials, with the involvement of Ryerson, arranged for the founding of a provincial organization called the Teachers' Association of Canada West. In spite of the reference to "teachers" in its title, in fact few classroom teachers were actively involved in its operation. Rather, the TACW (to be renamed the Ontario Teachers' Association in 1867) remained solidly under the control of state education officials for the rest of the century, and well into the 1900s, with a clear agenda of legitimizing and promoting increased professionalization, centralization, and bureaucratization in the minds of teachers across the province.[62] Concomitant with these ideological aspects, the Teachers' Association of Canada West also worked actively to regulate the credentials and behavior of its members. Speakers at annual conventions exhorted teachers to "long and severe application" of study in order to pass certificate examinations; if they were not prepared to "employ such diligence for improvement in their profession, they ought to leave it."[63] Equally, teachers were goaded at these conventions to accept the "need" for increased regulation within the "profession." For example, in the words of a "guest" speaker, "care must be taken to maintain and elevate the standard of the Teacher's qualifications; so that . . . the teacher is secured in what belongs to the dignity and efficiency of his profession."[64]

By the 1870s, provincial regulation of teachers had developed to the point that even their local associations, which to that point had been somewhat independent from direct governmental control, were taken over by the state. No longer were teachers free to meet under their own terms. In 1874, regulations were passed, stating clearly that

All masters and teachers in cities, towns and villages shall regularly attend the teachers' meetings, at such time, and under such regulations, as the Inspector shall direct; and they shall by study, recitation and general exercises, strive to systematize and perfect the modes of discipline and of teaching in the Public Schools.[65]

To be sure, there is no doubt that the sites of these local and provincial association meetings often served as sites for overt resistance on the part of some teachers who objected to this increasing regulation of their personal and pedagogical beliefs and practices.[66] Overall however, these associations, controlled as they were by state officials and those with similar outlooks, proved to be very influential in regulating the role of teachers, and teaching, in the province's schools.

Conclusion

As elsewhere in North America, the political and economic elite during the middle decades of the nineteenth century in Ontario were active in significantly altering the controls and structures of schooling—transitions that were not unrelated to the changing political, economic, and social events of the times. Increasingly, the provincial state assumed (or wrested) the regulation and control of teaching from the hands of local communities, in order to ensure that schools would, in the words of the school superintendent, fulfill the "wants of the age."[67] Moral regulation of the population—that is, moral regulation of a particular form—became the overall purpose of this newly restructured schooling system. Understandably then, in the minds of these elite, teachers clearly stood at the focal point of this change. In order that these new schooling objectives be achieved successfully, teachers themselves—those who would serve to instill these new values in the youth of the province—would have to be carefully trained and screened for this crucial social task.

Endnotes

1. During the first four decades of the nineteenth century, the present-day province of Ontario was entitled Upper Canada (as distinguished from Quebec, which was Lower Canada); from 1841 to the confederation of Canada in 1867, it was entitled Canada West, after which it became Ontario. All three titles will be used in this article. For the most part, these programs were both initiated and financed by the local community. While there was some provincial state provision for the operation of regional grammar schools, beginning in 1816, that provision was not extensive, and in fact diminished in effectiveness over the ensuing two decades that it was in force. J. G. Hodgins, *Documentary History of Education in Upper Canada*, Vol. 1 (Toronto: L. K. Cameron, 1894), pp. 102–104. See also Kari Dehli and Harry Smaller, "Introduction," *Ontario History*, Vol. 85, No.4 (December 1993), pp. 283–289.

2. See, for example, an advertisement in the *Bathurst Courier*, June 12, 1835, offering "liberal wages" for a teacher who can "teach English grammar well" (quoted in R. D. Gidney, "Elementary Education in Upper Canada: A Reassessment," in

Michael B. Katz and Paul H. Mattingly, eds., *Education and Social Change, Themes from Ontario's Past* (New York: New York University Press, 1975), p.16.

3. Norfolk Historical Society Collection, contract dated October 2, 1826, pp. 2761–2762. Quoted in Douglas Lawr and Robert Gidney, *Educating Canadians: A Documentary History of Public Education* (Toronto: Van Nostrand Reinhold, 1973), p. 27.

4. Quoted in J. G. Hodgins, *The Establishment of Schools and Colleges in Ontario, 1792–1910*, Vol. 2 (Toronto: L. K. Cameron, 1910), pp.107–108.

5. Hodgins, *Documentary History*, Vol. 5, p. 275.

6. This matter is discussed in some detail in John Harney, "Boarding and Belonging," *Urban History Review*, Vol. 2, 1978, pp. 8–37.

7. Quoted in Elizabeth Graham, "Schoolmarms and Early Teaching in Ontario," in Janice Acton, Penny Goldsmith, and Bonnie Shepard, eds., *Women at Work, Ontario, 1850–1930* (Toronto: Canadian Women's Educational Press, 1974), p. 185; Hodgins, *Establishment of Schools*, Vol. 1, p. 143.

8. Hodgins, *Documentary History*, Vol. 5, p. 279.

9. Ibid., Vol. 8, p. 300.

10. Ibid., Vol. 3, p. 269.

11. Ibid., Vol. 2, p. 37.

12. The most famous of these reports was undoubtably that undertaken by Reform Party member Charles Duncombe in 1836 (described below). However, John Strachan, Bishop of Toronto, and legislator Robert Baldwin Sullivan were among others to produce reports on education during the 1830s. For more detail on these events, see Bruce Curtis, *Building the Educational State: Canada West, 1836–1871* (London: Althouse Press, 1988), chap. 1.

13. Robert Murray, 1842; quoted in Susan Houston, "Politics, Schools and Social Change in Upper Canada," *Canadian Historical Review*, Vol. 53, 1972, p. 261.

14. Charles Duncombe, *Report on the Subject of Education Made to the Parliament of Upper Canada, 25th February, 1836* (Toronto: M. Reynolds, 1836; S. R. Publishers, 1966), p. 3.

15. Duncombe, *Report*, p. 19.

16. Ibid., p. 63.

17. Hodgins, *Documentary History*, Vol. 5, p. 270.

18. Ibid., Vol. 6, pp. 59–70.

19. Curtis, *Building the Educational State*, pp. 114–115.

20. Hodgins, *Documentary History*, Vol. 6, p. 301.

21. Ibid., Vol. 6, p. 268.

22. Duncombe, *Report*, pp. 63–64.

23. Hodgins, *Documentary History*, Vol. 6, p. 198.

24. Provincial Archives of Ontario, Record Group 2, Series C-6-C, Incoming Correspondence to the Department of Education (hereafter C-6-C), Robertson to Ryerson, February 26, 1855.

25. Hodgins, *Documentary History*, Vol. 9, pp. 57–58.

26. Provincial Archives of Ontario, Record Group 2, E-1, Box 1, Folder 1, Draft of circular, July 22, 1850.

27. Quoted in the *Toronto Globe*, August 9, 1865.

28. Alison Prentice, "Friendly Atoms in Chemistry: Women and Men at Normal School in Mid-Nineteenth-Century Toronto," in David Keane and Colin Read, eds., *Old Ontario: Essays in Honor of J. M. S. Careless* (Toronto: Dundurn Press, 1989), pp. 285–317.

29. Quoted in ibid., p. 301.

30. Quoted in ibid., p. 301.

31. Hodgins, *Documentary History*, Vol. 7, p. 96.

32. Prentice, "Friendly Atoms," p. 301.

33. Hodgins, *Documentary History*, Vol. 6, p. 62.

34. Ibid., Vol. 6, p. 62.

35. Ibid., Vol. 6, pp. 56–70; Vol. 9, p. 217.

36. Ibid., Vol. 5, pp. 272–273.

37. Ibid., Vol. 5, p. 274.

38. Harry Smaller, "Teachers' Protective Associations, Professionalism and the 'State' in Nineteenth Century Ontario." Ph.D. diss., University of Toronto, 1988, p. 78, n56.

39. During the last three decades of the nineteenth century, provincial-controlled normal schools were opened in three other regional centers of southern Ontario.

40. For example, of the 3,830 teachers employed in the common schools in the province in 1861, only 304 had normal school certificates. Annual Report of the Department of Education of Canada West, 1861, pp. 30–31.

41. Hodgins, *Documentary History,* Vol. 23, p. 75.

42. "The Questions and Answers by Candidates for First-class Provincial Certificates will be forthwith sealed in the presence of the Candidates, and transmitted to the Education Department." Ibid., p. 76.

43. Ibid., p. 75.

44. Ibid., Vol. 25, p. 8. It is probably no coincidence that, as the pressure to succeed at examinations built up over the decade, complaints increased as to incidents of teachers' cheating at these examinations. Finally, in 1877, the government was forced to conduct an inquiry into the matter. See, for example, Ontario Department of Education Annual Report, 1878, pp. 131–132, 134.

45. Duncombe, *Report,* p. 64; emphasis in the original.

46. Hodgins, *Documentary History,* Vol. 6, p. 206.

47. For further elaboration of these intrusions, and resistance to them, see, for example, Curtis, *Building the Educational State;* Harry Smaller, "Teachers' Protective Associations."

48. C-6-C, Merry to Ryerson, January 29, 1849.

49. Hodgins, *Documentary History,* Vol. 23, p. 80.

50. *Ontario Teacher,* Vol. 1, No. 6, June 1873, p. 172.

51. Ibid., Vol. 1, No. 2, February 1873, p. 52.

52. *Canadian Educational Monthly,* Vol. 1, No. 12, December 1879, p. 637.

53. John Dearness, "History of the Ontario Teachers' Association." Unpublished manuscript, Provincial Archives of Ontario, n.d. [1930s], chaps. 21, 23.

54. Quoted in J. G. Hodgins, *Historical and Other Papers and Documents Illustrative of the Educational System of Ontario, 1853–1868,* Vol. 5 (Toronto: L. K. Cameron, 1911), p. 3.

55. Quoted in Hodgins, *Documentary History,* Vol. 13, p. 71.

56. For further discussion of this aspect of early teachers' lives in Upper Canada, see Curtis, *Building the Educational State.*

57. See, for example, Smaller, "Teachers' Protective Associations."

58. Ontario Department of Education Annual Report, 1846, pp. 209–210.

59. *Journal of Education,* Vol. 3, No. 8, August 1850, p. 121.

60. R.G. 2, Series C-2, Drafts of Outgoing Correspondence of the Department of Education (hereafter C-2), Letter Book E, Ryerson to Thornton, July 22, 1850.

61. C-6-C, McDonald to Ryerson, July 9, 1850.

62. See, for example, Harry Smaller, "Gender and Status: The Founding Meeting of the Teachers' Association of Canada West, January 25, 1861," *Historical Studies in Education,* Vol. 6, No. 2, Fall 1994, pp. 201–218; Nancy Christie, "Psychology, Sociology and the Secular Moment: The Ontario Educational Association's Quest for Authority, 1880–1900," *Journal of Canadian Studies,* Vol. 25, No. 2, Summer 1990, pp. 119–143.

63. Hodgins, *Documentary History,* Vol. 23, p. 75.

64. Ibid.

65. *Journal of Education,* Vol. 27, No.11, November 1874, p. 172.

66. See, for example, Harry Smaller, "Teachers' Protective Associations," chap. 5.

67. *Journal of Education,* Vol. 1, No. 2, February 1848, p. 51.

Chapter Six
Good Teachers Are Born, Not Made
Self-Regulation in the Work of Nineteenth-Century American Women Teachers

Kate Rousmaniere

This chapter is a historical analysis of the notion that good teaching is an inherent quality that draws on natural attributes of the individual. In particular, I am interested in the effect that the popular meaning of the "naturally born teacher" had on nineteenth- and early twentieth-century women teachers as they first entered the occupation. By studying the journals of three nineteenth-century women teachers in New England and the student-teacher journal of a kindergarten teacher in Boston in 1904, I analyze the way in which these women experienced an interior regulation of their work: in the privacy of their own home after class, they wrestled with their own personalities and perceived character flaws, struggling to re-create their own thoughts and feelings to fit the popular image of what they had been taught a good teacher should be. According to these women, a good teacher was not only one who acted in certain ways, but one who veritably was a certain kind of person.

The popular notion of a "born teacher" has roots in nineteenth-century school reform literature that constructed teaching as nurturing work intended to develop children's personal, moral, and civic characteristics, and not merely to instruct children in letters and numbers. What nineteenth-century school reformers saw as the humanizing of schooling required also the adaptation of the occupational ethic of teaching from the impersonal delivery of information by untrained and itinerant male teachers to the personal nurturance of children's characters by a feminized teaching force. The notion of an innate attribute of caring and "goodness" in teaching played off of cultural images of nineteenth-century female moral purity, and it neatly corresponded with reformers' efforts to feminize the American teaching force. The very construction of teaching as personal work led all teachers, but women teachers in particular, to internalize and normalize cultural definitions into their own personal identities. The "good teacher," as defined by educators and broader culture, encompassed not only the classroom methods and skills of the practitioner, but also personal, moral, and spiritual qualities of the individual. Through popular and educational discourse, women teachers learned early in their careers to understand good teaching as a natural characteristic based in individual character. But, as new teachers learned in their first days and weeks in the classroom, a teacher's natural strengths were also her natural weaknesses and needed to be corrected by the teacher herself. Thus the emphasis on the individual personality of the teacher laid the weight of classroom problems on the individual personality, emotional makeup, and psyche of the teacher, and isolated the responsibility for the teacher's work away from the social and political context of the school and onto the individual teacher's own identity.

The emphasis of natural and personal qualities of teaching has placed an unusual pressure on teachers. In no other occupation are workers so driven to analyze, self-criticize, and evaluate their own personal behavior, identities, and motivations. In addition, the individualization of teaching has furthered the isolation and exceptionality of teachers' work. The tradition whereby learning how to be a teacher has been an intensely personal and individualized experience has shaped teachers' own perspective and critique of their work, leading teachers to value an isolated, individualistic model of teaching. Learning to become a teacher has been a distinctly individual process so that "becoming a teacher is reduced to an individual struggle" and not a development based on contextual or political elements. The glorification of individual effort has created certain "mythic images" of teachers, which resound in the historical culture of schooling, supporting what Willard Waller identified in the 1930s as the "rugged individual" icon of the American teacher. The individualization of teaching has thus maintained the status quo: problems in teaching are automatically identified as problems of the teacher, and not problems of the system; classroom troubles are experienced by teachers as personal inadequacies, rather than the consequences of the school organization or social forces.[1] Learning to teach has developed as a distinctly personal and individual process, one that is remote from the political and social determinants that actually shape the nature and character of teachers' work and children's learning. As Deborah Britzman argues,

the myth that teachers are self-made serves to cloak the social relationships and the context of school structure by exaggerating personal autonomy. . . . Propelled by the belief that the individual is responsible for what is in fact a product of complex social circumstances, the ideology of blaming the victim ignores the influence of social relationships and historical progression. In the case of learning to teach, the cultural myth of the self-made, isolated, expert teacher supports the ideology of blaming the victim and ultimately promotes a simplistic understanding of the operation of power in educational life.[2]

This paper is a study of the effect of that process on nineteenth- and early twentieth-century women teachers' early struggles to learn how to be a "good teacher." It is a study of the way in which teachers' interior experience of becoming a teacher was structured by the discourse of the good and natural teacher.

Teacher Training and the Study of Goodness in Teaching

The development of a notion of a "natural" teacher in the nineteenth century was intricately caught up in the development of a discourse of child-centered education and pedagogy. Inspired by the humanistic descriptions of child-centered pedagogies by Friedrich Froebel and Johann Pestalozzi in Europe, nineteenth-century school reformers in America advocated an expanded and humanized school system that dramatically changed the teachers' role from one of disciplinary power to moral exemplar. As promoted by early nineteenth-century school reformers, child-centered education placed the child's moral and civic development at the forefront of the classroom, thus corresponding with the designs of early republican discourse to create a new democratic nation with new citizens trained in moral and civic standards, social self-control, and industrious work habits.[3]

Reformers identified the character of the "good teacher" as the key to emphasizing moral character among students. It was not enough that teachers instruct in certain skills and behavior; they also had to model them, and to literally enact them in their very persons. This shaping of the new teacher was undertaken by the early teacher education schools, which offered the aspiring teacher not only classes in methods, but also in morals, ethics, and philosophy. The creation and monitoring of the appropriate teacher was also conducted by investigating teachers' backgrounds for appropriate gender, class, and cultural attributes, and by developing a method of "confessional technology" in teacher education to emphasize the reflective and self-regulating teacher who was driven by personal attributes of modesty and humility as well as intellect.[4]

According to teacher educators and school reformers, such a teacher was well prepared for the newly reformed nineteenth-century school, which promoted child-centered education and the nurturing of students' moral and personal development. Yet as Valerie Walkerdine and others have shown, the discourse of child-centered pedagogies actually disguised methods of control, primarily through their emphasis on the narrative of primary teaching as sensitive and enlightened mothering. The good teacher, argued Froebel, was like a "mother made conscious," who was naturally nurturing and self-sacrificing. Phrased and shaped as personal, caring relationships between the individual teacher and her children, the authority and directives behind the teacher were made invisible. The caring teacher actually disguised the objectives of the state to develop in students qualities of civic-mindedness, social self-regulation, and social and vocational skills and behaviors.[5] Students saw in the child-centered teacher only the nurturing individual behind her desk, and teachers saw only their own personal obligation to be nurturing. Teachers' identities as caring individuals was part of a broader cultural fabric, produced and reproduced by educational administrators, school structure, employment and personnel regulations, and teachers and students themselves for the purpose of maintaining a certain social order. The self-regulating citizen, argues Walkerdine, "depends upon the facilitating nurturance, caring and servicing, of femininity."[6]

How did teachers experience the process of becoming a good teacher who was naturally nurturing, self-restrained, and focused entirely on the needs of the student while simultaneously abiding by the expectations of the local school setting and the state? Ironically, the very identity of the natural, or born, teacher was created in much the same way that middle-class mothers were also taught about their innate abilities of maternity and mother love. Like middle-class mothers, women teachers were carefully guided in the ways of being natural, enmeshed in a powerful mythology about women's natural selflessness and omnipotently loving nature. Yet the aggrandized notions of female nurturance did not offer women any power; indeed, the sentimentalization of the nurturing female created a strange dynamic of public powerlessness for women, as cultural norms asserted the ideal of passivity for women, regardless of their circumstances. Both mothers and women teachers were valued for their apparently innate ability to undermine their own identities, and to replace selfishness with affection and virtue.[7] Women's responsibility to emphasize love and to ignore the problems presented by their immediate surroundings was exemplified in nineteenth-century popular culture by Louisa May Alcott's saintly Marmee in *Little Women,* for whom the trials of war, poverty, charity work, and motherhood still did not tear at the steel resolve of the ideal middle-class woman:

I am angry nearly every day of my life, Jo; but I have learned not to show it; and I still hope to learn not to feel it, though it may take me another forty years to do so.[8]

For women teachers in child-centered classrooms, too, their authority lay in their self-regulating passivity, both to the directives of school reformers and to the needs of the children. These themes were deeply interwoven in the training of a new corps of teachers by common school reformers. Horace Mann supported the entry of women into teaching in part because of financial exigencies, but also because of what he perceived as the optimum match of woman's natural character with the newly emphasized moral role of teaching. Mann viewed the woman teacher as "guide and guardian of young children" because in her natural state, affection was stronger than intellect.[9] Relying on the assumption that women had certain natural traits, Mann asserted:

Is not woman destined to conduct the rising generation, of both sexes, at least through all the primary stages of education? Has not the Author of nature preadapted her, by constitution, and faculty, and temperament, for this noble work?[10]

In Elizabeth Peabody's introduction to Froebel's text, republished in America, only the self-monitoring and self-regulating teacher allowed the child to develop freely. Indeed, it was the teacher's and mother's "instinct," which was "deeper than all thought," that inspired the ideal teacher, who was notable for "restraining her own self-will, and calling out a voluntary obedience."[11]

The first students at teachers' training schools in nineteenth-century America learned similar prescriptions about their future occupation of teaching. Mary Swift, who reported on her education at the Framingham (Massachusetts) Normal School in 1839, noted that teaching subjects was not the only job of the teacher. The teacher was also responsible for elevating students' "moral standards" by both instruction and modeling, by "both example and precept."[12] Females were particularly adapted to teaching because they possessed "more patience and perseverance."[13] Indeed the very qualities that were outlined for the good teacher were those associated with the ideal middle-class nineteenth-century woman, including a good reputation in the community, a "well balanced mind," interest in children, "nice moral discrimination," good health, and "patience, mildness, firmness, and perfect self control."[14] Teachers' personal qualities must not be merely adequate, but "perfect in everything."[15]

Of particular importance, recorded Swift, was teachers' ability to regulate their own actions, emotions, and personalities. Teachers needed to "ever be self-possessed," and to "rule their own spirits."[16] Yet like religious conversion experiences, such "moral feelings" could not be forced or falsified in teachers, and individual teachers needed to constantly study and reflect to ensure that their goodness had "its foundation in the heart. . . . It is not to be imitated, but must be possessed in reality, and made a consistent and constant part of character."[17] Good teaching, then, needed to evolve from the heart. If it did not originally reside in the heart, then aspiring teachers needed to encourage its authentic and not pretended presence.

The lessons taught to Mary Swift and her female colleagues at Framingham supplemented their broader social education in feminine self-restraint. Like mothers, teachers were taught to ignore the context and circumstances of their own lives, to repress their own emotions and fears, and to express only feminine love and generosity. Nineteenth-century women teachers were taught to monitor themselves constantly. Pedagogy was equated with their very personal selves, more so than with skills, the demands of the school institution, or students.

Nineteenth-Century Women Teachers' Experiences

The journals and letters of women teachers in the nineteenth century reveal recurring patterns of self-analysis and self-criticism as women teachers struggled to live up to the impossibly high standards—both personal and professional—that they were taught to believe should guide the teacher. Women teachers articulated lofty standards for the good teacher, and then immediately set about criticizing themselves for not reaching those standards, usually identifying their own personal character as the problem.

The pressure on teachers in nineteenth-century country and urban schools was intense. Although the experience of teaching in a town school in the East was in some ways radically different from the experience of teaching in the Western frontier, mid-nineteenth-century women teachers in both settings experienced common problems presented by students of diverse ages and capabilities, the personal pressure of local parents and school officials (some of whom they might be boarding with), supervisory inspections, and the day-to-day trials of maintaining classroom order, instructing the curriculum, and keeping the schoolhouse clean and maintained.[18] Gail Hamilton, who taught at the first public high school in Hartford, Connecticut, in the 1850s, literally broke down under the pressure.

I am so tired. I gave up entirely this morning. Sent my class out at half-past eleven, and had a cry. I am not sick, nothing in particular is the matter, but I am so tired, tired of learning lessons, tired of teaching them, tired of going to school at nine o'clock every day, tired of never visiting anybody, tired of going going from one thing to another just as fast as I can, tired of being in a whirl all the time, tired of school, tired of everything—almost.[19]

Martha Barrett, a teacher in Massachusetts in the mid-nineteenth century, also confided in her diary of her weariness from teaching: "My school seems more troublesome than ever before and I feel almost discouraged. I wish I was never obliged to leave my home and friends."[20]

But the pressure of such physical strains did not absolve teachers from their duties. Indeed, teachers often blamed themselves for being miserable, and admonished themselves simply to keep working harder, and keep analyzing and criticizing their own behavior and motivations. Martha Barrett began her very first day of teaching by reflecting on her own behavior and efforts, already questioning her abilities: "Well. I have commenced my school and spent one day in it and as evening is coming on I sit down to review it. What have I done aright this day? What wrong? What left undone? These are questions I must put to myself daily." Over and over again, Barrett expressed concern that she might not be "the means of doing [the students] much good," and she identified a number of personal areas that she needed to monitor, including her health, her studies, and her "continual progression" as a teacher. "I must try to make them all respect me. I must have more learning. I must devote myself more to books, and not superficially. I must plunge deep in to the sciences till they become familiar things." But improved skills were only part of Barrett's concern: good teaching meant that she perform her "whole duty," not just intellectual labors.

After the first few months of teaching, Barrett expressed increasing self-doubt that she might be able to accomplish any of her goals: school was "troublesome," she missed her family and friends, and she was "almost discouraged." Barrett turned these problems back on herself; her unhappiness was her own fault:

What have I done amiss in the year that has just past [sic]? Many, many things, alas! I fear the wrong overbalances the right, the good. I have learned something, added to my stock of knowledge, but is my heart any better? That is the great question, and I fear to answer it.

Thus, learning new knowledge or tasks was not enough: it was the development of the personality that made the real difference in teaching, according to Barrett. The nurturing of her own native talents was crucial, although she worried whether or not she had any: "I hope I have not mistaken my vocation," she confessed, and she longed for the "talent of teaching" that she observed in a friend whom all his students "loved." Her friend's success was due apparently to his natural talent or gift as a teacher, while every problem that Barrett experienced as a teacher was, she believed, her own fault and seemed to indicate that she did not have the natural talent for the work. Even sheer exhaustion was her own fault: "O dear I am tired. I never was made for a teacher." Ironically, Barrett did not see the break in logic between her own doubts that she was a natural teacher and her belief that a good teacher could "mould and train" others. The creation of character, discipline, happiness, and knowledge in others was her task alone: "All that depends on myself." As a teacher, she needed natural talents in order to create talents in others.

Emily Rice, who taught in Buffalo, New York, in the same period, expressed a similar value that teachers should work harder to "gain the love of those under our charge" and to "lay a good foundation for coming years" so that her students would "go forth into the world noble, virtuous and good, becoming good citizens and promote the good of their fellow creatures." In setting up such lofty goals for the teacher, Rice, like Barrett, immediately questioned her own abilities to accomplish them: "Time is hastening and each moment is one less to improve." In particular, Rice chastised herself for not understanding the "human mind" and wished she "could read the human heart better [and] I should know how to encourage and discourage the youthful creatures that are daily under my care." She recognized her own weaknesses, including the times that she spoke without thinking. She struggled to improve herself, "to know and govern myself that I may better teach and know others," and to accomplish this by being "more active" and "more industrious, letting no time pass without something being gained by it." By setting up "strict hours of study," Rice promised to constantly remind herself of the golden rule to "try try again."[21]

Frances Merritt Quick, a teacher in Framingham, Massachusetts, in the 1850s, also articulated incredibly high standards for the perfect teacher, and then flagellated herself for not being able to reach those standards. The classroom teacher literally needed to be "faultless, to have quick perceptions and a clear judgment," and to know "the inner and outer life of her scholars." Teachers must be born with "an out-going power reaching to every fibre and touching those little secret springs of action" in a child, "rousing" the child's "faculties to a systematic action." As a teacher, Quick felt she could not be content unless she was working with such "untiring devotion and self-sacrificing spirit." There was a sharp contrast between these ideals and Quick's own teaching: she believed her own mind was missing many of those natural qualities that she asserted were necessary in a teacher.

How little I have accomplished for the good of those under my charge! . . . All my efforts, or nearly all, seem to me to be wrongly-directed or else of little avail. My faults of mind and character are a great obstacle to my teaching. . . . There are still many things which trouble me—a heart which still clings to its sinful idols, a want of deep, affectionate earnestness in seeking the welfare of souls, . . . a selfishness, a want of self-renunciation and self-dependence. When I feel that I am not working with that untiring devotion and self-sacrificing spirit in my school.[22]

As a teacher, Quick admitted remorsefully, "I never feel satisfied with what I do or say."

Like her fellow teachers, Quick felt she could never live up to the expectations of the job. What they lacked was not skills or knowledge so much as what they believed to be natural capabilities that would allow them to be good teachers. Constantly evaluating themselves, they found themselves lacking, believing that whatever accomplishments they had were still unperfected, or that they should have been developed "years ago."[23] Most painfully, women teachers simply doubted their own natural abilities as communicators and as the moral guardians that they believed all good teachers to be: Emily Rice believed she was "not capable of doing justice to the young mind." Her contemporary, Arozina Perkins, who taught in Iowa in the 1850s, stated it even more directly, betraying deep pathos and dismay when she confessed that she felt "utter weakness and incapacity to accomplish aught that is good."[24]

Women Teachers in Progressive Schools

Teachers in a later period were not relieved of the burden of personal perfection. Indeed, the child-centered education of Froebelian kindergartens and Pestalozzian-influenced elementary schools pressured teachers to reflect upon and analyze their role even more deeply. In particular, the emphasis on child-centered learning in such classrooms led teachers to question their very presence in the classroom: if student-centered learning was the goal, then the teacher was most effective when she was essentially invisible. Such goals were admirable, yet they placed teachers, and particularly new teachers, in a confusing position as they wondered about their role in the classroom and, in particular, about their responsibilities to maintain or enforce discipline. Mary Rousmaniere's journal of her observations and student teaching in Froebelian kindergartens in Boston in 1904 betrays this particular anxiety about her abilities as a teacher and her concerns about where, when, and how she should exert her own presence in the classroom.[25]

From her first day observing kindergarten, Rousmaniere was concerned with the extent of her role in shaping her students. The best lesson, she observed, was to begin with the students' ideas and then to follow their interests, rather than "to squelch them and begin in your own topic in your own way." The problem remained, however, that the teacher needed to tactfully maneuver the subject toward the objectives of the classroom, while still maintaining their interests as central. She considered that it "must take a good deal of ingenuity and tact . . . to lead them around to your subject without apparently forcing them in any way." Kindergarten teaching was a constant balancing of the teacher's own presence with the freedom of the children, and only close study of children would give teachers an idea of which individual child needed which kind of approach: "It must be hard, too, to know how far to help and where to begin to insist on their doing it all themselves—some children will lean on you and take all the help you will give them, these must be thrown back on themselves." Close study of the children was necessary to "grow to really understand them" and to respond accordingly as a teacher.

After observing two classrooms for a few months, Rousmaniere began her student teaching. On her very first day as a student teacher, she confessed her concerns about control and freedom: "I'm afraid they rather did things as they liked instead of as I liked—you don't want a class of puppets, but at the same time they must understand that you're there to guide them and to be obeyed." Later, she raised a similar directive about balancing the curriculum between students' experience and the teacher's broader objectives, noting that she must "bring things to child in the form of his experiences but must at the same time liven, broaden, and deepen his experiences."

Woven throughout her broader concerns about teaching were Rousmaniere's own anxieties about her own abilities, particularly her abilities as a controller or disciplinarian.[26] Discipline problems were always her own: "The marching is pretty poor and straggling as yet. . . . I must be more strict about the talking. . . . free play—*very* poor—my fault because I hadn't thought it out at all and the children were all uneasy and fidgety." With particularly difficult students, Rousmaniere blamed herself: little John "does talk continually and I must stop it." On another day "Willie had a toothache and cried most of the lesson and Thomas was . . . silly. I was stupid which was the main trouble I suppose, but it certainly was a desperate half hour." The next week, Thomas was "silly" again, "and just sat there giggling, he's done this for several days, so I finally sent him to Miss Reilly. . . . I'm afraid I'm poor, indeed, at discipline." Finally, "Miss Potter sent Thomas away—it does seem as if my children were especially in evidence, and I'm afraid it's because I haven't been strict enough with them in my class. I'm going to be a bear tomorrow and squelch everything for a while!" A "bear" she was some days later, when she disciplined both Thomas and Willie. Gradually, Rousmaniere seemed to be coming to terms with the question of her authority in the classroom. "I certainly did feel mean doing it but I must somehow make him realize that it's wholesome for them to obey." Rousmaniere took a different tactic with a little girl who misbehaved and then refused to apologize. Adopting a more nurturing approach, she took little Mary onto her lap until "she finally said she would do as I asked her to."

Rousmaniere's concerns about control and discipline in the child-centered classroom are examples of the invisible controls of child-centered education. Well trained and well versed as a progressive educator, the teacher created an environment within which children were to learn how to regulate themselves, and in which they learned that it was "wholesome" for them to obey. In order to reach this stage, Rousmaniere went through her own self-analysis and self-regulation—first criticizing herself, and then learning how to assert herself while justifying her control and normalizing her discipline of the children. Throughout the process, she took the personal responsibility for the classroom problems, blaming herself for failing to recognize what was in effect a terribly contradictory and difficult situation. Indeed, the task that faced Rousmaniere was to maintain control by her very absence, to assert by remaining passive, and to control her students by controlling herself.

The concluding comment by her Froebelian instructor in the margin of her student-teaching notebook represented the tension between control and freedom that progressive kindergarten educators promoted: "Tell the children to do the thing they wish to do, then they'll mind." Such advice was philosophically sound, but in practice Rousmaniere wrestled with the tension, and tended to blame herself for not accomplishing what in many respects seems an impossible task: providing freedom within structure.

Conclusion

The individual self-analyses of teachers like Gail Hamilton, Martha Barrett, Frances Quick, and Mary Rousmaniere preceded what was to become a full-fledged project of educational professionals in the early twentieth century. Researchers in the emerging fields of educational administration and psychology took on the study of the critical characteristics of what made a good or successful teacher. Beginning in 1906, a series of national studies tried to identify and determine the relationship between effective teaching and teachers' academic achievement, their cultural, class, and ethnic background, and their "personality traits." By the 1920s the methods of surveying and measuring teachers was adopted by many American school districts for the purpose of evaluating teachers' performance. The projects betray the persistence of educators' concern with the question of whether the good teacher was born or made. Moreover, the methods of analysis exemplified the now traditional practice of subjecting the most intimate part of teachers' lives to systematic surveying, monitoring, and subsequent advising.

Using newly developed methods of questioning and cataloguing of responses, educational researchers systematically probed teachers' and teacher-education students' family backgrounds, grades, and rates of absenteeism in high school, college, teacher education, and student teaching; physical health, appearance, speech, age, extracurricular activities, reading habits, and hobbies; handwriting, marital status, and family responsibilities. They developed and administered tests that evaluated "mental keenness," "sympathy," "public opinion," and emotional history.[27] The test results remained the same: the most significant determinant for effective teaching had less to do with intelligence or academic training and more to do with "personality traits." Or as one researcher worded it: those personal qualities called "temperamental make-up" were more important for teaching than "intellectual make-up."[28]

Such studies must not have surprised most educators, but it bolstered a stream of new advice literature that reminded teachers that their road to success in teaching was paved with their own attributes of good citizenship and upright character. Clearly, all successes and failures in the classroom could be attributable to the teacher, argued a Vermont superintendent in 1919. One did not have to be a scholar to realize that "good teaching personality is the outward expression of genuine, refined, sympathetic and virile manhood and womanhood."[29] Good teaching required a good attitude, a continually positive outlook, a generous spirit, selflessness, sympathy, judgment, self control, enthusiasm, and the ability to overcome difficulties without complaint.[30]

The most successful teachers are those who take a happy attitude toward their work of teaching. They fail to see the drudgery of a necessary task, and always radiate enough sunshine about an assigned lesson to encourage pupils to want to study and prepare it.[31]

The reverse was also true: poor teaching was the result of a deficient personality, or of an individual who simply did not maintain a positive and enthusiastic attitude about the work, or who was not genuine, refined, sympathetic, virile, happy, or radiant. In particular, a bad teacher was one who was so "selfish" as to join a labor union, which lowered the interests of teaching to mere finances and greed.

By the early twentieth century, then, there was an emerging institutionalized discourse that defined the good teacher as a good individual who stood alone, self-restrained and self-monitoring, disinterested in financial rewards, oblivious to particular organizational or political problems in the school, and, universally, constantly available and energetic. So pronounced was the emphasis on the personal behavior and integrity of the public school teacher, that public officials like Herbert Hoover asserted that "the public school teacher can not live apart." A teacher literally could not separate teaching from "daily walk and conversation." Constantly in the public eye, the teacher "is peculiarly a public character under the most searching scrutiny of watchful and critical eyes." The teacher's life, Hoover concluded, "is an open book."[32] So, too, has the teacher's very identity and character historically been a subject of public scrutiny and debate. Not only have teachers investigated their own goodness, but the public, too, has dissected teachers' personal identity and behavior in search of clues for the origin of the good teacher. That origin has always resided in a peculiarly singular and isolated individual. The "rugged individual" of the American teacher was a self-monitoring and self-sufficient identity who was still directly subject to the interests and concerns of the organized educational community and the larger society.

Endnotes

1. My thoughts for this paper have been informed by contemporary analyses of teachers and teacher education, in particular Deborah Britzman, *Practice Makes Practice: A Critical Study of Learning to Teach* (Albany: State University of New York Press, 1991), p. 86; Deborah Britzman, "Cultural Myths in the Making of a Teacher: Biography and Social Structure in Teacher Education," *Harvard Educational Review*, Vol. 56, November 1986, pp. 442–456; Deborah Britzman, "The Terrible Problem of Knowing Thyself: Toward a Poststructural Account of Teacher Identity," *Journal of Curriculum Theorizing*, Vol. 9, Spring 1992, pp. 23–46; Hilary Burgess and Bob Carter, "Bringing Out the Best in People: Teacher Training and the 'Real' Teacher," *British Journal of Sociology of Education*, Vol. 13, 1992, pp. 349–359; Madeleine Grumet, *Bitter Milk: Women and Teaching* (Amherst: University of Massachusetts, 1988), pp. 31–58. For related analyses of the disciplining of American students through self-control, see Barry M. Franklin, "Self Control and the Psychology of School Discipline," in William F. Pinar, ed., *Contemporary Curriculum Discourses* (Scottsdale, AZ: Gorsuch Scarisbrick, 1988); and David Hogan, "Modes of Discipline: Affective Individualism and Pedagogical Reform in New England, 1820–1850," *American Journal of Education*, Vol. 99, November 1990, pp. 1-56.

2. Britzman, "Cultural Myths in the Making of a Teacher," pp. 452–453.

3. Carl F. Kaestle, *Pillars of the Republic: Common Schools and American Society, 1780–1860* (New York: Hill and Wang, 1983), pp. 66–74.

4. Dave Jones, "The Genealogy of the Urban Schoolteacher," in Stephen J. Ball, ed., *Foucault and Education: Disciplines and Knowledge* (New York: Routledge, 1990), pp. 57–77.

5. Carolyn Steedman, "The Mother Made Conscious: The Historical Development of Primary School Pedagogy," *History Workshop*, Vol. 20, Autumn

1985) pp. 149–163; Valerie Walkerdine, *Schoolgirl Fictions* (New York: Verso, 1990), pp. 18–27; Valerie Walkerdine, "It's Only Natural: Rethinking Child-Centered Pedagogy," in Ann Marie Wolpe and James Donald, eds., *Is There Anyone Here from Education?* (London: Pluto Press, 1983), pp. 79–87.

6.   Walkerdine, *Schoolgirl Fictions*, p. 56.

7.   Adrienne Rich, *Of Women Born* (New York: Norton, 1982), pp. 1–38; Grumet, *Bitter Milk*, pp. 31–58; Jan Lewis, "Mother's Love: The Construction of an Emotion in Nineteenth Century America," in *Social History and Issues in Human Consciousness,* Andrew E. Barnes and Peter N. Stearns, eds. (New York: New York University Press, 1989), p. 217.

8.   Quoted in Rich, *Of Women Born,* p. 28.

9.   Quoted in Jurgen Herbst, *And Sadly Teach: Teacher Education and Professionalization in American Culture* (Madison: University of Wisconsin Press, 1989), p. 75.

10. Quoted in ibid., p. 28.

11. Quoted in Grumet, *Bitter Milk,* p. 42.

12. Cyrus Peirce, *The First State Normal School in America: The Journals of Cyrus Peirce and Mary Swift* (New York: Arno Press, 1969), pp. 81–82.

13. Ibid., p. 87.

14. Ibid., pp. 91–92.

15. Ibid., p. 102.

16. Ibid., pp. 134, 188.

17. Ibid., p. 137.

18. For descriptions of nineteenth-century teachers' work in rural and urban settings in North America, see Alison Prentice and Marta Danylewycz, "Teachers' Work: Changing Patterns and Perceptions in the Emerging School Systems of Nineteenth and Early Twentieth Century Central Canada," *Labour/Le Travail,* Vol. 17, Spring 1986, pp. 59–80; Wayne E. Fuller, "The Teacher in the Country School," and James W. Fraser, "Agents of Democracy: Urban Elementary-School Teachers and the Conditions of Teaching," in Donald Warren, ed., *American Teachers: Histories of a Profession at Work* (New York: Macmillan, 1989).

19. Selections from Gail Hamilton's journal quoted in Sandra Fowler, "The Character of the Woman Teacher during Her Emergence as a Full-Time Professional in Nineteenth Century America: Stereotypes vs. Personal Histories," Ed.D. diss., Boston University, 1985, p. 125.

20. Selections from Martha Barrett's journal, quoted in ibid., pp. 96–105.

21. Selections from Emily Rice's journal, quoted in ibid., pp. 128–132.

22. Selections from Frances Quick's journal, quoted in ibid., pp. 140–144.

23. Quoted in ibid., p. 166.

24. Quoted in ibid., p. 167.

25. Mary S. Rousmaniere's observation and student teaching journal is in my possession, given to me by Rousmaniere's niece, Mary Morain. Mary S. Rousmaniere was my great-aunt.

26. Kate Rousmaniere, "Losing Patience and Staying Professional: Women Teachers and the Problem of Classroom Discipline in New York City Schools in the 1920s," *History of Education Quarterly,* Vol. 34, Spring 1994, pp. 49–68.

27. The first study of note was Junius Lathrop Miriam, *Normal School Education and Efficiency in Education* (New York: Teachers College Press, 1906). For reviews of the significant studies, see Federic B. Knight, *Qualities Related to Success in Teaching* (New York: Teachers College Press, 1922); Grover Thomas Somers, *Pedagogical Prognosis: Predicting the Success of Prospective Teachers* (New York: Teachers College Press, 1923); and Ervin Eugene Lewis, *Personnel Problems of the Teaching Staff* (New York: Century, 1925). See also George E. Carrothers, *Physical Efficiency of Teachers* (New York: Teachers College Press, 1925); M'Ledge Moffett, *The Social Background and Activities of Teachers College Students* (New York: Teachers College, 1929); Clara Robinson, *Psychology*

and the Preparation of the Teacher for the Elementary School (New York: Teachers College Press, 1930); "What Teachers Want to Read About," National Survey of the Education of Teachers, U.S. Office of Education, Vol. 5, Special Survey Studies, 1935; Bruce Robinson, "The Teacher's Own Problems," *Understanding the Child,* Vol. 4, 1934, pp. 3–6.

28. Elizabeth Hunt Morris, *Personal Traits and Success in Teaching* (New York: Teachers College Press, 1929), p. 2.

29. Walter H. Young, "The Personality of the Teacher," *Education,* Vol. 39, Fall 1919, p. 375.

30. Ibid. See also John Raymond Shannon, "Personal and Social Traits Requisite for High Grade Teaching in Secondary Schools," Ph.D. diss., Indiana University, 1927, p. 79; C. O. Davis, "Our Best Teachers," *School Review,* Vol. 34, December 1926, pp. 754–759; Roscoe Pulliam, *Extra-Instructional Activities of the Teacher* (New York: Doubleday, 1930).

31. Webster P. Reese, *Personality and Success in Teaching* (Boston: Graham Press, 1928), p. 118.

32. Quoted in J. Frank Marsh, *The Teacher Outside the School* (New York: World Book, 1928), p. x.

Chapter Seven
Teacher Dismissals and Local Conflicts in Danish Schools, 1908–1933

Hanne Rimmen Nielsen

This article is a study of the gender politics of teacher dismissals in Danish village schools in the early twentieth century. In this period the village schools went through a process of modernization and professionalization. The dismissal cases reflected both the increased demands on teachers' qualifications, following the professionalization process, and the intensified attempts of the local school authorities to enhance their influence on school matters.

The dismissal cases are interesting because they make visible some of the conflicts in the everyday life of schools in relation to the teacher's role. In these cases, social norms and pedagogical ideals are formulated quite explicitly in a way that is rare in most sources of school history.

The dismissal cases can also be used to explain differences in the demands on the genders. Were the male and female teachers simply judged by different standards—for example, that the schoolmistresses had to be especially motherly? Or is it rather the case that male and female teachers behaved differently and were consequently exposed to different types of criticism? What was the role of professionalization and rising standards of qualifications—were the dismissed teachers simply incompetent educators and nothing else? Essentially, the dismissal cases show that the schoolmistresses, even more than the male teachers, internalized certain norms to a kind of encompassing moral regulation. Most important, maternal and modest behavior was internalized and regulated in this way. The state did not have to regulate the women—they regulated themselves.

The Politics of Professionalization
The Danish village school went through a modernization process in

the late nineteenth century. Elements of this process were the professionalization of teachers, a partial feminization of the educational system, the diffusion of new pedagogical ideals, and an increase in school attendance.[1]

The teacher of former times had been a "peasant among peasants." Now teaching was established as a profession in the modern sense of the word. The Act on Teacher Training of 1894 increased the qualifications required of teachers. Teacher training was always to take place at a training college, and the theoretical and pedagogical requirements were considerably expanded. The Education Act of 1899 increased teachers' salaries and granted them a more independent position vis-à-vis the local community. The teachers themselves were also active in organizing and professionalizing themselves. The Association of Danish Teachers, founded in 1874 by discontented village schoolmasters, worked for the double purpose of achieving an improvement in the working conditions of teachers and advancing the cause of general education.

The Act on Teacher Training of 1894 placed male and female teachers on an equal footing and established that training requirements should be identical, except that the women were to be trained in needlework. But the 1890s was also the decade that introduced a totally new women's education that quickly became popular in the countryside—namely, the education of infant-school teachers. The infant-school teachers were always women, and they received a shorter education that especially qualified them for teaching smaller children, as well as for teaching needlework to the older girls. The infant-school teachers soon became very popular in the countryside, partly because the population explosion in the countryside necessitated the establishment of infant-schools, and partly because the infant-school teachers personified the new pedagogical ideals that spread in the same period.

Carolyn Steedman has shown how a new ideal of motherliness exerted its influence in the English educational system of this period. She argues that the feminization of teaching intersected with new ideas about child-centered education to create an ideal type of woman teacher who was passive and self-sacrificing, like a "mother made conscious."[2] In Denmark, too, there was a partial feminization of the educational system, strongest in the towns, less strong in the countryside. The proportion of village schoolmistresses increased to 25 percent of the total number of village teachers in 1905.[3] The new ideal of motherliness was especially strong in the education of infant-school teachers.[4]

Also central to the process of professionalization was a policy for the dismissal of teachers who were deemed incompetent. Prior to 1908, teachers could be dismissed only for "incompetence" and for "other reasons" that included indecency and criminal offenses. The Act on Teachers' Salaries of 1908 introduced a new provision on dismissals, section 8, which stated that a teacher who "had entered into such a bad relationship with his teaching post that the results of school activities are considerably reduced" could be dismissed on the initiative of the local authorities.[5]

To understand the workings of section 8, it is necessary to begin with a short introduction on the administrative apparatus of the Danish school system. The local administration of schools was in the hands of the parish council (sogneråd)—that is, the locally elected municipal council. Women were eligible for inclusion in this council after 1908. The parish council elected the education committee (skolekommission). The two bodies divided the school administration between them so that the parish council handled financial and building matters and the education committee was responsible for instructional matters. The local vicars were assigned a central role as chairmen of the education committees. At the regional level, the rural deans, as chairmen of the local education authorities (skoledirektion), had considerable influence on school matters. The clerical dominance in supervision of schools remained virtually untouched until 1933. At the national level, the ministry of education exercised the ultimate authority in school matters. But, as the example of section 8 shows, the power of the ministry was not unlimited in all respects.

The Act of 1908 released a wave of dismissals. In March 1925 the minister of education, Nina Bang, informed the parliament that a total of thirty-nine teachers had been dismissed in accordance with section 8 since 1908. From 1926 to 1933, the number of dismissals was about ten, according to my own examination of the records of the Ministry of Education. The total number of dismissals in the period between 1908 and 1933 can thus be assessed at about forty-nine.[6] Most of the dismissals affected village schoolmasters, which indicates that they were generally in a more visible and exposed position than teachers at town schools. The distribution along gender lines was also unequal: only four of the forty-nine were women. It should be noted, though, that a good many more section 8 cases were brought against schoolmistresses, but they were given up for various reasons.

The reasons for dismissing male and female teachers were different. The male teachers were most often dismissed according to section 8 or for "other reasons" (indecency and criminal offenses), while the schoolmistresses were much more exposed to being dismissed under section 18 (the so-called "incompetence" provision).[7] Roughly speaking, then, the male teachers were dismissed because of their involvement in local conflicts and their violations of moral and sexual norms. The female teachers were dismissed because of incompetence. However, all this was only the tip of the iceberg compared with the total number of instituted cases and the threats under section 8. The real significance of section 8 was the fear and self-discipline among teachers that it inspired.

The decisive point about section 8 was that the ministry could not prevent a dismissal if the local school authorities were in favor of dismissal. Thus, section 8 must be seen as a concession to strong, popular, and political forces who for many years had been demanding more local and parental influence on the management of schools. This demand should also be related to the peculiar Danish Grundtvigian tradition of popular education.[8] Thus, section 8 had two aspects: professionalization and local influence. The two aspects could work together, but they could also be contradictory—for example, if local forces wanted to dismiss a highly competent but unpopular teacher.

The teachers originally accepted the new provision, partly because removal of incompetent teachers was a necessary consequence of professionalization and partly because they were offered concessions in return—that is, increased salaries. But the teaching profession had never imagined that section 8 would be used and misused to the extent it was. The detested section 8 consequently became a matter of dispute for many years, until a new law of 1933 introduced a milder provision for dismissals. The dismissal cases are central to understanding how the teachers were positioned in the changing social and political circumstances of this period.

A Just Dismissal?

In August 1912, 140 men and women in the rural parish of Faardrup in southwest Zealand made a petition to the local school authorities. In the petition, they requested the removal of Miss Christiane Fold as schoolmistress of the infant-school at Faardrup. The reason stated was that "several parents with children in the school have learned that they have been inspired with fear so that they are not accessible to learning."[9] This was the beginning of a dismissal case brought against the schoolmistress who was fifty-four years old. It ended with her dismissal a little more than a year later.

The Faardrup school was situated in the small parish of Faardrup, a typical rural community dominated by middle-sized farms. The school had two teachers, the head teacher, Mr. J. M. Pedersen, who taught the older children, and Miss Fold, who taught the small children. Miss Fold had taught at the infant-school at Faardrup since it was founded in 1901. Like many older schoolmistresses, she had received no formal teacher training.[10] Both teachers lived in the school buildings and were socially integrated in the local community.

Six months before the petition of dismissal was submitted, the local education committee had addressed the superintendent, the rural dean, C. V. Bondo, on behalf of the villagers. He had held an extra visitation in Miss Fold's classes and had concluded that the school could be assessed as a good second-class school—that is, it was of an average standard. But at the same time, he had directed the schoolmistress to be more careful with her arithmetic teaching and more gentle and kind toward the children. Later the rural dean held that she had complied with this, but both the education committee and the parish council were of the opinion that the dean's instructions had been without result.[11]

After the villagers' petition, the Faardrup parish council and the education committee took up the case, and a formal case of dismissal was brought against Miss Fold. As section 8 of the Act on Teachers' Salaries laid down, two joint meetings between the parish council and the education committee were held, on August 14 and September 4, 1912. Miss Fold attended the last meeting and presented a written statement in her own defense. Both meetings expressed the unanimous wish that the schoolmistress be dismissed. The reasons stated were the following: "dissatisfaction with the schoolmistress who is thought to be too harsh, that her teaching is too mechanical, that it advances too slowly, particularly in arithmetic, and that the children are inadequately prepared to be admitted to the main school" (the school for children older than ten).[12]

In her written statement, Miss Fold repudiated the accusations. The complaint had come "unexpectedly and undeservedly," and she did not find that a bad relationship existed; on the contrary, there was a good and friendly relationship between the villagers and herself. She did not think that it was true that she had inspired the children with fear. On the contrary, her relationship with the children was intimate and loving. However, she admitted that she had beaten a very disobedient child with her open hand on a single occasion. Concerning the allegation that her teaching was inadequate, she maintained that this was a vague and disputable accusation that could be made against many teachers. She described her teaching methods and mentioned that the rural dean had repeatedly expressed his satisfaction with her.[13]

The rural dean, C. V. Bondo, chairman of the local education authority, supported the schoolmistress. He characterized the complaint as an abuse of section 8. He suspected that the complaint came from a few men who had very idealistic and pretentious concepts of what could be expected of a teacher. The dean himself was satisfied with the teaching of the schoolmistress. She was perhaps a little quick and nervous, but she was a decent person. The dean also obtained a statement from the male teacher at the school, J. M. Pedersen, who declared that although there had been some disagreements between himself and the schoolmistress, he thought that it would be an injustice to dismiss her. He had been "quite satisfied" with her teaching even if arithmetic was a weak point. Nor did she beat the children.[14]

Neither was the Ministry of Education enthusiastic about the dismissal case. The ministry demanded that a third joint meeting be held. This was made possible by section 8 in cases of doubt, and the indication was that the request for dismissal was questionable. On the other hand, it was the ministry's opinion that the dismissal could not be avoided because of the formulation of section 8. The new joint meeting was held on March 6 and resulted merely in the local bodies insisting that the schoolmistress be dismissed. No new arguments were put forward.[15]

The discussions continued for several months. Dean Bondo defended the schoolmistress in several letters, but was unable to make any impression on the villagers. The ministry made further inquiries, but even if the officials probably regarded the dismissal as unjust, they did not feel authorized to take effective steps to prevent it. Finally, on November 14, the ministry wrote to the local education authority announcing that the schoolmistress would be dismissed on December 1, 1913, with an annual pension of 520 kroner, amounting to half of her annual salary.

At Miss Fold's departure from the school, local women gave her a coffee service as a memento of her friends in the parish. The story of this incident was reported with biting sarcasm in the journal of the Association of Danish Teachers, *Folkeskolen* (The Primary School).[16] The journal explained the case of Miss Fold in Faardrup by pointing to suddenly arisen public feelings, rumors that had blackened the reputation of the schoolmistress, and individuals who had succeeded in whipping up a hostile attitude against her.[17] It had been rumored that the schoolmistress had beaten a girl who was hard of hearing. There had been accusations that "the schoolmistress was unable to teach the children anything," that "she refused to let them go to the lavatory," and that "she played cards." Among the 140 persons who had signed the petition against her were some who later admitted that they did not know the schoolmistress very well or that they had nothing against her.

About Miss Fold's relations with the villagers of Faardrup before the case, *Folkeskolen* explained that she had apparently been quite popular. At any rate she had been a frequent and welcome visitor in their homes, and the villagers themselves gave examples of her helpfulness toward them and her friendliness toward the children. About the background of the case the journal explained:

A couple of years ago a rumour sprang up in the school district that the daughter of a farmer had to be escorted to school because she was afraid of the schoolmistress. . . . The explanation was that Miss Fold, who is

definitely a methodical person, probably grumbled when a child was
late and when permission to go to the lavatory was asked too often. Some
people from the free school in the parish were also against the schoolmistress,
and when a member of the education committee was particularly
responsive to the rumours, the petition against the schoolmistress was
drawn up.[18]

In many ways the case against Christiane Fold was typical of later
dismissal cases against schoolmistresses. "Incompetence" and "harshness" were among the most common reasons for dismissals. But it
was also typical that the case was entangled in a web of local in-
trigues, personal antipathy, and rumors. Local disagreements were
also at the bottom of two other dismissal cases that were brought
against teachers in the same region.[19]

In several dismissal cases the schoolmistresses were middle-aged
women who were accused of inadequate teaching or harshness. Some
of them lacked the competence and self-confidence that formal
teacher training could have given them. They were described as
"strict" in their treatment of the children and some of them were
opposed by local people from the free schools, people with more
liberal views on education and discipline. In spite of their apparently close relationship with the villagers, these schoolmistresses were
not truly popular or respected. They never succeeded in becoming
fully integrated into the local community. From the perspective of
professionalization, they belonged to a group of older, not formally
qualified teachers who could not meet the new, rising standards. In
relation to the new pedagogical ideal of motherliness, they held an
older understanding of the role of the female teacher.

As Carolyn Steedman has suggested, it is possible to identify
two different concepts of motherliness in the everyday life of schools:
"The official texts speak of a contained liberality, the freedom for
children to move and discover as they might in a good bourgeois
home. But many teachers, like many working class parents, know
that it is much better if they are all sitting down, getting on with
something."[20] Miss Fold herself saw her relationship with the children as "intimate and loving." She probably did not see any conflict
between this intimate and loving relationship on the one hand and
the need for order, discipline, and occasional punishment of the

children on the other. It is not clear to what extent she had actually beaten the children, but verbally at least she distanced herself from corporal punishment. However, this was not enough for the villagers of Faardrup. It is evident from the case that their ideal schoolmistress should be both a competent teacher and an affectionate mother to her small pupils.

In spite of opposition by the Association of Danish Teachers, a formally qualified schoolmistress was appointed to the teaching post at Faardrup. The new schoolmistress, Karen Marie Frederikke Petersen, had until then served as a substitute teacher in the office. She was twenty-eight years old and had graduated from the training college in Vordingborg in 1912. According to one newspaper, she was the daughter of a farmer close to the school who was an ardent supporter of section 8. Irrespective of these rumors, chances were that the villagers of Faardrup would have been satisfied with their new schoolmistress: she was young and well educated and already known by people in the parish. The new schoolmistress would have to do, though, without congratulations from and the respect of her colleagues in the Association of Danish Teachers.[21]

The Cases

Today, it is almost impossible to decide what was reasonable in individual dismissal cases. The public debate tended to focus on the more questionable cases. But, from the documents, many of the dismissals seem to have been for good reasons. The dismissals were often experienced as unjust by the accused teacher and by the teacher community as such. But from the perspective of the local population, the cases reflected simply reasonable objections to a teacher who was not in harmony with local views on pedagogy, discipline, morals, religion, or politics. The schoolmistresses in particular were squeezed between new professional and pedagogical requirements, power and conflict in the local community, and norms of female behavior.

The dismissal cases point in several directions, but here I want to focus on the role of gender. Were there any systematic differences between the cases against men and women? What can the dismissal cases tell us about the social norms that regulated the behavior of the schoolmistresses in the local communities?

More male teachers were dismissed than schoolmistresses. One reason was that there were simply more male than female teachers. Another reason was that the complaints about men and women were different: while men teachers were judged on actual acts, women teachers were pressured to behave in certain ways with such rigor that they tended to leave the occupation before they were even "caught."

The cases of dismissals I have examined can be divided into three categories that help to clarify some of their most important aspects: cases about pedagogical qualifications and discipline; cases about local conflicts and "quarrelsomeness"; and cases concerning moral and sexual norms.[22] This grouping is not without problems, as the categories tend to blend together. But they all seem to have to do with local authority to judge teachers based on gender norms.

Gender and New Pedagogical Ideals

Both male and female teachers were judged according to the increased requirements in qualifications and the new pedagogical ideals that spread after the turn of the century. Older teachers with inadequate qualifications or with disciplinary problems came into the limelight. The cases that involved male teachers were mostly about disciplinary problems. Brutal teachers were looked upon with increasing disgust, but it was also seen as a problem when the teacher was unable to maintain discipline. A combination of bad teaching, insufficient discipline, and strained relations between school and home were frequent reasons in these cases.[23]

Among the schoolmistresses, a particularly exposed group were the many teachers without formal teacher training who had been appointed in the 1880s and 1890s as infant-school teachers. They were being replaced by qualified teachers very slowly, in part because it was difficult to get the qualified schoolmistresses to apply for the posts in the countryside. In addition, it was much less expensive to employ unqualified teachers. The Act on Training of Infant School Teachers of 1892 meant the introduction of a totally new category of schoolmistresses, the infant-school teacher, "a specialized, but experienced schoolmistress with a short and cheap education."[24] The debate preceding the act provides documentation that the schoolmistresses were increasingly judged on the basis of the new pedagogical ideal of motherliness. The education lasted one year and presupposed that the students had a sound knowledge of ordinary school subjects. The education particularly stressed pedagogical training and practical teaching ability. From a reading of the training college testimonies on the students, the historian Adda Hilden describes the new type of teacher:

When you read the testimonies and references you will find that the words practical, lively, understanding, conscientious, kind, and loving were especially positive adjectives; without the practical grip on handling a group of children, an infant-school teacher was badly off. And without the ability to establish a tie between herself and the small children, she would not be able to manage this kind of work. Competence was of course highly valued, but mostly in connection with a vivid narrative skill and gifts for guiding children.[25]

The case against Miss Fold and similar cases provide examples that the requirements had increased and that the concept of the ideal schoolmistress had changed over time. In fact, this appears from the very first section 8 case against a schoolmistress in 1909. In this case, the teaching of the schoolmistress was criticized as being "heavy and sluggish." Another aspect of the case was a conflict between her and the parents regarding teaching methods. The schoolmistress wished to use the so-called "phonetic method" in reading lessons, but the parents strongly objected.[26]

The main reason for the dismissal of another teacher, Miss Marie Pedersen in Randlev, according the education committee and the parents, was that she "lacked the ability, with understanding and love, to take care of the small children." Thus, it was the harsh treatment practiced by the schoolmistress that explained "the strong feeling against her and the wish to replace her with another teacher who, with skill, but also with kindness and much more understanding love, would take care of the small ones."[27]

Many cases against older schoolmistresses were about bad teaching and incompetence, often caused by infirmity or nervousness on the part of the schoolmistress. This does not mean that the older schoolmistresses were generally disliked or regarded as unskilled. But the ideal schoolmistress was increasingly compared favorably to the young, educated infant-school teacher.

However, the advance of infant-school teachers did not solve all problems. Dismissals and complaints affected the infant-school teachers much more than the primary school teachers. This was due to the few formal requirements made of infant-school teachers and their hard working conditions in village schools. The teaching of small children was toilsome, and so was the needlework with the older girls. Remarkably, many cases were about problems in needlework teaching. Many schoolmistresses taught more than forty hours a week, and they were overburdened and worn down at an early age. Moreover, they received low wages and were frequently offered very poor housing conditions. In all respects they were placed at the bottom of the school hierarchy.

The individual schoolmistress was often badly prepared to deal with the attacks. Almost always, she was placed in an isolated position, cut off from both other schoolmistresses and from any network of local women. Moreover, on account of dominant norms of behavior, women very seldom dared to raise their voices in the public sphere of local society. This meant that the schoolmistress who suffered an attack often had to ask for the help of male friends, such as the vicar or the male teachers of the local association of teachers.

Female members of the executive committee of the Association of Danish Teachers also took part in the fight against section 8. On the whole, however, the village schoolmistresses were poorly organized. The League of Village Schoolmistresses, founded in 1910, worked within the Association of Danish Teachers to secure the seats of women representatives. The league did not regard the dismissals as particularly a woman's issue. Probably they thought that they served their cause best by joining forces with the male teachers in fighting section 8. The low profile of the schoolmistresses could also be connected to the fact that most dismissals and complaints affected infant-school teachers. The relationship between this group and the female primary school teachers was not very good, and in 1913 the infant-school teachers founded their own organization, the League of Infant-School Teachers.

Marie Hansen, the spokeswoman of the infant-school teachers and a member of the executive committee from 1915, was one of the few women who defended their interests in *Folkeskolen*.[28] In sharp, often sarcastic articles, she described the arbitrariness and the exposed position of the infant-school teachers. They were the only group of teachers who could not "flee from" section 8 because they were cut off from applying for posts in the towns. And, referring to the abovementioned case against Marie Pedersen in Randlev, she delivered the following ironic commentary entitled "When an infant-school teacher does her duty":

The daily press has recently announced that an infant-school teacher in Jutland has been dismissed because she tried to get herself some peace at work. At the same school, the male teacher has been dismissed because he would not do his job. Would it not be a good idea to inform potential applicants what is demanded from people employed in this parish? . . . To the announcement on the infant-school teacher office should be added: "The schoolmistress must put up with anything that the children in the main school can think of by way of teasing and disturbing the small ones. Any complaints will result in the immediate dismissal of the schoolmistress."[29]

Local Conflicts and "Quarrelsomeness"

In the period after 1908 a number of cases were conducted against male teachers who had become involved in local conflicts of a political, religious, or personal character. Such cases could be about, firstly, that the teacher was in opposition to the locally dominant party (such as the Liberal Party) or the dominant religious movement (such as the Home Mission). Secondly, the cases could be about more personal power struggles.[30] Cases involving local conflicts affected male teachers more frequently than schoolmistresses. This can be interpreted to mean that men much more than women were regarded as opinion-makers and cultural leaders in the local community.

In local society, the male teachers generally performed far more public and organizational functions than the schoolmistresses. The women were considered suited to perform church and social functions on vestries, child welfare committees, relief funds, the YWCA, and nursing associations. The sphere of action of the men was far wider and extended to political and economic offices in parish councils, the local Liberal committee, cooperative societies, dairies, savings banks, and so on. Obviously, men and women encountered different local expectations, although the different public roles could also be explained by a socialized reticence on the part of the schoolmistresses. In any case it is clear that male teachers had a more prominent public role than schoolmistresses, and that the men therefore ran more of a risk of making powerful enemies in the local community.

However, in some cases, schoolmistresses also became involved in local conflicts. One example was the much discussed Randlev case.[31] The case began in 1912 when education authorities took steps to dismiss the male teacher of the school at Randlev on account of incompetence and drunkenness. The immediate occasion was a complaint from the schoolmistress of the school. During a public meeting about the case, some of the villagers suddenly suggested that the schoolmistress, Miss Marie Pedersen, also be dismissed. The official reason was stated to be her nervousness, her lack of self-control, the bad relationship between her and the other teacher, and, finally, the general sentiment at the meeting. However, the case was weakly founded, as Miss Pedersen, though not formally qualified, was recognized as a skilled teacher. Later, due to a procedural error, the ministry decided to turn down the case against her. But the case agitated the public mind strongly in the small parish and divided the villagers into two camps. The case was about pedagogical principles and about differing views on children and schooling. Many thought that the schoolmistress was too strict, too demanding, and even unkind in her treatment of the children.

Other elements in the case were not so much about the teacher as about local politics. Farmers and adherents of the free school were against the schoolmistress, whereas the smallholders and workers generally supported her because they wanted to strengthen the public school for economic and ideological reasons. Finally, the case was also about gender politics, as it made visible the vulnerable position of women in the public debate and the organizational weakness of the schoolmistresses. The case lasted for almost five years (1912 to 1916); it was raised twice and ended with a prolonged action for slander in court. The schoolmistress was finally allowed to stay in her office, but the case had heavy personal costs for her. She died, ill and worn out, at fifty-four years of age, in 1926.

In another type of local conflict, it was the personal qualities of the schoolmistresses, their "quarrelsomeness" or "obstinacy," that were seen as the problem. In the case against the infant-school teacher at Haarslev in 1913 and 1914, the villagers and parents complained of her self-willed behavior and lack of cooperativeness.[32] It was revealed that the teacher had taken a dislike to three girls whom she taught needlework. In several ways she had harassed the girls and, moreover, she had refused to consider all peace efforts. The case ended with the teacher getting a severe reprimand from the ministry. The case exemplifies some common problems: the hostile relationship between school and home that existed in many places, the reactions of an overburdened teacher, and, finally, the conflict between the ideal of motherliness and the actual behavior of schoolmistresses.

Another case of quarrelsomeness concerned the relationship between the schoolmistress and the leading male teacher at a school. In the so-called Masnedsund case in 1916, the most important complaint against the schoolmistress, Miss Cathrine Agerskov, was her "quarrelsomeness" and her resistance to submit to the principal of the school.[33] The principal requested that she be dismissed and was backed up by the local education authorities as well as the ministry. According to the documents of the case there were errors on both sides—the principal was probably just as quarrelsome as the schoolmistress, and he did not deny that, on several occasions, he had abused her in front of the children—but it was the schoolmistress who paid the price and who was judged more harshly. She was called "mentally disturbed" and "unbalanced," while the principal had an "impetuous temperament." The decision was predictable, because the authorities had to back the leadership of the principal. But the case also involved obvious questions of gender politics. Conflicts between a male principal and the subordinate schoolmistresses were part of the everyday life of many schools. The schoolmistresses were placed under a monopoly of male leadership at all levels of the public school. The question of leadership was also raised by the schoolmistresses in their struggle to get access to the superior posts in the public school system. After 1916, schoolmistresses were formally admitted as principals at town schools and head teachers at village schools.[34]

Normally the schoolmistresses were not exposed to overt

discrimination. However, it should not be overlooked that in all conflicts, they faced a massive wall of male administrators and politicians. From several cases it appears that the schoolmistresses often had difficulties in making their views known. In at least two instances, disagreements between the schoolmistress and the local vicar (who was also the chairman of the education committee) were so serious that the cases resulted in the dismissal of the teacher.[35] In this type of case, the male administrators typically referred to the teacher's "nervousness," which was regarded as an extenuating circumstance. However, nervousness could also work as an effective argument against taking the schoolmistress seriously.

There are a few cases of schoolmistresses getting into trouble because of their religious or political attitudes. In 1916, Miss Due, a teacher in the small town of Skagen, was dismissed because she had joined a religious sect. The crucial question was whether she had been agitating for her opinions at school. She denied this, but was dismissed after all.[36] The dismissal in 1920 of Marie Nielsen, a teacher in Frederiksberg near Copenhagen and a well-known communist, was a case that attracted extensive coverage by the press. Marie Nielsen was dismissed because of her illegal political work, which had resulted in imprisonment for half a year. She was the editor of a communist newspaper that had encouraged the use of violence.[37]

These two dismissals did not reflect widespread popular opposition to the schoolmistresses, unlike the cases against male teachers. Both Miss Due and Miss Nielsen received support from the parents of their schools. But the dismissal of Marie Nielsen was clearly part of a local and party political power struggle, as is evident from the fact that it was decided in the town council with Conservative votes in opposition to Social Democratic votes.

The teaching profession offered extensive support to Miss Due, but not to Marie Nielsen. She was generally regarded as being too far to the left to deserve any support. However, these cases made many teachers consider the moral problem of whether it was possible or desirable to separate school work and personal attitudes. To most, the answer was no. They agreed with Miss Johanne M. Sørensen, who did not believe that "it was possible to put on a pedagogical smock at school and bring up children to the opposite values of what you bear in mind and publicly work for."[38] Most of them were ready to submit to commonly accepted demands on the attitudes and moral obligations of teachers.

Moral Conduct, Honesty, and Sobriety

It is an interesting question whether the demands on the moral conduct of schoolmistresses were greater than or different from the demands on male teachers. In legislation, it was an acknowledged fact that "the personal affairs of a teacher could be of such a nature that they render impossible his continuance in the office because they reduce the necessary esteem and confidence on the part of the population."[39] The personal affairs in question could be, for example, lack of sobriety, economic fraudulence, serious criminal offenses, or sexual offenses such as indecency and adultery.

A fairly large number of cases against male teachers were about indecency, adultery, and drunkenness, whereas that category of offense was almost absent among the schoolmistresses. I have come to the conclusion that the norms concerning the schoolmistresses were probably so rigid that most of them chose to conform. Moreover, a schoolmistress of questionable moral conduct would probably have felt compelled to leave the school long before a formal dismissal case was brought against her. This was moral regulation at its most systematic: the state did not even have to regulate the women; they essentially regulated themselves.

Frequent reasons for charges against male teachers were indecent behavior toward pupils, adultery (that is, a sexual relationship with a local married or unmarried woman), drunkenness and gambling, and, finally, disorder of pecuniary affairs. To my knowledge, comparable cases were in no instance conducted against schoolmistresses. Below, I discuss a few cases involving schoolmistresses, but these cases are all of a different, less obvious character. Some of the women were victims of rumors rather than persons of tarnished morality.

One case that attracted a lot of attention was the dismissal of the infant-school teacher Mrs. Nielsine Jensen, in Vinding near Vejle in 1927.[40] Mrs. Jensen was accused of "fraudulent conversion"—in plain words, theft—after a deficit had been established in her needlework accounts. According to the schoolmistress, the deficit resulted from the fact that several poor pupils had received materials free of charge. She was dismissed in accordance with section 8, but later she won an action for slander at court. The case demonstrates how vulnerable the female teachers were to attacks on their morals and how difficult it was for them to defend themselves. As the Association of Danish Teachers pointed out, the schoolmistress was dismissed on sheer circumstantial evidence. In this as in other cases, there was an element of personal aversion to the teacher, of rumors and "women's wiles" at work. Finally, the case also points to fundamental problems in the way needlework teaching was organized at Vinding and other places. *Folkeskolen,* for example, printed an article from a schoolmistress who described needlework teaching on the basis of her own experiences. She explained that it was almost impossible both to manage the teaching and at the same time keep the needlework accounts.[41]

When a male teacher was dismissed because of "drunkenness" he would probably have been guilty of a considerable abuse of alcohol. Mr. Andreasen at Randlev is a good example. His drinking was often accompanied by card-playing and other excesses in public arenas. The so-called Hvalsø case, however, was about something quite different. In this case, the schoolmistress was accused of drinking at a private party, thereby ruining her reputation through a single, ostensibly dishonorable act.

The Hvalsø case started in March 1914 when the schoolmistress, Miss Arnfeldt, and five others went to have dinner at the local inn after a gymnastic meeting.[42] At that occasion, they also had some Madeira to drink and the next day it was rumored in town that Miss Arnfeldt had gotten drunk. After the "affair," the schoolmistress herself chose to leave the private school where she was employed. Later, she took legal action against the vicar who had spread the rumor. Miss Arnfeldt lost the action for slander, but even if she had won the case, she would probably not have been able to restore her honor and reputation fully. The fact is that a woman's lost virtue or honor could never be restored. Even more than the schoolmistresses in the Randlev and Vinding cases, Miss Arnfeldt was judged by a concept of female honor, because the accusations against her were about morals and indirectly about sexuality. It has been shown that in agricultural society, female honor was normally bound up with sexuality and with modesty and that women could damage their reputations merely by taking legal action and thereby allowing a public discussion of their honor.[43] In the Hvalsø case, both the reputation and the occupation of the schoolmistress were ruined, perhaps forever.

Moral self-regulation is probably the best explanation of why so few allegations of immoral behavior were actually made against schoolmistresses. According to other sources, the schoolmistresses were forced to submit to very strict norms of moral and sexual behavior if they wished to secure a future in the narrow, local communities.[44] Scattered evidence suggests that a schoolmistress experiencing an attack on her morals would choose to leave the school before a case of dismissal was actually brought against her. In 1903, a schoolmistress in southern Jutland transferred to another parish after reports that she was the mistress of the local vicar. This teacher too seems to have been primarily the victim of rumors, in this instance caused by her support of the vicar in the heated national conflict over that district bordering on Germany.[45] In another instance, *Folkeskolen* told the story of a schoolmistress who was threatened with section 8, but "she has now become engaged, so the case will probably be solved in a way satisfactory to all parties."[46] Whether the schoolmistress was also satisfied with this "solution" is not clear from the evidence.

In the same way, schoolmistresses who had an illegitimate child often chose to leave their jobs in order to avoid a public case. The number and fate of these schoolmistresses is unknown, but they were probably exposed to severe condemnation. The first publicly known instance of a schoolmistress having an illegitimate child was the Inger Merete Nordentoft case from 1946.[47] The special thing about this case was that Miss Nordentoft was a principal, a former chair of the association of schoolmistresses in Copenhagen, and a well-known communist. Moreover, the case took place in Copenhagen, where views were more liberal than in the countryside. In the end, Inger Merete Nordentoft was allowed to stay in her position, but not until a heated debate had taken place. During this debate, it was widely claimed that the authorities should dismiss her. Many older schoolmistresses, too, thought that she ought to resign, one of the reasons being the reputation of the profession.

The debate on the Nordentoft case also revealed that there was "a small group of schoolmistresses with children we have had to cheat to get."[48] The usual procedure was to go away during pregnancy and later to return from "sick leave" with an "adopted" child. In the countryside, there were probably geographical and religious differences over what could be tolerated. As regards the male teachers, the minister of education stated during the parliamentary debate on the Nordentoft case that seven male teachers had been dismissed because they had had an illegitimate child. On the other hand, no schoolmistresses had been dismissed for this reason. According to the minister, this showed that no boundary had been drawn between men and women.[49] However, another interpretation could be that generally schoolmistresses had to be more reticent and discreet in their sexual behavior than male teachers because of the prevalent double standard of morality. If they behaved modestly and discreetly there was no reason to dismiss them.

It was expressly forbidden to dismiss a female teacher who got married.[50] But marriage could result in new problems for a schoolmistress if she chose to keep her job. In the section 8 case against Julie Vallentin in 1921, it was an important charge that she had neglected her school work after she had had a daughter. The villagers' complaint stated that the schoolmistress had left the children alone in the school in order to cook and help her husband with his work. Moreover, she had brought the baby with her and nursed it during lessons. In another case against a married couple, both employed as teachers at the small school at Salby, the complaint stated that the schoolmistress was not always in school with the pupils and that she neglected her duty to supervise her own children.[51] Such complaints probably reflected real difficulties for many schoolmistresses who tried to combine marriage and work.

Great demands were made on the moral conduct of both male and female teachers, but the demands were different and in some ways probably heavier on the women. The human and emotional costs caused by the strict norms of behavior must have been considerable. One solution for many unmarried schoolmistresses was probably to channel their motherly feelings into their school work. However, it was a tragic irony that motherliness was demanded of a group of women who themselves had been denied the right to motherhood. Another solution was to marry and in fact increasing numbers of village schoolmistresses did so. Marriage gradually became one of the most important ways to secure integration into the local community. In this way, the motherliness of schoolmistresses was established in a double sense.

Conclusion

In the period between 1908 and 1933 a number of schoolmistresses were dismissed from their posts in Danish public schools. Some were no doubt hopeless as teachers, and others got into trouble because they were unable to comply with the increased requirements and the new pedagogical ideals that stressed the motherliness of the schoolmistress. Most important, the dismissal cases show that the schoolmistresses internalized norms of maternal and modest behavior to an encompassing moral regulation.

The notion of the ideal schoolmistress was internalized through certain mechanisms ranging from the norms learned during teacher training, to the strict social control of behavior in narrow, local communities, to the ultimate threat of dismissal and loss of honor and reputation. The dominant ideal emphasized the skill, diligence, and responsibility of the schoolmistresses. They were expected to be motherly and gentle in their treatment of the small children. Preferably, they would be able to maintain discipline without resorting to corporal punishment. No stain could be attached to their moral conduct, and, in a sense, this demand for modesty or celibacy seems to contradict the ideal of motherliness. The schoolmistresses were expected to commit themselves to matters of local society, but within certain limits. Particularly, self-asserting or independent behavior was not regarded as desirable.

The actual behavior of the schoolmistresses shows that they had in fact internalized these ideals and norms. Many of them were ambitious and wanted their school to "stand forward as the best." Motherliness existed as an element of their own socialization, but it could also work as a compensation for biological motherhood. Strong religious feelings could alone promote an austere sexual morality. And the feminist attitudes of many schoolmistresses led them to public commitment, but primarily within certain limited fields such as education, the church, and social work. The project was to combine the conflicting norms and thereby achieve integration and acceptance in the local community.

However, the dismissal cases also demonstrate that most of the schoolmistresses offered resistance when attacked. Several of them chose to defend themselves publicly, thereby ignoring norms of ideal female behavior. But the isolated position and weak organization of these women were serious obstacles to effective resistance. Their situation often resembled that of Christiane Fold, who was compelled to "silently accept her fate and defend herself in a humble statement."[52]

Endnotes

1. Joakim Larsen, *Bidrag til den danske Folkeskoles Historie 1818–1898* (Copenhagen, 1899) is still the best survey of this period. See also Ning de Coninck-Smith, "Skolejubi-læ(r)erne". Et bidrag til skolejubilæernes historie," *Historie og Samtid,* Vol. 3, 1989, pp. 69–74. For the struggle over school attendance, see Gunhild Nissen, *Bønder, skole og demokrati. En undersøgelse i fire provstier af forholdet mellem den offentlige skole og befolkningen på landet i tiden ca. 1880–1920* (Copenhagen, Institut for dansk Skolehistorie, 1973); and Bodil K. Hansen, *Skolen i landbosamfundet ca. 1880–1900* (Sorø: Landbohistorisk Selskab, 1977).

2. Carolyn Steedman, "Prisonhouses." *Feminist Review,* No. 20, 1985, pp. 7–21; and Carolyn Steedman, "The Mother Made Conscious: The Historical Development of a Primary School Pedagogy," *History Workshop,* Vol. 20, Autumn 1985, pp. 149–163.

3. In 1905 there were 3,748 male teachers and 1,208 female teachers in Denmark. The female teachers included 337 "ordinary" teachers, 606 infant-school teachers, 64 infant-school teachers without a certificate, and 185 winter teachers. *Statistiske Meddelelser,* Series 4, Vol. 27, No. 1, 1908.

4. Adda Hilden and Erik Nørr, *Lærerindeuddannelse. Lokalsamfundenes kamp om seminariedriften. Dansk læreruddannelse 1791–1991,* Vol. 3 (Odense: Odense Universitetsforlag 1993), pp. 143ff.

5. On provisions of teacher dismissals, see Henrik Lehmann, *Haandbog i Lovgivningen om den danske Folkeskole* (Copenhagen: Systematisk Fremstilling 1909), pp. 356–365; and Henrik Lehmann, *Haandbog i Lovgivningen om den danske Folkeskole* (Copenhagen: Kronologisk Fremstilling, 1914), pp. 68, 337, 394–395. Generally, very little has been written about dismissals of teachers. Erik Nørr, *Skolen, præsten og kommunen. Kampen om skolen på landet 1842–1899* (Viborg: Jurist- og Økonomforbundets Forlag, 1994), pp. 330–338, discusses ten dismissal cases between 1868 and 1884. A. Barfod, "De saerlige Regler om Afskedigelse af Laerere i den danske Folkeskole," *Nordisk Administrativt Tidsskrift,* Vol. 17, 1936, pp. 155–178, gives a survey of dismissal cases conducted against teachers between 1908 and 1936. An account of the teachers´ struggle against section 8 is chronicled in Stinus Nielsen, "Kampen mod § 8 og § 33. Den danske lærerstands retsstilling gennem 75 år," *Danmarks Lærerforening 1874–1949,* (Århus: Danmarks Lærerforenings Hovedstyrelse, 1949), pp. 184–194.

6. *Folkeskolen,* 1914, pp. 134, 226; *Rigsdagstidende,* 9, Folketingets Forhandlinger (The Proceedings of Parliament) 1924–1925, column 6624–6625 (March 28, 1925). In the Archives of the Ministry of Education I have found a survey of the thirty-nine cases between 1908 and 1925; see July 17, 1926 "The Parliamentary Committee on the bill concerning the administration and supervision of the educational system wants access to all documents in the section 8 cases." In the Archives I have also identified ten cases covering the period 1926 to 1933.

7.   A counting on the basis of the records shows that from 1916 to 1933 ten female teachers and fifteen male teachers were dismissed in accordance with section 18; eight female teachers and twenty-six male teachers were dismissed for "other reasons." These figures are subject to some uncertainty, but they convey a certain impression of the distribution.

8.   The clergyman N.F.S. Grundtvig (1783–1872) gave name to the Grundtvigian movement, a popular religious and cultural movement with a strong influence on the peasant population. A bright Christian faith and an educational program founded in the national and historical tradition were two of the elements of the Grundtvigian movement. The Grundtvigian movement served as the starting point for an extensive private school sector, comprising free schools and folk high schools. The Grundtvigian pedagogy stressed the free development of the child, much in accordance with the maternal pedagogy. Locally, the Grundtvigian free schools and the public schools were often involved in ideological struggles. However, the Grundtvigian pedagogy also influenced the public school system and was a important factor in spreading the maternal ideology. The literature on Grundtvig and the Grundtvigian movement is vast. Introductions to the person and the period can be found in Hal Koch and Bjørn Kornerup, eds., *Den danske Kirkes Historie,* vols. 6–8 (Copenhagen: Gyldendal, 1954–1966). The free schools and folk high schools are discussed in A. Ankerstrøm, *Friskolen gennem hundrede Aar,* vols. 1–3 (Odense: Skandinavisk Bogforlag, 1946–1949); and Ernst J. Borup and Fred Nørgaard, eds., *Den danske Folkehøjskole gennem hundrede Aar,* vols. 1–2 (Odense: Skandinavisk Bogforlag, 1939–1940).

9.   Quoted from *Folkeskolen,* 1913, p. 473. The documents of the case against Christiane Fold are in AO 2650, the Archives of the Ministry of Education, the National Archives in Copenhagen. All details of this and other dismissal cases referred to in this paper are located in the Archives of the Ministry of Education (hereafter: National Archives), unless otherwise indicated. About the school at Faardrup, see Johs C. Jessen, *V. og Ø. Flakkebjerg Herreders Skolehistorie. Blade af den danske Skoles Historie fra ca. 1690 til vore Dage* (Slagelse, n.p., 1938), pp. 113–116.

10. *Danmarks Folkeskole,* 1910, pp. 42–43. Jessen, *V. og Ø. Flakkebjerg,* pp. 115–116.

11. The rural dean Bondo on behalf of the local education authority, Letter to the Ministry, October 5, 1912. The education committee and the parish council, Letter to the Ministry, September 18, 1912, National Archives.

12. The education committee and the parish council, Letter to the Ministry, September 18, 1912, National Archives. *Folkeskolen,* 1913, p. 473.

13. Christiane Fold, Letter to the parish council and the education committee, September 3, 1912, National Archives.

14. The rural dean Bondo on behalf of the local education authority, Letters October 5, 1912, and January 30, 1913. J. M. Pedersen, teacher of the main school at Faardrup, Letter to Dean Bondo, January 12, 1913, National Archives.

15. The parish council and the education committee, Letter to the Ministry, March 14, 1913, National Archives.

16. *Folkeskolen,* 1914, p. 36.

17. *Folkeskolen,* 1913, pp. 473–474; 1914, pp. 16–17.

18. *Folkeskolen,* 1914, p. 16.

19. Jessen, *V. og Ø. Flakkebjerg,* pp. 171–172, 210.

20. Steedman, "Mother Made Conscious," p. 159.

21. *Folkeskolen,* 1914, pp. 81, 228. *Odder Dagblad,* June 24, 1914.

22. I have examined the majority of cases of dismissals and complaints against schoolmistresses (1908–1933), accessible in the National Archives, and all the cases against male and female teachers dealt with in *Folkeskolen.*

23. Ning de Coninck-Smith, "Paa den mest ryggesløse Maade," *Den jyske Historiker,* No. 56, 1991, pp. 71–90. As regards other cases in this category, see

Folkeskolen and the Archives of the Ministry of Education. The survey in July 17, 1926, is also very useful.

24. Hilden and Nørr, *Lærerindeuddannelse,* p. 204.

25. Ibid., pp. 195–196.

26. Schoolmistress in Lejrskov, Malt, Dismissal in accordance with section 8, 1910, National Archives.

27. *Odder Dagblad,* December 5, 1913.

28. *Folkeskolen,* 1913, p. 566; 1914, pp. 32–33.

29. Marie Pedersen, "When an infant-school teacher does her duty," *Folkeskolen* 1913, p. 566.

30. The following cases were very much debated at that time; see *Folkeskolen:* Mr. Schrøder in Oudrup, 1910, Mr. Juhl in Bjerge, 1910, Mr. N. Nielsen Vad in Tørring, 1914, Mr. A. Olesen in Bønnerup, 1914, Mr. Fogtmann in Gislinge, 1916.

31. Marie Pedersen in Randlev, section 8 case, 1913, National Archives. Judgment of December 4, 1916, in Record of Judgments of Hads-Ning District 1915–1920, the Regional Archives of Northern Jutland, Viborg. Articles in *Folkeskolen,* 1912–1916, 1926, and the local newspaper, *Odder Dagblad,* 1912–1916, 1926.

32. Schoolmistress in Haarslev, Case of complaint, 1913, National Archives.

33. Cathrine Agerskov in Masnedsund, Dismissal in accordance with section 18, National Archives. Articles in *Folkeskolen,* 1916, and *Købstadskolen,* 1916.

34. As regards the female head teachers, see Hanne Rimmen Nielsen, "Mine Hvid, Samsø—Den første kvindelige førstelærer," *Den jyske Historiker,* No. 62, 1993, pp. 62–94.

35. Schoolmistress in Gyrstinge, Dismissal on account of "Insubordination," 1917, National Archives; Julie Vallentin in Rugsted, Dismissal in accordance with section 8, National Archives. The case against Julie Vallentin is also commented on in *Folkeskolen,* 1922, pp. 55, 57, 67.

36. The case against Miss Due in Skagen is treated in several articles in *Folkeskolen,* 1916, and *Købstadskolen,* 1916. The case is apparently missing in the National Archives. There are other dismissal cases about leaving the national church in the National Archives, but there are also examples of schoolmistresses who were allowed to remain in their jobs after leaving the church; see *Folkeskolen,* 1922, p. 806.

37. Several articles in *Folkeskolen,* 1920–1921, 1926, and *Købstadskolen,* 1921.

38. *Købstadskolen,* 1921, p. 2.

39. Lehmann, *Haandbog i Lovgivningen,* p. 360.

40. Articles in *Folkeskolen,* 1927, 1928, 1929. The case is apparently missing in the National Archives.

41. Karen Jensen in Hatting, *Folkeskolen,* 1927, pp. 653–654.

42. Articles in *Folkeskolen,* 1914, 1915. On the private school at Hvalsø, see *Danmarks Folkeskole,* 1910, p. 444.

43. The concept of female honor is discussed in Lisbeth Nielsen and Poul Porskær Poulsen, *Kæltringer og skikkelige folk i Gødvad sogn. Et midtjysk sogn og dets mennesker, belyst gennem herredsretten 1858–1890* (Odense: Landbohistorisk Selskab), 1991, pp. 83–86, 139–141.

44. Knud Peder Jensen, *Nåden og skammen* (Copenhagen: Gyldendal, 1985), pp. 128–132, describes the falling in love of a male and female teacher at the same school, their cautious behavior, and the gossip that affected them after all.

45. The fate of Marie Landtreter, Skærbæk, is treated in Gottlieb Japsen, *Pastor Jacobsen fra Skærbæk og hans foretagender* (Åbenrå: Historisk Samfund for Sonderjylland, 1980), pp. 170–184.

46. *Folkeskolen,* 1924, pp. 582–583.

47. The I. M. Nordentoft case is the subject of Poul Hammerich, *Skindet på næsen. Første bind af En Danmarkskrønike 1945–1972* (Copenhagen: Gyldendal, 1976), pp. 157–180.

48. Cutting from the newspaper *Land og Folk* 1946, File on the Nordentoft case, The

Women's History Collections, The State Library, Århus. *Rigsdagstidende,* Folketingets Forhandlinger (The Proceedings of Parliament), 1945–1946, column 6346ff (Debate on the Nordentoft case). See also Adda Hilden, "Stærk som døden—en uægteskabelig historie fra 1800-tallets slutning," *Historiske Meddelelser om København,* 1993, pp. 33–51, about a female teacher in Copenhagen who had an illegitimate child in the 1870s.

49.   *Rigsdagstidende,* Folketingets Forhandlinger (The Proceedings of Parliament), 1945–1946, column 6380.

50.   Lehmann, *Haandbog i Lovgivningen,* pp. 356–365, pp. 362, 260.

51.   Julie Vallentin in Rugsted, Married teacher couple in Salby, Case of complaint, National Archives.

52.   *Folkeskolen,* 1913, p. 473.

Chapter Eight
Moral Regulation and the Nineteenth-Century "Lady Teacher"
The Case of Catherine Streeter

Marjorie Theobald

On February 15, 1883, Mrs. Catherine Streeter, first assistant teacher at the Sandhurst State School, was sworn in as a witness before the royal commission into public instruction in the Australian colony of Victoria.[1] Though eighty-six witnesses were called, Streeter was one of only nine women to give evidence, and the reason for her presence was soon apparent. The commissioners wished to know her opinion upon the current practice of teaching girls and boys together in the public elementary schools, which were the subject of their inquiry. For her part, Catherine Streeter was unequivocal. She believed that the mixing of the sexes in class made the girls "bold and forward, . . . wanting in modesty"; mixed schooling led to "roughness and rudeness, . . . writing of love letters, and meeting after school." The generality of male teachers were, in her opinion, not fit to teach the older girls; they made too free with them, putting their arms around the girls' waists in class and flirting with them during recess time. The male student teachers she singled out for particular censure. At this distance it is not possible to know how the commissioners reacted to her evidence, but they did invite her to describe how she had put a stop to such behavior in her own schools over the twenty years of her teaching experience. Again, Streeter did not hesitate:

I was obliged to do it by my own strength, by my own will. . . . I never allowed them to sit in the same seats. I never allowed them to play together, or even to speak in school. . . . I separated them in different blocks of seats. . . . I separated them perfectly during play, by keeping the boys all at one side of the yard, and the girls at the other. . . . I punished any who broke the order.

To the question "Would you send [your daughter] to these mixed schools?" Mrs. Streeter replied, "No, I would not."

Catherine Streeter also raised before the commission a case of immorality in which she had become embroiled in a previous school at Ballarat, like Sandhurst a prosperous gold-mining town, one hundred kilometers northwest of Melbourne. Here is her telling of the incident:

There was first an investigation, and I found that certain parties were afraid to give their evidence unless they were forced to give it on oath, and then we applied for a Board to the Minister, which the Minister granted. The Board was appointed and it only consisted of three gentlemen. Two or three days before the sitting of the Board, a friend came and cautioned my husband and me that the decision of the Board was premeditated. We then employed a barrister and . . . the evidence was taken on oath, and it seemed very clear, but the finding of the Board was in opposition to the evidence, as I think you will find by referring to the evidence, which must be in the hands of the department. For instance, I was found guilty of insubordination, but there was no charge whatever made against me.

Though he was not named on this occasion, her protagonist in the affair was William Cox, head teacher of the Ballarat school, against whom she had brought unspecified charges of immorality. We learn only that, in her opinion, Cox was one of those who was inclined to lay his hands upon the girls while teaching them in class.

The perception of state elementary school teachers as "moral workers" is not new; indeed this perception underpinned the whole revisionist project in the field of the history of education in the 1970s and 1980s.[2] Nor indeed was the notion of women as moral arbiters of the sexual economy new in the nineteenth century; women on working-class doorsteps and in middle-class drawing rooms had considerable power to monitor and regulate the relationships of those around them. As "lady teachers," however, women like Catherine Streeter gained access to the state's burgeoning capacities to know about its citizens, and to regulate them in new ways. The notion of women teachers as willing agents of moral regulation has proved conceptually uncomfortable for feminist historians, who have preferred to look for existential gains as women entered the teaching profession.[3] I will argue that a close reading of the Streeter case need not lead to recriminations, but to new and interesting connections between educational system-building, moral regulation, and individual subjectivities.

There are traces of these connections in the evidence that Catherine Streeter gave before the royal commission in 1883. Two tightly interwoven themes carry Streeter's sense of herself through her encounter with the commissioners. Firstly, her accounting of power, of her efficacy as a technician in the schoolroom, is embedded within a melodrama of sexual danger; secondly, there is an insistent subtext of loss, of power and status diminished. "You were at one time the head teacher of a state school?" the male commissioners inquired, signaling and dismissing contingency, humiliation, and the hard work of assembling the self in the lives of Victoria's lady teachers.

I will begin by sketching in the larger topography of educational system-building as it shaped the subjectivity of the nineteenth-century lady teacher. Indisputably, Catherine Streeter's chilling certainty as moral arbiter did not diminish as the state systematically dismantled the possibilities for women teaching in the nineteenth century. Born Catherine Sheppard in Ireland in 1842, she had entered the teaching service in Australia in 1858 under very different circumstances from those that produced the royal commission of the early 1880s.[4] As a (Catholic) teacher in the St. Mary's Catholic denominational school in Geelong, her employer was the local school committee (under the tutelage of the priest, Dean James Hayes) and her salary was paid by the Denominational School Board, one of two boards that administered state-subsidized schools until 1862. At mid-century, the habit of going to school had yet to be established. As attendance was not compulsory and fees were charged, church, state, and private providers were obliged to compete in a free market of education that made the formation of an orderly teaching service impossible. Educational boundaries were shifting and permeable in ways that would become unthinkable later in the century. Highly educated teachers, capable of grafting onto the elementary curriculum the "middle-class" subjects of mathematics and classics, formed alliances with local committees and parents, moving easily between the dual boards, the church grammar schools, and their own private enterprise schools. A similar traffic developed among women capable of teaching the female accomplishments of music, modern languages, and painting.

In the 1850s, Victoria was an immigrant society. The discovery of gold in 1851 had triggered the transformation of Melbourne from a small outpost serving a pastoral hinterland into a prosperous, cosmopolitan city. For the next two decades, a significant source of teacher supply was the well-educated immigrant, male or female, who had no difficulty in passing the "literary examinations" instituted by both boards in the 1850s. This lateral recruitment of staff was in marked contrast to the vertical recruitment and training of student teachers, themselves parsimoniously educated in state schools, which characterized the service by the end of the century. It is salutary to realize that, in the first two decades of its existence, the state teaching service in Victoria had more highly educated, idiosyncratic, and ungovernable teachers, male and female, than at any other time.

Both Catherine Sheppard and her husband, Julius Streeter, became teachers under these conditions, as did several other members of their families. Both had claims to gentility; they were referred to as "well-bred" in the minutes of evidence generated by the affair at the Ballarat school in 1878.[5] Julius had moved between the sectors, from the Presbyterian Ballarat Grammar School, to his own private secondary school, and then into the state system; Catherine was almost certainly "moonlighting" at the "Ladies' Seminary, Yarra St., Geelong, conducted by the Misses Sheppard." Both had prepared candidates for the civil service examinations and for the University of Melbourne matriculation examination.

The strongest evidence of Catherine Streeter's standing in the hothouse society of nineteenth-century Victoria—and indeed of her robust sense of self—comes down to us through her remarkable career as a portrait painter, pursued with great tenacity thoughout her thirty-six-year stint as an elementary school teacher.[6] Her departmental record notes cryptically that in 1867 she passed the examination for a license to teach drawing in elementary schools, but her training as an artist developed well beyond the requirements of her employer. Her commissioned portraits include Mother Xavier Maguire, founder of the Mercy Sisters' Geelong mission, the Rev. William Quick, a founder of Queen's College at the University of Melbourne, and Sir Anthony Colling Brownless, chancellor of the same university. She exhibited regularly, attracting good reviews, and in 1879 her painting entitled "Portrait of Manfred" gained an honorable mention at the Paris International Exhibition. She continued to exhibit, and at the age of fifty-eight, while first lady assistant at a large Melbourne school, studied at the National Gallery School. Her growing reputation as portrait painter to the middle classes of Melbourne also helps to explain her selection as a witness before the Rogers Templeton commission in the early 1880s.

Well-educated middle-class immigrants like the Streeters could be lured into the state teaching service only with the promise of reasonable remuneration. Though the point cannot be elaborated here, the regulations developed to encourage entrepreneurial activity by head teachers (the key elements were fees and the teaching of "middle-class" subjects), with the result that successful husband and wife teams in large urban schools could and did earn in excess of £1,000 per annum—more than the sum required to lure the first professors of the University of Melbourne away from the ancient universities of England and Ireland. Thus in the middle decades of the century, Victoria developed what Carole Hooper has described as "an effective, and administratively supported, system of higher education within government schools."[7] Official discourse celebrated the entrepreneur school teacher. In 1866, chairman of the Board of Education, Sir James Palmer, commented approvingly: "Accomplished masters . . . who are classical scholars, and have a knowledge of French and German, and have received a college education, will always be appreciated, and will derive, and most deservedly so, a high remuneration."[8]

Remarkably, in the same decades there were no regulations excluding women from the rewards of this government-subsidized entrepreneurship, though from the beginning their base salaries were less than the equivalent male rate. Women head teachers could and did earn aggregate salaries far in excess of many of their male colleagues. Victoria's women teachers too were subject to the market forces that shaped the policies of the educational state, but they were positioned differently from men. The discourses that surrounded their presence in the schools had little to say about their natural endowments as teachers, and even less about their availability as cheap labor. The educational state forged its alliance with women on other grounds entirely. The presence of women teachers in Victoria's classrooms was legitimated by a persistent discourse of moral danger, curiously at odds with the official discourse that insisted that the state-funded elementary school was productive of public and private morality.[9] Dissonance between women and the public sphere ensured that, throughout the nineteenth century, there were more boys than girls in the state schools, even after compulsory attendance destroyed parental choice. While sons might be committed to the rough and tumble of the publicly funded school, daughters were a different matter. It was girls who were withdrawn at the slightest hint of moral transgression, and moral transgression was routinely detected in the arrival of an unmarried male teacher. In small country schools parents preferred a married couple (often designated head teacher and sewing mistress); and in urban centers, they preferred separate girls' departments staffed and headed by women. As the educational state was obliged to purchase respectability through a female presence in its classrooms, the lady teacher too had her market value. This parental preference for the teaching family also explains why marriage, child-bearing, and domestic duties were not at first constituted as incompatible with elementary school teaching. Indeed the lure of the aggregated family income, invisible in official calculations of teachers' incomes, made elementary school teaching additionally attractive in the nineteenth century.

The autonomous female departments headed by women were the crucial link between subjectivity and system-building. Mrs. Mary Jenvey, head teacher of the girls' department of a large Melbourne school and acknowledged as the top woman in the Victorian system, had appeared before an earlier royal commission in the 1860s to explain the technicalities:

[Q.] What is the relation that exists between the female teacher and the head teacher of a school?—[A.] I am the head, as far as my school is concerned.

[Q.] Then is there any relation whatever between the head male teacher and the head female teacher?—[A.] Not the slightest . . . .

[Q.] What was your net income last year?—[A.] Three hundred and sixteen pounds, from all sources.

[Q.] Net?—[A.] Yes.

[Q.] That is for yourself?—[A.] That is for myself.[10]

The incomprehension of the all-male commission face to face with a female member of the urban head teacher elite prompted Jenvey to elaborate on her situation at the Church of England–affiliated St. Mark's school. She was at the time under suspension by her local committee over the distribution of the very lucrative fees, and her testimony affords an insight into women's access to the speculative market that the educational state had created by the mid-1860s. Jenvey had taken the school when it was very run down and made it profitable: "It was a kind of speculation that as soon as I could make it a profitable school the profits should be mine; but as soon as it became profitable, first one percentage was taken off and then a larger one, so that I feel myself very much ill-used indeed." She claimed that as a result of her suspension, most of her 150 girls were being kept home in protest by their parents. Not surprisingly, Mary Jenvey, like Catherine Streeter, regarded the mixing of boys and girls as "very inexpedient." And, like Streeter almost twenty years later, she advised that if the sexes were to be mixed a female teacher should be employed, on the grounds that "boys suffer less under a mistress than do girls under a master."

In this manner the system shaped an elite of teaching matriarchs, respected by parents and inspectors alike, who were accustomed to wielding power; but it was power embedded in the melodrama of sexual danger that Catherine Streeter invoked before the royal commissioners in 1883. Though its own regulations were silent on the matter, the new Board of Education, which replaced the dual boards in 1862, began a covert war of attrition against these separate female departments, ostensibly on the grounds of "rational" school organization but actually on the grounds of economy. It was reluctant to allow separate departments in schools established after that time, and upon each forced amalgamation in an existing school the female head teacher was demoted to first assistant, with considerable loss of salary and status. Though Catherine Streeter's career in these years can only be sketched in from the minimal details on her teacher record, the head teachership of the girls' department at St. Mary's appears to have eluded her. In 1870, when the average attendance of girls rose to forty, she won the right to be paid the base salary of a headmistress under a clause designed to compensate the first female assistant in schools that had been amalgamated.

Throughout the 1860s, women teachers routinely formed alliances with parents to invoke the threat of mass withdrawal of female pupils if classes were to be mixed, on some occasions departing with the female pupils to begin a private school."[11] Indeed the women teachers found other powerful allies in the 1860s. The same royal commissioners who took the evidence of Mary Jenvey wrote in their report:

We think that the mixing of children of both sexes is objectionable, except in schools where ample accommodation exists, together with such an amount of efficient supervision as can be only rarely provided; and therefore that it is advisable to provide separate schools for boys and girls, at least wherever one hundred and fifty children of each sex are in attendance at the school.[12]

The Board of Education quietly ignored this recommendation, although women demoted from head teacherships were created first assistants above the highest ranking male assistants in recognition of their onerous duties as senior woman in mixed schools. The *coup de grace* against the separate female departments was delivered by the regulations flowing from the Education Act of 1872.

The Victorian Education Act of 1872, sometimes known as the "Free, Secular, and Compulsory Act," created a department of education under a minister of the crown, which centrally administered staffing, curriculum, and textbooks. The act withdrew effective power from local authorities and parents, withdrew state aid from church schools, separated secular instruction from religious instruction, abolished fees, and mandated attendance at school. The Victorian Act, emulated by the other Australian colonies over the next twenty years, gave to the phenomenon of state elementary schooling its essential characteristics for over one hundred years.[13]

The impact of the 1872 Education Act upon teachers has received little systematic attention from historians. Though its main focus was religious and constitutional, the act also dismantled the entrepreneurial possibilities of the previous regime. Again, it is not possible to explicate fully the reasons here, but the key measures were the centralization of control over teachers, which destroyed the grassroots alliances between teachers and parents, and the abolition of fees, which limited the extra earning potential of the urban head teacher. This was a pivotal moment in the delineation of the elementary school teacher, as men began to leave the service for more lucrative occupations at a time when compulsory attendance fueled a voracious need for teachers. For the last quarter of the nineteenth century, the department's dealings with its female teachers must be read in mirror image, for they reflect the struggle to recruit and reproduce a male teaching elite in the vastly changed circumstances ushered in by the 1872 act. Official discourse quickly abandoned the celebration of the entrepreneur-teacher, and began instead to speak of disinterested public service and professionalism. This was not entirely empty rhetoric. In a strategy designed to attract and retain men, the Public Service Act of 1883 constituted Victorian state school teachers, male and female, as public servants. Hailed at the time as a victory for the teaching profession, this strategy had consequences that were possibly unintentional, but nonetheless insidious for Victoria's lady teachers. In effect, they were thrown into the state-controlled sector of the white-collar labor market at precisely the time when it was being transformed into a respectable bailiwick for middle-class men outside the uncertain pursuit of wealth in the marketplace.[14]

The consequences for women were soon apparent. In 1885, the public service commissioner, who now controlled the fate of Victoria's state school teachers, issued the first classified roll for Victoria's state school teachers, promising an orderly teaching service, with progression through the ranks based on seniority, literary qualifications, and merit. Though the classified roll was a disturbing document for all teachers, women had special cause to feel betrayed. For the first time, women teachers lost the right to be head teachers in any but the smallest country schools. Everyday understandings that women should not be in authority over men, permeable to negotiation and subversion, passed into legislation with the decision that women could not be heads of schools with an enrollment of under 50. Women were excluded from the first class of teachers, which consisted of 37 men, corresponding roughly to the number of large, urban schools in the first class. The 28 most highly qualified women in the service, the teaching matriarchs, were clustered in the second class. Without any explanation, there were only 6 places allotted for women in the third class, while there were 132 for men. This constituted an almost insuperable block to promotion for the 82 women in the fourth class. By far the largest group of female teachers, 780, were classified in the lowest, or fifth, class, and their chances of promotion were remote. This was not the final indignity. Again without explanation, a further group of 240 women and 36 men were placed in a newly created division at the bottom of the fifth class and designated "junior assistants." In this group were many who had been classified teachers before the Public Service Act of 1883, the longest-serving among them being Mrs. Kate Bell, who had been teaching since 1856.

In this manner, the construction of a male elite in the profession of elementary teaching passed into legislative possibility. Yet the destruction of the teaching matriarch was not quite complete. In November 1889 the Gillies government legislated to remove married women from the public service and therefore from the teaching profession. They were not again allowed equal access to the teaching labor market until the Teaching Service (Married Women's) Act of 1956. For the majority of young women who entered teaching in the first half of the twentieth century, the department had installed a revolving door. Women who remained single grew old in the infant room, paid to be exemplar of the ever-present mother with children who were not her own. In the calling of the elementary school teacher, the construction of a male teaching elite was a *fait accompli.*

This then was the web of educational state-building, material circumstances, and discursive practices within which Catherine Streeter was obliged to shape and reshape her professional and personal identities. Unlike the women who entered teaching after the marriage bar was in place, the teaching matriarchs of the nineteenth century experienced their oppression as contingent, humiliating, and grounded in the everyday politics of school life. When we read Streeter's actions against this larger topography of system-building, her angry *mission civilisatrice* begins to make sense. Streeter experienced in full the dislocation of the school system as the 1872 act was implemented. Administrators faced the dual problems of dismantling the defeated church/state system and implementing the compulsory clause. As a Catholic school, St. Mary's was closed in November 1874. With her Catholic colleagues, Streeter faced the prospect of life in the *de facto* Protestant schools that masqueraded as neutral territory under the benign patronage of the state. Streeter's next school, Redan State School in Ballarat, came into existence as a direct result of the act, enrolling over 500 children in three make-shift premises by February 1874. Streeter was appointed first assis-tant in December of that year, shortly after the school moved to its new premises. Twelve months later she was transferred to Soldier's Hill State School, where she remained until May 1878, when it too was struck off the roll and re-established in new premises in Macarthur Street, Ballarat. This brings us full circle to the affair at the Macarthur Street school in that year.

The splendid new school proclaimed in red brick and gable the triumph of the educational state over denominationalism, over local interests, and over families. The Macarthur Street school and its coun-terparts in the major cities and towns of Australia were more than an architectural expression of the triumph of the state. Australia's first generation of powerful educational administrators—notably Will-iam Wilkins in New South Wales and John Hartley in South Aus-tralia—saw the new state schools as crucibles for their credo of rational school management. They had chafed under the restrictions upon their power in the previous era of church and local participa-tion, and they had exercised a powerful influence over the centralist form that the new legislation took. From the center, their power radiated out through an inspectorate, through the head teacher, and finally through his "subordinates." While the new state education departments tolerated outward architectural diversity, the ground plans of their new urban schools had in common those features that marked out a system of mass education in transition from monitorialism to the classroom as we understand it today.[15] In the nomenclature of the times, the ground floor plan of the model school consisted of large schoolrooms up to sixty-five feet long by twenty feet wide housing up to two hundred children, served by smaller adjunct classrooms with stepped galleries where children could be withdrawn for "simultaneous" class instruction. This first generation of educational administrators did not abhor the large congregations of children assembled in the urban school; on the contrary, it quickly became an article of faith that large schools were superior to small schools, bringing to bear on the individual child the power of the prevailing moral climate.[16] Architectural plans reflected the now official ban upon separate boys' and girls' departments in Victoria, although this was not so in other states, where segregation by sex remained official policy if numbers allowed. The retention of the huge schoolrooms, even into the twentieth century, also reflected the continuing reliance upon the cheap labor of student teachers, who could not be put in authority over classes without the constant supervision of the head teacher or first assistant. Drawing ambiguously upon the ideas of British educationalists David Stow, James Kay-Shuttleworth, and Samuel Wilderspin, Australian educational administrators demarcated a new space within which childhood could be shaped afresh in the changing circumstances of the urban, industrial society. Relationships between adult and child were abstracted from everyday life, where the proprieties of class, gender, and age were deemed to be under siege. In the mass school systems that developed, adult authority over children became theater, reenacted every day through a common set of practices which over the years took on a patina of inevitability. So pervasive did this technology of the state school become that it cast all other forms of organization as "alternative," a nomenclature that to this day carries a suggestion of children out of control.

What Catherine Streeter did in 1878 was to capture this elaborate technology of moral regulation and turn it against the opaque certainties of adult male sexuality itself. On June 1, 1878, nearly seven hundred children, eight teachers, and eight student teachers moved into the new Macarthur Street premises. They were by no means new to each other, for they were the staff and pupils of Soldiers' Hill State School, a Presbyterian-sponsored school under the pre-1872 regime, over which headmaster William Cox had presided in substandard accommodation for many years. Under Cox the staff descended in strict hierarchical order from first to seventh assistant, their salaries diminishing with their status. For the historical reasons already sketched in, Catherine Streeter, as first assistant, ranked second in command, above the most highly qualified male assistant, though she did not preside over a separate female department. Her husband, Julius, was third assistant on a considerably lower salary, though he had been teaching the senior class for many years. Despite these optimum conditions for the implementation of rational school management, a mere two months after the move to the new premises relationships between the staff were disorderly to a point where the Education Department felt obliged to hold an inquiry.

Catherine Streeter and her husband tripped the mechanism that brought Inspector Holland to the scene in August 1878. The Streeters' complaints against William Cox were not, at first, the stuff of high drama, though they are familiar fare to anyone who has used the school records of the period: among other things, the Streeters alleged that Cox had been critical of their teaching within earshot of the children, thus diminishing their status in the eyes of their pupils; he had reminded them that they were his "subordinates" and not his "coadjutors" in the school; he had made it known that he did not want a husband and wife team on his staff; he had transferred Julius Streeter "in an abrupt and insulting manner" from the position of sixth class teacher to the position of third class teacher; and he had opened a letter addressed to Mrs. Streeter. This was a ritual battle over status and subjectivities played out again and again by teachers of the former regime in the changed circumstances after 1872. Inspector Holland diligently inquired into the charges—his minutes of evidence are still in existence—and while he found fault with both sides, especially with regard to brawling in front of the children, by and large his report exonerated William Cox, with whom, he pointed out, ultimate authority in the school resided.[17] Nevertheless, Holland concluded his report with the comment that, in his view, there were "some other grounds for dispute beyond this which neither party is willing to state." He found it impossible to say who was to blame in the first instance.

There were indeed "other grounds for dispute" between William Cox and the Streeters, and this subterranean narrative of the sexual—anathema to the moral regime of the state school—was brutally exposed in the second inquiry held into the affair in November of the same year, this time before a board of inquiry with barristers present on behalf of both parties.[18] As bachelor teachers, William Cox and Julius Streeter had been "on intimate and friendly terms" before the Streeters' marriage in December 1877; indeed Streeter had lived in Cox's home. In early 1876, Sabina Williams, a servant in Cox's household, wrote to the Education Department informing them that she was pregnant by Cox, and that he had "abandoned" her. Before the board of inquiry in November 1878, Julius Streeter had testified that he had advised Cox not to marry her, and that subsequently Cox had paid her off. The affair was, in Streeter's words, "pretty generally known in the town and talked about in public places." There was a departmental inquiry at the time, though no action was taken against William Cox, apparently on the grounds that Sabina Williams was in no way connected with the Macarthur Street school.

Relationships between Cox and the Streeters were still sufficiently amicable for Cox to act as best man at their wedding on the morning of December 22, 1877, and for the three to go in the afternoon to the school picnic in the country some miles outside Ballarat. The domain of the sexual, symbolized by the Streeters' wedding, was customarily given quasi-legitimate expression on the social occasion of the picnic, which provided a bounded temporal and geographic space in which the forbidden sexual dimension among those in regulated daily contact could be played out in ritual games of physical contact between the sexes. William Cox, who, it was hinted by one witness, was somewhat the worse for alcohol from the wedding party, joined in a game of "kiss in the ring" with the girls and allegedly chased and pulled to the ground a seventeen-year-old girl named Harriet Nicholls.

Upon her marriage, Catherine Streeter herself was drawn inexorably into the domain of the sexual. She became pregnant soon after her marriage and, when she was away on sick leave for a few days in June, a lascivious rumor was put about that she had already given birth to a child. The Streeters later accused Cox of instigating the rumor, precipitating a comic-book brawl between the two men that must thereafter have loomed large in the folklore of the school. The Streeters' baby was born in October. Catherine Streeter came into possession of these three pieces of information about Cox—the Sabina Williams affair, the incident at the picnic, and his casting of Streeter herself as a loose woman—in the context of her deteriorating professional relationship with him at the school. With Inspector Holland, I conclude that it is impossible to know at this distance which was cause and which was effect.

The ill-feeling between William Cox and the Streeters, which had rendered the school virtually unworkable, came to a head in September 1878 when Catherine Streeter threatened to write to the department concerning the "assault" upon Harriet Nicholls if Cox did not ask for a transfer to another school. In her telling of events, William Cox believed that he could not withstand a second inquiry into his conduct and agreed to go. Ironically, both Cox and the Streeters were gone from the Macarthur Street school before the affair was placed on the public record by the second official inquiry in November 1878.

Before the board of inquiry in November the "facts" were not in dispute, though they were presented differently by the various parties. Cox refused, on the advice of his lawyer, to answer questions about his relationship with Sabina Williams. In the present context, the inquiry should be read as both theater and artifact of moral regulation in a particular historical context. Canadian historian Bruce Curtis has argued that the rapid spread of state school systems, preceding as they did other forms of governance in many localities, was crucial to nineteenth-century state formation. He suggests that the voluminous reports of inspectors and other functionaries from the localities to the center vastly expanded the state's capacity to "know" its citizens and hence to render them governable. Curtis characterizes this as a "new tutelar relationship between state and citizen, a relationship of intellectual, moral and paternal guardianship."[19] With Philip Abrams, Curtis argues for a dual conception of the state on the one hand as a set of institutions, buildings, and functionaries, and on the other as a process—the state in action—which he characterizes as a continuous quest for legitimacy in the domination of one class (and sex?) over another. Thus Curtis's conceptualization of the state allows for contestation and ambiguity—and indeed for the possibility that state formation and the fortunes of individual protagonists may go on in a symbiotic relationship. As Curtis would be the first to admit, the positioning of women in the processes of state formation remains problematical for historians, though he has suggested that the intersection of "regimes of gender relations" with "regimes of knowledge/power" will be discoverable in social and political praxis, rather than in sexed bodies or in distinctive women's ways of knowing.[20] The sexual politics that Catherine Streeter played in her own interests at the Macarthur Street school suggests just such an intersection of gender and power in praxis—in this case, the calling into discourse of male sexuality itself through the knowledge-producing regimes of the educational state.

Streeter's aggregation into "truth" of the moral pollution at the Macarthur Street school was certainly strategic and perhaps duplicitous. Hers was not innocent knowledge. She had known of William Cox's lascivious behavior at the school picnic since December 1877 yet, mysteriously, the charge blossomed into one of sexual assault only when the girl in question, Harriet Nicholls, came to her house with the new version of events shortly after the Streeters' defeat at the Holland inquiry in August. Armed with this unsubstantiated charge, Streeter had no compunction in forcing Cox out of the school. Streeter was rubbery in the extreme as to when she had first learned of the Sabina Williams affair: on one occasion it was before her marriage; on another it was six months after her marriage. Yet knowledge of this affair was central to her case against Cox, a case that was rapidly assembled after the Holland inquiry exonerated the headmaster in August. In essence, Streeter testified that she had sensed in the school from the time of her arrival a low moral tone:

I heard when I was [at the Macarthur Street school] a few months that there was a great deal of scandal talked about Mr. Cox and though I scarcely knew Mr. Streeter I went to him and said that Mr. Cox should get a hint about it if he did not know about it. It was talked of about town. I consider it had the effect of making the boys and girls too free with each other, the male pupil teachers showed a freedom towards the grown girls. I considered that they all knew it and it had a bad effect upon the children.[21]

Streeter's accounting of this miasma of male sexuality polluting the Macarthur Street school, this narrative of unmarried men laying siege to female virtue, enabled her to invoke the lady teacher as indispensable moral worker:

I saw the freedom amongst the pupil teachers and the grown girls and I separated them. I think this freedom was the result of the scandalous reports and in mentioning it to Mr. Cox he told me to put it down but he gave me no assistance in doing so.[22]

In the end, the men closed ranks against Catherine Streeter. The board of inquiry, like Inspector Holland's investigation before it, exonerated William Cox. Only Samuel Figgis, in a dissenting report, was prepared to concede to Catherine Streeter a superior moral instinct by virtue of her sex. In his view, her "matured judgement and womanly instinct" uniquely qualified her to define "the line of decorum to be observed in the intercourse between young and unmarried teachers of both sexes." The majority report found that, on the evidence of the other members of staff, there was no "uneasy feeling or tone" in the school, nor did the witnesses admit to knowing about the Sabina Williams affair. The charge of "immoral behaviour and indecent conduct" at the picnic was also dismissed, largely on the grounds that Harriet Nicholls had appeared unperturbed at the time and had waited eight months to tell her story of sexual assault. The board found Cox to be "deserving of mild censure" and the Streeters to be "deserving of severe censure," a verdict that Catherine Streeter deplored before the Rogers Templeton commissioners a few years later. Nor was William Cox's career unduly affected by the events of 1878. He was transferred as headmaster to the nearby Maryborough State School, followed Patrick Whyte as head of the prestigious model school in Melbourne in 1886, and by 1895 had returned as head of the Macarthur Street school. In the official history of the Victorian Education Department both William Cox and the Macarthur Street school are accorded pioneer status in the triumphal narrative of state education, though there is no mention of Catherine and Julius Streeter.[23]

Afterword

When Catherine Streeter left the Macarthur Street school at the end of 1878 she was appointed head teacher at Scarsdale, a school of nearly four hundred pupils twenty-five kilometers from Ballarat. In that year she was the only married woman in the Victorian state service to be head teacher in authority over her own husband. Such an appointment was no longer possible after the Public Service Act of 1883 confined women to the headships of schools with fewer than fifty pupils. On January 1, 1883, Streeter was transferred as first assistant to Sandhurst State School in central Victoria, where she was teaching when she gave her evidence before the royal commission of 1883. Her testimony captures something of the everyday politics surrounding the status of the first lady assistant under the regime ushered in by the Act of 1883:

> *The position of the first assistant [she said] is very indefinite, and depends altogether on the will or whim of the head teacher. In the school I am at present teaching in, there are two male teachers teaching the senior classes, while I am teaching the upper fifth or third class in the school. . . . I would have been sent to teach the infants in Sandhurst if I could sing, and I was very glad I could not sing.*[24]

In November 1883 Catherine Streeter returned to Melbourne, replacing Mary Jenvey as first assistant at the prestigious Carlton State School, a plum position which ensured that she was placed among the top twenty-eight women on the first classified roll of 1885. She nevertheless joined forces with the Melbourne teachers, male and female, who began to organize in protest over the administration of the Public Service Act of 1883. She was present in October 1885 at the meeting that approved the constitution of the first teachers' union and was elected to its council as a representative of the second-class teachers.[25] Though the early records have been lost, she was almost certainly a member of the militant Victorian Lady Teachers' Association, formed in the same year to fight the manifest injustices done to women by the classified roll of 1885. Her teacher record for this period notes that she was again teaching the senior classes, where her duties included "extra and advanced subjects."

With advancing age Catherine Streeter apparently lost nothing of her fire. She was officially censured twice in 1891, once for "the infliction of undue punishment upon a male pupil," and once for insubordination to the head teacher. This censure was accompanied by a warning that, unless she complied immediately with the instructions of the head teacher, she would be suspended and her case referred to the Public Service Board. In the same year an inspector noted: "I am not favourably impressed with Mrs. Streeter's teaching and class management, nor does it seem to me that she renders loyal service and effective help to the Head Teacher." The Public Service Amendment Act of 1889, which legislated to remove married women from the service, did not require that women already married should resign. Catherine Streeter taught for another five years when she was compulsorily retired, with all other married women, as a retrenchment measure in the economic depression of 1894. Her record ends with the information that she had taught for thirty-five years and eighty-two days, and that she retired on a pension of just over £192. The Victorian Lady Teachers' Association wrote in its report for 1894 an epitaph for the teaching matriarchs of nineteenth-century Victoria:

A most valuable section of our teachers has been compelled to retire, the majority of the married ladies and those ladies who had served for thirty years, most of them being in the prime of their life and powers. It has been a sad blow to our association, as many of them have been members of it from its foundation, and several were among the promoters. The sudden removal of these experienced teachers cannot fail to have a most detrimental effect on our schools.[26]

In 1921 Catherine Streeter moved to the northern state of Queensland for the sake of her health, and there she continued to paint, holding an exhibition of her work in 1923. Her uncompromising self-portrait, painted in these years, depicts an elderly woman, easel and brush in hand, still painting. She died in 1930. A manuscript autobiography has not been located.

Women's history emerged in the 1970s as a political process to restore to women their own past; no matter how disturbing that past might be, women's history has always been, quintessentially, an act of celebration. For this reason, the lady teacher as willing agent of the regulatory state has presented conceptual difficulties that we have chosen to ignore. We do not approve of the Catherine Streeter who emerges from the vignettes of her teaching life, preserved among the voluminous documentation of the educational state. Streeter and her kind have been left stranded in the shallows of the ridiculous. If Catherine Streeter had not taken her stand against William Cox at the Macarthur Street school in 1878, would she now be safely ensconced among the lady teachers respectfully retrieved from obscurity in recent decades? Certainly, this essential lady teacher will no longer do. It is time to ask new and interesting questions about gender, power, and subjectivities, and the nineteenth-century lady teacher, uniquely interactive with the state, is a promising place to start. I have tried to show that Catherine Streeter's story may be interrogated to yield important connections between her sense of self, the material circumstances of her life, and the larger structures that both confined her and offered her the promise of an independent professional life. It was Streeter's existential dilemma to confront the power of men, bravely, without the words to name her own confinement within a discourse of sexual melodrama that still has its seductive appeal today. We have something to learn from the teaching matriarchs of nineteenth-century Australia.

Endnotes

1. *Victorian Parliamentary Papers 1884,* Royal Commission . . . into Public Instruction, Minutes of Evidence, pp. 307–311.
2. For an overview of "revisionism" in the history of education, see Carl F. Kaestle, "Historical Methods in Educational Research," in Richard M. Jaeger, ed., *Complementary Methods in Research in Education* (Washington, DC: AERA, 1988).
3. See, for example, Alison Prentice and Marjorie Theobald, eds., *Women Who Taught: Perspectives on the History of Women and Teaching* (Toronto: University of Toronto Press, 1991).
4. All details of Catherine Streeter's teaching career are from her teaching record (Department of School Education Archives, Melbourne) unless otherwise stated.
5. Victorian Public Record Series (hereafter VPRS) 892, No. 888, Board of Inquiry report, p. 11, Victorian Public Record Office (hereafter VPRO); all details of both inquiries into the Streeter case are from this special case file unless otherwise indicated.
6. Details of Streeter's career as a painter are from Veronica Filmer, *Painters of the Past: Colonial Art and Geelong* (Geelong: Geelong Art Gallery, 1991), pp. 44–46; and Joan Kerr, ed., *Dictionary of Australian Artists: Painters, Sketchers, Photographers, and Engravers to 1870* (Melbourne: Oxford University Press, 1992), pp. 721–722.
7. Carole Hooper, "Vision Unrealised: State Secondary Education in Victoria, 1850–1872," *History of Education Review,* Vol. 19, No. 1, 1990, p. 1.
8. *Victorian Parliamentary Papers 1867,* Royal Commission on Public Education 1867, Minutes of Evidence, p. 37.
9. I have developed this idea in Marjorie Theobald, "Discourse of Danger: Gender and the History of Elementary Schooling in Australia, 1850–1880," *Historical Studies in Education/Revue D'Histoire de L'Education,* Vol. 1, No. 1, 1989, pp. 29–52.
10. Royal Commission 1867, Minutes of Evidence, p. 284.
11. I have written about this phenomenon in Marjorie Theobald, "Women's Teaching

Labour, the Family and the State in Nineteenth-century Victoria," in Marjorie Theobald and R. J. W. Selleck, eds., *Family, School and State in Australian History* (Sydney: Allen and Unwin, 1990), pp. 25–44.

12. Royal Commission 1867, Report, p. 25.
13. For a useful overview of Australian education, see Alan Barcan, *A History of Australian Education* (Melbourne: Oxford University Press, 1980).
14. For the transformation of the public service in these years, see Graeme Davison, *The Rise and Fall of Marvellous Melbourne* (Melbourne: Melbourne University Press, 1979).
15. I am greatly indebted here to Lawrence Burchell, *Victorian Schools: A Study in Colonial Government Architecture 1837–1900* (Melbourne: Melbourne University Press, 1980).
16. My thinking here owes much to the following: R. J. W. Selleck, *James Kay-Shuttleworth: Journey of an Outsider* (Portland, Oregon: Woburn Press, 1994); Ian Hunter, *Rethinking the School: Subjectivity, Bureaucracy, Criticism* (Sydney: Allen and Unwin, 1994); Bruce Curtis, *Building the Educational State: Canada West, 1836–1871* (London, Ontario: Falmer Press/Althouse Press, 1988); and Andy Green, *Education and State Formation: The Rise of Educational Systems in England, France and the USA* (London: Macmillan, 1990).
17. VPRS 892, No. 888, Report of Inspector Holland.
18. VPRS 892, No. 888, Board of Inquiry, Report and Minutes of Evidence. The following account is based on this document unless otherwise mentioned.
19. Bruce Curtis, *True Government by Choice Men? Inspection, Education, and State Formation in Canada West* (Toronto: University of Toronto Press, 1992), p. 8.
20. Bruce Curtis, "Gender in the Regime of Statistical Knowledge/Power." Paper presented to the ANZHES/CHEA Conference, University of Melbourne, 1993.
21. VPRS 892, No. 888, Board of Inquiry, Minutes of Evidence, p. 7.
22. Ibid., p. 22.
23. L. J. Blake ed., *Vision and Realisation: A Centenary History of State Education in Victoria* (Melbourne: Education Department of Victoria, 1973), Vol. 2, p. 809.
24. Royal Commission 1884, Minutes of Evidence, p. 310.
25. *Australasian Schoolmaster,* Vol. 6, No. 77, November 1885, p. 266.
26. *Victorian Lady Teachers' Association, Tenth Annual Report,* November 1, 1892, p. 1.

Chapter Nine
Fashioning a Self
Gender, Class, and Moral Education for and by
Women in Colonial Bengal

Himani Bannerji

> *Woman was not created to be the ignorant slave or the plaything
> of man. As it is the purpose of a woman's life to do good to others,
> and to live for them, so does a woman live for herself. And the
> serious responsibilities that are entrusted to her demand not only
> a sympathetic heart, but also a cultivated head.*
> —Krishnabhabini Das, "Reply to the Protest against the Edu-
> cated Woman." Sahitya, *1904*

> *We call this "moral regulation": a project of normalizing, render-
> ing natural, taken for granted, in a word "obvious" what are in
> fact ontological and epistemological premises of a particular and
> historical form of social order.*
> —*Philip Corrigan and Derek Sayer,* The Great Arch, *1985*

Nineteenth-century Bengal is characterized by its preoccupation with
social reform, much of which concentrated on women.[1] Immediately meant for bettering the lot of women, it also aimed at reorga-
nizing fundamental social relations and forms of consciousness struc-
turing the family and lives of women among the middle classes.[2] A
reconstructive contestation resulted between the colonial state and
the Bengali male intelligentsia whose object was "the new Bengali
woman." But from the last decades of the century women themselves sought to contribute to this formative process of their social
subjectivities and agencies. The issue of education attracted much
attention, being the most well articulated and definitively ideological area within the scope of social reform. Controversies raging around
women's education, and the "educated woman," alias *bhadramahila*
(the gentlewoman), signaled far beyond the immediate social prob-

lems of women and served as a complex signifier of the common sense of the middle classes.[3] Seen thus, the various social reform projects of the century could be interpreted as marking moments in a battle for hegemony in which a class, or a class fraction, elaborates an ideological stance in its bid to become morally, culturally, and politically a dominant force within the civil society or the everyday life. They marked a stage in what Gramsci has called "the passive revolution," attempts at transforming the common sense of classes prior to, or along with, assuming a directly political role. The important question for us while dealing with social reform is what role women themselves, of their own volition, play in this "passive revolution." How did women fare in the "self-making" of their classes, and of themselves, and what modes did they adopt in this necessary task of fashioning selves and society?

Although most public facilities were not available to women, the print media, creating a bridge between the public and the private, offered them a wide communicative space. These women were already "educated," far beyond the literacy stage, the older ones mostly at home, and many of the younger ones in girls' schools. Magazines established by the male reforming intelligentsia, such as *Bamabodhini*, held space for women writers under the heading of *Bama Racana* ("Women's Writings"). But there were also other magazines such as *Bharati*, along with *Antahpur, Sahitya, Mukul, Sakha, Pradip*, and others, all of which created an extensive sphere of social influence and a field of participation for the rudimentary women's intelligentsia of the time.[4] Through an exploration of the content of these magazines we can arrive at some understanding of the type of social subjectivity and agency that middle-class Bengali women sought to create for themselves.

In the pages of these magazines the women writers and their women readers build up an extensive network and a general fund of communicative competence. They work up "women's issues," "women's approaches," and invite pieces on new themes, or hold essay competitions from among the readers. Thus it is difficult to see them as solely male-identified and an isolated mimic intelligentsia, as Sumanta Banerjee seems to suggest in his book *The Parlour and the Streets*.[5] They use the journal/magazine to create another social, moral, and cultural space for and by women, which is dis-

tinct from the domestic culture of the women's inner quarters
(andarmahal). Obviously both the society of women in the
andarmahal culture and that of the magazine producers shared forms
of patriarchal consciousness with their male counterparts. But
beyond and through their "women's educational agenda" and acceptance of "femininity," these women sought a guidance role within
society as a whole, as "women" members of propertied classes. As
Krishnabhabini Das put it:

*Especially, since the education of male kind ["purush jati"] depends
essentially on women's education and sense of morality, and since we can
directly see how a man's character depends on his home life, especially on
his mother's example, then who can deny that higher and quality education for women, lies at the root of national progress and morality?*[6]

This sentiment and argument, expanding in concentric circles
from the self-improvement of the woman, through her son, to the
nation, are found consistently and centrally in the works of all the
women writers who provide material for this essay. They are
Swarnakumari Debi, Gyanada Nandini Debi, Sarala Debi,
Hironmoyee Debi, and Krishnabhabini Das. This essay seeks to
locate their educational proposals within a larger problematic of formative relations between gender, class, and colonialism. The exploration centers on the nature of social subjectivity and agency,
assumed and recommended by these articles, and their implications
for the hegemonic aspirations for their class or class fraction. Through
this, the essay intends to show how "cultural," in the broadest sense,
"class" is and as such how deeply gendered is the agenda of "class"
and "classified" the construction of gender.

The special type of subjectivity that women have within a class
topography can be captured conceptually by adapting Louis
Althusser's notion of ideological interpellation.[7] Women of propertied classes are simultaneously empowered by their social location
and subordinated to the class's patriarchal, gendered organization.
From this perspective it can be said that women as members
of the middle class were "summoned" by Bengali nationalism's
"emancipatory" calls to become "social actors," hence their presence
on the stage of education.[8] Thus, the "dominant ideology" of the

reforming male intelligentsia calls on women to function as class subjects, while this subjectivity itself is sought to be contained, managed, truncated, and inauthenticated by the repression of their full social being through patriarchy. The women intelligentsia of the time are themselves not unaware of this double-edged situation. Their texts are therefore structured through complicity and antagonism, convergence and contradiction, making them simultaneously objects and subjects of their own discourse.

Studying an ideological process so woven with complex mediations of unequal relations of power, we need to be specially attentive to the processes of conceptual negotiation and moral syncretism which involve various adaptive, cooptive, exclusive, and innovative strategies. We have to note traces of collaboration that are highlighted by the very marks of resistance. We need to look both for values and symbols, interpretive devices and epistemologies, which share and advance patriarchal (local and colonial) class terms and hegemony, while waging an "inner struggle" against patriarchy within the same class space. The hegemonic agenda is invariably an agenda of morality, of values expressed through both ideas and practices.[9] It is through the creation, re-creation, and the diffusion of a set of norms and forms that the necessary "consent" can be built.[10] Thus one of their main consent-producing devices, as of colonialism, is "education," and the contents of these women's magazines offer an informal or noninstitutional aspect of that moral education.

Framing a Method

Women's education in the nineteenth century, and well into the twentieth, had little to do with economic functions, needs, or development of professional expertise among women. As Meredith Borthwick puts it, "Whereas education for males was directly related to the pursuit of employment, female education had no economic function."[11] The magazines make it clear that the main public use of women's education lies in its very nature as a private acquisition. Its ability to create appropriate personalities, familial-social relations, and households, and offer a moral basis for the everyday life of the *bhadralok* or the gentry, provides its justification. Women's educational projects are thus always phrased in terms of both social and moral "betterment," and the totality of this "betterment" is consistently expressed as the welfare of the family. "Proper" child-raising, character-building, and conjugality, as the core of the familial life, supply the occasion and the legitimation for a noninstitutional, home-based education among the women of urban propertied households, especially in the households of the professionals and the bureaucrats.[12] Even when "schooling" is considered, it is not in terms of acquisition of knowledge, profitable or otherwise, but rather in terms of betterment of the family. The general sentiment is phrased by Krishnabhabini Das:

There are some who raise objection to women's education on the ground that women lose their womanly virtues through the influence of education. They compete in everything with men and pay no attention to housework, etc. But if they [those who object] were to open their eyes they could see that this belief is wholly erroneous. In spite of the great amount of progress made in women's education in America, women there are neither inattentive to their homes, nor ignorant of child-care. In fact they are able to do both child-care and housework with great regulation and discipline, thus increasing happiness within the home, and facilitating the progress of their nation. Of course a few women, wearing men's clothing, abuse their independence and higher education, but does it make any sense to be outraged about women's education and independence in general by the examples of a few?[13]

In her essay "Jatya Jiban O Hindu Nari" ("Life of the Nation and the Hindu Woman"), she reiterates the nation's dependence for its future improvement on women and their organization of family life.[14]

If a society needs to develop new forms of "class consciousness" or subjectivities, this can be done in a fundamental way only by reworking the family form. The sexual-social division of labor that characterizes the family is of a piece with gender organization and division of labor that mediate the mode of production as a whole. Therefore, what we concretely understand as "class," its subjective, cultural moment, is vitally expressed and constructed through familial gender relations, for example in socialization to masculinity and femininity, mothering, conjugality, and so on. It is not surprising that these form the very topics for the new educational project outlined by the women intelligentsia.

Education is always a moral proposal, and the concept of morality allows us to be social and personal at the same time. It is only fitting that the educational proposals for and by women are primarily conceptualized in moral terms—of "educing" or cultivating moral sentiments of the woman and her family. This agenda is not simply a spontaneous expression of common sense, but also a well-thought-out ideological position, which has substantially reconstructed and rearticulated the found elements of common sense. This elaborates "appropriate" social norms and forms for certain sections of the middle classes and aims to create "social" individuals, identities, and subjectivities within historically constructed relations.[15] An examination of these women's texts, therefore, must be attentive to both common sense and ideology and their changing relations. It is the ability to mediate, manage, and contain these divergent elements of common sense that makes or mars the success of an ideology and charts the direction and cultural form of hegemony.[16]

In the middle of such fluidity different ideological positions emerged, each putting forward a contested claim as a candidate for hegemonic ascendancy. The women reformers of Bengal build their own ideological claims on two levels: that of ethics and that of practical management—in the realm of ideas and of social reproduction. They are always speaking about the "ises" and "oughts" of the social life of women and men of propertied classes. These generalizations reflect an empirical knowledge of lives and experiences of women around them and their own material conditions of life and feelings. Within the purview of their general ideological direction, to quote Corrigan and Sayer:

Certain forms of activities are given the official seal of approval, others are situated beyond the pale. This has cumulative, and enormous, cultural consequences for how people identify . . . themselves and their place in the world.[17]

Andarmahal and Griha

The language of social reform in the nineteenth and early twentieth centuries in Bengal is inscribed with the discourse of "crisis." Allusions to "continuity and change," "tradition and modernity," "these new times," all involve the management of changing social relations of gender and social/sexual division of labor outside and within the family. For example, Tapan Raychaudhury makes this idea of "new times" and "encounter" between "the East" and "the West" the point of departure for his whole interpretive and historical exercise. The "encounter," he points out, means "a change." "It is a part of modernization," "the revolution in their world view." He also notes that the "changes occurred" not just through the "adoption of cultural artifacts, like specific elements in western life habits and belief systems. . . . The contact was a catalyst. . . . It induced mutations in inherited ways."[18]

Tanika Sarkar remarks on the extreme and unprecedented nature of this "change" brought about by the colonial encounter in the following terms: "For the first time, since Manua perhaps, and in a very different sense from him, family life and womanhood directly and explicity emerges as a central area of problematization."[19] A few pages later she points out "a compulsive, almost obsessive probing of tension spots . . . all the traumas of a woman's life were brought out and examined, nothing was taken for granted."[20]

The contents of the magazines under investigation assume a miscellaneous air unless we thematize them to establish a focus. This thematization is provided by the obsessive concern regarding women and the family, which involves a reconstruction of basic relations of social reproduction implicating not only the established sexual division of labor but also a changing cultural-moral dimension. This is expressed in speaking about the familial social space in two different ways, as *andarmahal* (inner quarters) and *griha* (home/household), and about the main creator-organizer of this home space, who is a woman. She is singled out as *grihini* (the mistress of the home/homemaker), which means both a *bhadramahila* (gentlewoman) and a mother. An emerging typology of the "sentimental, morally-educative motherhood" of a gentlewoman subsumes social relations peculiar to the ideal space of the *griha*. These two typologies of *grihini* and the *bhadramahila* mother-homemaker, who is both an educator and a nurturer, are more than that of a domestic laborer or a biological reproducer, just as *griha* is qualitatively different from a physical dwelling space. The aim of education, as propounded in the magazines, is to enunciate, and elaborate on, these concepts, and to construct these typologies in their fullness and to socialize them through practical advice and know-how.

The model of the ideal home or *griha* that emerges from the magazine pages, and to which the concept of the *bhadramahila* is integral, offers a critical insight into the changes in conceptual and actual organization of the familial social space in nineteenth-century Bengal. The two words *andarmahal* and *griha,* indicating a physical social domain and a sentimental moral space, are often used interchangeably. Both are used merely to indicate a private sphere as opposed to the public workplace or the world outside. This use simply attends to a demarcation between two physical or architectural spaces and functions within them, but ignores the qualitative difference between them with regard to the forms of social reproduction and their attendant morality. But as the writers of these magazines reflect on the changes in their social space, and construct the ideal "home," the newness of the concept of *griha* (home/hearth) and its qualitative difference from the notion of *andarmahal* (inner quarters) stare us in the face. Sharing many of the reproductive social functions, these terms yet mark or represent different moments in the organization of social relations and social vision. They indicate a very different relationship to *bahir,* or the public and the outside world. The earlier stage of *andarmahal,* which simply indicates an architectural and physical-social domain in women's care (which is the constant habitat of women, children, domestic servants and the nocturnal habitat of adult males), serves as a contrast to *griha,* the affective-moral private space, namely "the home," which forms the central project of thoughts on women's education.

The main difference between *andarmahal* and *griha* is that the former indicates a separate physical domain for women, appropriate to a more differentiated type of sexual division of labor, with very little indication of any direct normativeness or emotionality. The latter is a concept of morality and affect rather than a direct expression of a division of labor. It speaks to the moral, emotional social relations appropriate to a distinctly narrower and more fused social space presided over, created by, a central female figure. Though both realms refer to the private, it is conceived more in terms of an emotional and moral, rather than of a physical, privatization. Lacking an architectural correlate, which divides up the physical space into two parts of living quarters, private and public, the social inferiority of the *griha* is mainly expressive of a state of mind, a moral ideological venture of the colonial middle classes, rather than a functional place on earth. It is here that the male intelligentsia's self-consciously advanced moral (thus social) projects regarding "mothering" and "conjugality" are supposed to be operationalized. This *griha* has to be "achieved" through a process of ideological clarification, rather than found in daily living. It necessitates a conscious, practical socialization. The concept of *griha* thus encapsulates the ideal type of moral harmony desired in the lifestyle of the *bhadralok* (the Western-educated urban gentry).

What these magazines bring out is that this master concept of "the home," implying familial life, surrounded by ideological clusters of a new social design, and moral imperatives, provides the main destination of women's education. In Swarnakumari Debi's reminiscences in "Sekele Katha" ("The Story of Old Times"), for example, we find a description of a gradually vanishing *andarmahal* being replaced by a more "modern" form, which is presumably the ideological-material basis for *griha*. Swarnakumari Debi offers us a view of life in the women's quarters in earlier times that conveys a sense of everyday life. We catch a glimpse of a whole social domain of women when she says,

In our "antahpur," in those days, reading and writing, like eating, resting and worshipping, were daily rituals among women. Just as every morning the milk maid brought the milk, the flowerwomen supplied the flowers, and Deben Thakur came with his almanac and rolls of astrological charts, to foretell the daily auspicious and inauspicious details, just so a bathed and purified, white-robed and fairskinned Baishnabi Thakurani appeared within the interior of the household radiant with the light of knowledge. She was no mean scholar.[21]

Or:

I remember the days when the flower woman came to sell books—what a commotion it created in the women's quarter! She brought a few new books published in "Battala" poetry, novels, tales of fantasy—and increased the size of sister's library. As in every room there were dolls, other

*toys, clothes, so there were books in trunks. When I grew up I thumbed
through them.*[22]

This *andarmahal* simultaneously expanded and contracted with
the notion of *griha,* which was constructed from and through the
moral design of social reform, whose object was women.
Swarnakumari Debi herself describes this transition and links it to
the return of her father, Debendranath Thakur, from the foot of the
hills of the Himalayas. Both the narrowing of the household from a
larger social domain to a focused moral design as well as its expansion in breaking the segregation between the domains of social
reproduction (the inner/the outer, male and female worlds) become
clear from her following statements. She begins by drawing the
reader's attention to Debendranath's stature as a "social reformer,"
not to be encompassed within the conventional view of him as a
"religious reformer."

We can testify to the fact that it is through him that women's
higher education received its foundation (in Bengal). He was the
first to reform the custom of child marriage, and carefully attended
to the project of creating civilized clothing for women.[23]

Not content with that, he discarded the idol of shalagram and
initiated everyone into the Brahmo religion,[24]

*He also removed mean female-rituals, prevalent through India, one by
one from the women's quarter. He came up with a "mature age" of
marriage . . . and put together a marriage ritual. From my middle sister onwards all weddings in this household are performed in his way.
When his infant daughters reached the proper age he started their education by using an improved method. He hired a "pundit" for us. After
completing the second primer we began to learn Sanskrit. "Mems" (white
women) started coming into the women's quarter. At the time when our
household was being thus improved, Keshab Babu became my father's
disciple. For the first time, a non-kin male entered from the outside
world, into the women's quarter, unpenetrated by even the rays of the
sun.*[25]

This evolution in the ideological-moral dimension of the
familial social space, described by Swarnakumari Debi, illustrates

the difference put forward above between *andarmahal* and *griha*. It also spells out a new social division of labor in the male reformer's involvement with women's daily lives and rituals, and an equally new relationship to *bahir* (the outside), which comes into the house as adult kin and nonkin males and white women.

In Gyanadanandini Debi's "Stri Shiksha" ("Women's Education"), written in 1882, we get what amounts to a manifesto for women's education written by a woman.[26] This advocates and displays the beneficial results of the desegregation of the sexes and of a rigid sexual division of labor, and shows how education is both the cause and the result of this process. It elaborates an educational content in which Gyanadanandini incorporates affective-moral functions into women's household tasks. Like Krishnabhabini Das, she also redefines and recodes the conventions of gender. In the extreme practicality of itemization of education, we see the construction of the home of the *bhadramahila,* linen by linen, and relation by relation. The principle of organization of the text, in which household chores and conjugality are transparently integrated, becomes evident if we see these chores as moral/sentimental codes. Thus it is that Gyanadanandini can speak of conjugality (so new a theme in Bengali homes) and childcare in the same breath with tailoring, recipes, clothing and ornaments, nursing and healthcare involving a knowledge of anatomy, physiology, hygiene, chemistry or accounting. This fits in with Krishnabhabini's statement that women will be better, not worse, homemakers, mothers, and wives if they are educated.

The Sentimental Educative Mother and Her Child

This construct of the *griha,* "the home" (practically "the hearth"), is centered around or radiates from the figure or construct of the sentimental, educative mother, who is one of the many mother figures at this time in Bengal. Her traits are those of the *bhadramahila* or gentlewoman. She is not the *bibi,* the caricature of the educated/ Westernized woman, but rather her reversal, a figure self-consciously fashioned from all the benefits of education and cultural exposure, available in the new social context. Not diabolic or inverted, as is the *bibi* (a symbolic representation of the fallen times of the *kali yuga*), who is perceived as a masculinized female, she is sweet, moral, capable of reason and learning—a creator rather than a destroyer of homes. Embodying the new moral code advocated by women themselves (in conjunction with their reforming male counterparts), the *bhadramahila* mother is an individual nurturer of the body, an educator of the sentiments and morality. In this scheme of motherhood, physical reproduction is socialized through a new morality. This is compounded from notions of sentimental education and childhood produced in Enlightenment and utilitarian England and Europe from theories of the German kindergarten educationalist Froebel, Rousseau, utilitarian social reformers, and social Darwinism, in conjunction with indigenous values and practices based on ideas of innateness of motherhood.

Together with this sentimental-educator mother is born "the sentimental child," who subsequently becomes the basis for a whole literary genre of childhood reminiscences—for example, Rabindranath Thakur's "Chhelebela" ("Childhood"). This construct of "the child," individually nurtured by mother and mother nature, provides the basis of a personal *bildungsroman*, developed in secular autobiographies and biographies. This child is always male, while every female child is typed on "the mother." The required educational content for women (and girls) is directed at "his" developmental process. Krishnabhabini Das's essay "Kindergarten" captures the essence of this mother-child relation. As she put it, "Mothers are the natural teachers" of children (male); the real education of children begins in her lap. Since this process begins at birth, the distinction between education and socialization is obliterated.

A child has an inkling of his mother's love or her nature through his senses, and this love slowly enters into the child's half-asleep soul as mother holds him to her bosom or puts him into his cradle with great care, and breastfeeds him as soon as he wakes. In this way a mother's selfless love, joy and gratitude enters the child's soul and lay the foundation for a sacred, noble and exalted human nature. It is through this affectionate interchange of mother and son that a sense of the spiritual first awakens in the human [male] heart.[27]

Both Krishnabhabini and Gyanadanandini also speak of the

mother's educational role in terms of teaching children to play, sing, and so on.

In mother's sweet and simple songs and games of house keeping are spent the child's first three years. At four the child should go to a kindergarten. But of course boys learn from their mother all of what the kindergarten could teach, for them their home is the school. They need not go any where else.[28]

The above passages should be read in the context of changes in the mode of physical and social reproduction as conceived by the notion of *griha* and its contrast with the ways of *andarmahal*. The authors both speak to a single female nurturing figure, a biological parent, personally and daily engaged full-time in child-raising.[29] This duo of mother and child is remote from child-raising in the context of the *andarmahal*'s joint family, where child-raising is done by different female kin figures—grandmothers and aunts, older female siblings, and also by female and male servants. No allusion is made here to these actual sources of nurture and socialization, which actually existed (and still do) in middle-class Bengali everyday life. The construct of *griha* has no space for these extra actors on its ideological stage. It is the mother and father (wife and husband), and the child, that provide figures for the icon of this new "holy family." And of course all interactions are emotionally/psychologically individualized.

In Sarala Debi's short autobiographical sketch of her childhood, we find this same approach to childhood, a time of growth read through the construction of individual nurturing and sentimental care, all embodied in the presence or absence of the mother.[30] She reads her life among her siblings and the joint family through the same frame of a "sentimental mother-care" as did the intellectual men of her time. And she was unusual in that she demanded this care, the realization of the ideal type of nurture, which was meant for boys. She herself did not identify with the maternal nurturer of the ideology but rather with the male nurtured.

What these women authors wanted and missed indicates the difference between *andarmahal* and *griha*, both in terms of ideology and practice. It may be claimed that the concept of *griha* anticipated the nucleation of urban middle-class families and its moral regulation and captured a tendency of change in the pattern of social reproduction among the urban propertied classes. The *andarmahal*, on the other hand, has no particular reference to the individual in terms of conceptual forms or social relations of his/her psychic, moral life. But rather it is a "domain" of social reproduction, indicative of women's daily practical functions and location within a general patriarchal mansion, without imposing duties with regard to shaping of a moral masculinity and a personal nurturing femininity. In fact, the bulk of this upbringing for boys was previously actually done by men, both kin and servants.

The poet Rabindranath Tagore in his reminiscences speaks of a childhood spent in the domination of male servants and other male mentors, as though it was his terrible personal fate. But existing texts give evidence of an ordinary daily life, where not just he, but all male children of the upper castes and classes, routinely grew up being fed, bathed, and clothed by male servants, returning to the *andarmahal* only at night to sleep. They were inducted into a male life and conduct by older men of various classes, learning to command and obey. But Rabindranath, like Sarala Debi, read the workings of the division of labor between *andarmahal* and *bahir* through the ideological lens of *griha*, a sentimental small unit, where a woman, the very same woman, should be always involved in caring for (male) children.

Women's Ambivalence and Male Experts

Since the organization of *andarmahal* and *griha* are both gendered and patriarchal, it is not surprising that the women writers display an ambivalence, bordering sometimes on antagonism, regarding both. On the one hand they deplore the segregation, and what they consider to be the social unimportance of women in the former; on the other, they resent the Pygmalionlike role that men seek to play in shaping women's and family life in the *griha* and its morally regulatory form, *garhastha* (domesticity/conjugality). In Gyanadanandini's "Stri Shiksha," Swarnakumari Debi's "Strishiksha O Bethune School"[31] and "Shekele Katha," Krishnabhabini Das's "Striloker Kaj O Kajer Mahatya,"[32] and articles submitted for essay competitions by women for *Bamabodhini* under the title of "What Advantages

May Accrue Should Women's Education Become Common in this Country, and What Disadvantages Result from Its Absence?,"[33] we find much evidence of this ambivalence regarding both the segregated social space of the *andarmahal* and the new, relatively fused one of *griha*. In their reflections on "then" (as *andarmahal* social organization seemed an older form) and "now" (the *griha* of the new *bhadramahila*) these writers are at times nostalgic or angry about the loss of a social domain for women, outside of direct male interference. In an essay entitled "Amader Hobe Ki?" ("What Will Happen to Us?") Krishnabhabini Das projects such a resentment when she says,

Even in terms of freedom our mothers and grandmothers lived in a better state. As everyone knows, hindu women were in enclosure for a long time, but even so they had a full right to pilgrimages, worshipping at holy sites, and other religious rituals of religion, and travelling. But on account of this "little or half education" we are about to lose this pleasure of our distinct [or separate] lives. Now Bengali young men are furious at the very mention of women's pilgrimages, they don't believe in worshipping "dolls." Well then, explain to them [women] why such things are bad, and what religion really means, and take them elsewhere and show them nature's beauty, and you will see in what a short space of time they rid themselves of superstition.[34]

Her essay on "Swadhin O Paradhin Narijiban"[35] ("Independent and Subject Life of Woman") repeats her accusations about male encroachments in all areas of "modern life," as instructors and judges of women. Swarnakumari Debi's "Shekele Katha," while hailing the reforms introduced by her father in the women's quarters, actually evokes a nostalgia about the happy bustling women's world in her description of the bygone days.

But this ambivalence precludes a return to the past through a forward-looking thrust. Women authors welcome the end of the segregation integral to the earlier domain but regret the loss of a limited control over their own lives. Their underlying standpoint is one of a quest for influence and power for women over their own lives. Having once broken through the older barriers, they resent new forms of male control. Thus empowerment through education becomes their rallying cry to self-creation. Though it coincides with the reforming male agenda, women go beyond the male prescription in demanding a full right to higher education for women, not just the "little learning" handed out to them in order to serve a new patriarchal purpose.

Krishnabhabini wrote of this male redefinition of women's lives, about the normalization of a new patriarchal morality, and about how women had to be contented with a partial education, while facing continuous male criticism for their unwitting ignorance. She pleaded for a higher and "useful" education that would end women's *paranirbharata* (dependence on others), and spoke against these male judges, censors, and experts.

Lately Bengali men have become completely puffed up in the arrogance of their education and civilization. They lecture everywhere about "Swatantrata" (independence/freedom/self-distinction), but, even in their dreams, they can not conceive of the fact that the bud of national independence and civilization must first quicken in characters of that nation's individuals. How each parent treats his/her children, or young men their mothers, sisters and wives, tells us about that nation's civilization and progress. If any other nation looks into our lives what will it say about the shameful things that exist in hindu families. . . . [36]

She echoes the sentiment of many of her peers when she says,

Whenever there is the talk of righting the wrongs of hindu women, and establishing their equality with men, many [men] refer to the scriptures and speak of their status as the goddess (Devi). But where do we see any respect for this goddess?[37]

Women's ambivalence about the male reforming agenda is thus not a sign of their refusal of change, a case of the "reluctant debutante."[38] Their aim is "real emancipation," the right to self-definition and to exerting a social-familial influence and control. Not only Krishnabhabini, in essays mentioned above, or in "Karjya Mulak Shiksha O Jatya Unnati" ("Useful Education and National Progress"), but also Hironmoyee Debi in her various social scientific articles and observations on Newnham College, where she studied, puts forward a strong demand for making women's education a "real" social and personal achievement, not simply a cosmetic expression of the new gentry's lifestyle. Even Swarnakumari Debi, after her nostalgia for "those days," advocates a "serious education" of philosophy, spiritual thought, classical literature, and so on, for women, which could be possible in the new social context. Women such as these repeatedly stressed the need to go forward with the enlightened male section of their class, rather than to retreat into the past. This, however, did not signal the end, but rather an augmentation of a gender struggle.

All the women writers agree that this loss of a functional domain for women should be replaced and recouped by extending "real educational" facilities to women. Only this would provide them with the required information, morality, and cultural practices to create an informed self, a good son, a good home, and "mother" the nation. This implied an expansion of women's activities rather than seclusion and segregation, and meant taking on some of what was considered a male role. This meant becoming intellectuals and teachers—mental producers and practical implementers, not just physical and emotional nurturers. Nether *Jenana* education (gender-segregated female education) nor *Jenana* living were considered as solutions for counteracting women's subordination. It is their genuine concerns for women's intellect, morality, and authority that make the writers deplore these customs, not just a submission to the dictates of the "enlightened" male reformers. Not only do women feel that they should have the right to "come out" and be in "mixed company," but they also wish to construct and enforce new terms and conditions for their own emergence and emancipation. The new prescription of feminine moral education therefore contains in itself a double edge of demands, which spells out both containment and emancipation of women. Typified by the educating mother figure, it contains in itself all at once the sternness of moral authority and a sweet sentimentality.

Moral Education and the Natural Laws of Feelings

These contrary dimensions of power and submission, sentimentality and moral education, intuition and rationality are revealed at their best in the essays on child education and child-raising.

They contain an injunction for a mother's unqualified love and dedication to her child, but also insist on a role of guidance and discipline. Gyanadanandini's "Kindergarten" or Krishnabhabini Das's essay by the same name, or her essay on "Sandare Shishu" ("Child in the Family"), for example, are organized around the apt metaphor of the gardener and her garden. Plant imageries, and other imageries of natural life and growth associated with the child, are accompanied by the image of a mother as an intelligent and informed gardener who knows the nature of life forms and plants. She trains them cooperatively, intelligently, "for their own good," by pruning and gently directing. The mother is thus the first teacher of the child, who must know better than the child what his real emotional and moral nature is, and thus produce the finally desired result.

These essays, while stressing sentiments, are materialist and social in their emphasis. Discussing principles of human nature and reason, with the help of Rousseau, Froebel, Helvetius, and others, they posit a clear relationship between body and mind, senses and intellect, individual and society, thus integrating physical reproduction with social, moral, and intellectual education. They discuss how knowledge arises in the first instance from sensory impressions. Putting forward the proposition that "whatever enters the mind is through the senses," they go into details of toys, for example, "to suspend a coloured ball or rattle over the child's cradle," to a series of games observed in detail that instruct children while they delight in their senses. Throughout, the mother learns about the child, and can trace in his developing lineaments the physiognomy of adulthood:

As the embryo of a fully grown tree lies hidden in the seed, which in time becomes a huge tree with roots, as the seed of life within an egg matures into a bird with wonderful limbs and wings in the due course of time, so in the child or the infant lies the possibility of a whole human being.[39]

Though no one can go against a natural law, these natural laws of emotions, morality, and intellect (of the whole human nature and the individual nature of the child) can be studied and understood. Kindergarten philosophy and social Darwinism are both attractive because they offer the mother different but related kinds of knowledge into the natural laws appropriate for a child's education. Here, in the emphasis on information and instruction to the mother, we see a superaddition to the themes of maternal love and feminine intuition that makes her a practical scientist and a moral philosopher. Though her "natural" predisposition offers her a willingness to serve others and love her child, they in themselves are not enough. A mother herself needs to be educated in moral philosophy and practical sciences for her precise duty of mothering. Her natural disposition merely provides her with a head start in matters pertaining to children's education and social morality. But that is only the base or the starting point. Krishnabhabini claims that

A woman can effortlessly learn [Froebel's philosophy] and use this knowledge in a short time, and show great results. A child is the dearest treasure of the mother, who will be more attentive to and successful in his education.[40]

She goes on to develop an elaborate instruction plan for her which is far from naturally available to her. As Krishnabhabini sees it, better at child education than "a most learned man," a woman is a natural teacher, but that is not enough. For a woman to be simultaneously a nurturer and an educator, she absolutely needs to acquire knowledge, which is produced by the type of mental cultivation that gives her strength and help in this matter.

This instructional logic that connects the natural with the moral/intellectual, and places women centrally in the realm of social construction, is stated succinctly in the following statement:

Nature has vested in women the responsibility for people's health, and their moral and mental health lie hidden within their physical condition. Therefore, it is only by understanding the laws or dictates of nature and following them that one can devise a design for children's physical, moral and mental health.[41]

This construct, which combines intuitional mothering with the attributes of a teacher, therefore reworks a patriarchal, service ideology into a relatively autonomous and stern form. If loving is the attribute of a mother, then moral authority and discipline mark the teacher. This implies a permission for emotionality for both the mother and the child, while curbing the excesses. It introduces a sentimental discipline that lies at the heart of a new notion of morality. The new education deplores corporal punishment, for example, but instead achieves a restraining effect through a sustained and reasoned appeal to conscience, and personal love. Gyanadanandini in "Stri Shiksa" offers an example of how to discipline a child through a firm, loving patience, and points out the discipline-inducing nature of adult-directed "children's games" (devised as a part of the educational plan by the instructors). The end in view is always social adjustment or norm induction—that is, control and discipline. The randomness of play is undercut by the fact that it is the parent or the school that decides when a game begins or ends, or what rules to follow: "Children must have much joy in these games, but they must obey the rules of the game and the school."[42]

"No one can join or break the game at will" or the rules of "the home." Through this training process children are inducted into a "gentleman's conduct." Good manners, politeness, obedience, rule maintenance, and thrift all fall within this province of "feminine" method and the goal of schooling. This new ideological venture into personal-moral education rests inevitably on another new ideological notion, that of the "individual." It presupposes a private realm of individual conscience, which is in harmony with a social or a collective conduct.

Motherhood, Reform, and Revolution

The novelty and daring implied in this conception of motherhood, which both consents to a gendered/patriarchal service role and turns it around to gain social control, do not become fully evident unless we examine accounts of the actual lives of women as presented by various reformers. Rammohan Roy's description of women as physically abused household drudges,[43] Vidkyasagar's portrayal of women as objects of male sexual and social repression, and Rasasundari Debi's description of her daily life and secret attempts at education[44] all show how radical a departure this teaching role for women is.

But we must also note that this was a reformist, not a "revolutionary" enterprise. Though the women intelligentsia proposed to counteract their submission through gestures of reform, these same gestures were made within a patriarchal class parameter that further entrenched the conditions of their submission. Even as they gain a limited degree of familial power by being the delegated agents of class socialization, they are caught in an ambiguous scheme of over-all gender organization. This mother-child relation, which expands to include male-female family relations in an educative mode, and confers to the woman the status of an adult and to the man that of a child, is not in the long run as empowering to women as it initially appears to be. The tyranny of being governed by the needs of the child, to be educated and moral, primarily in order to nurture the *bhadralok*, or the male gentry, or to cultivate fortitude and courage in order to nurture the heroic sons of Indian nationalism, all show the double-edged nature of such an ideologically interpellated form of subjectivity.

Sarala Debi's essays on women's role within nationalism pro-vide the best examples of women's subordination to patriarchal poli-tics. Gender controversies created by "less political" women writers offer a greater radical possibility than that of patriarchal imperatives of Bengali nationalism and its myth of aryan hindu womanhood found in her writing and in her invention of nationalist rituals for women based on them. The ritual of *Virashtami* (Heroes' Day), to be celebrated by women, for example, was a morale boosting for males, rather than an opportunity for women to be "heroes" in their own right. This dilemma, inherent in nationalist ideologies of moth-erhood, is emphasized by Jasodhara Bagchi, speaking of the con-struct of the mother goddess and the feminized cultural symbolic constitution of Bengali nationalism. According to Bagchi, "It was ultimately a way of reinforcing of a social philosophy of deprivation for women. It was a signal for women to sacrifice everything for their menfolks."[45] She goes on to say:

The nationalist ideology, therefore, simply appropriated this orthodox bind on women's lives by glorifying it. This renewed ideological legiti-macy made it even more difficult for women to exercise their choice or autonomy in the matter.[46]

The typology of the sentimental and educative motherhood is, however, quite distinct and different from these nationalist typologies.

The self-improvement and dedication of a highly educated mother obviously does not call for self-sacrifice. Neither does it hark back to goddesses and heroes. This is probably why it serves as a favorite typology for middle-class women with a practical moral project, though sometimes the boundaries between dedication and sacrifice are blurred.

The boundaries between self-improvement and self-sacrifice are most clearly drawn in the works of Krishnabhabini Das. Sharing with others, male and female, a general urbanity and emphasis on the practical, daily dimension of motherhood and mothercraft, her ideological position leaves room for an ego for women and encourages a basic sense of "self." She makes an efficient use of the openings that are to be found in the concept of a moral, educative mother, to escape from the first circle of patriarchal containment. In the essay "Amader Hobe Ki?" ("What Will Happen to Us?"), she deplores complete self-abnegation preached to women as the basis for male exploitation. Discussing *matrittwa* and *satittwa* (motherhood and wifehood) as expressions of a destructive and exploitive power of middle-class Bengali young men over women, she comments:

> But as the beautiful flower when put into a child's hand lies immediately torn in the dust, as jewels are ground to dust in the hands of a mad man, so does that great virtue [woman's selflessness] lie trodden underfoot when put into "unworthy [man's] care."[47]

Krishnabhabini notes a growing misogyny among the males of urban propertied classes, and a great hypocrisy among male reformers and nationalist leaders who preach various virtues to Bengali women, including the fortitude and courage of Roman mothers. But she notes with sarcasm, "Many Roman mothers, such as Cornelia, pass in front of our eyes among hindu women, but how many Caiuses, or Tiberiuses, appear in the midst of Bengali families?"[48] She attributes women's selflessness not to an innate virtue but to a forced submission to patriarchal ideology and economic dependence over centuries, and mentions the ease with which men gain control over, or the possession of, women in Bengali society. After all,

> she [the wife] knows that husband is the only recourse for a hindu woman.

Whether that husband is honest or dishonest, kind or cruel, he remains the object of a hindu wife's worship. Following him is the foremost religious conduct enjoined to her. Probably just for that very reason ignorant, churlish young men return that bottomless love, devotion and faith with such cruel arbitrariness.[49]

She turns the patriarchal notion of women as "natural mothers" on its head:

That nature has given women the higher role of being the "mother of the world," is a notion that has to be understood in its real meaning. To make it come true, so they truly live up to that high calling, requires an equally advanced education.[50]

The various constructs of motherhood in nineteenth-century Bengal can be situated within this slide between self-sacrifice, self-dedication, and self-improvement. Underlying this range of shifts and transfers is a basic manipulation of a social epistemology. We are confronted with the classic mode of arguing about human nature in terms of nature and reason, and relatedly with arguments pertaining to the "nature of women" and "women as nature." The notion of a self-sacrificing mothers rests, for example, on the premise of a "natural motherhood" innate in women, and an intrinsic, essentially feminine nature of the female psyche. This equation between women and nature, considering women as guided by instincts, emotions, and intuitions, rather than rationality, led to both a positive and a negative valuation.[51] Women were regarded as both weak, frail, and sentimental, as well as strong embodiments of primal sexual power.

Femininity, Nature, and Reason

Speculations regarding feelings or instincts of women, the essential meaning of "femininity" and other related themes fill the world of male social thought. But of interest to us is that both pro- and anti-reform schools share much in common by subscribing to an argument by nature, and the innateness of a gender-coded consciousness. Thus reform and reaction share a similar epistemology regarding women and human nature, and it is their different manipulation of the nature-reason opposition that determines their respective views on women's education. Principles of enlightenment were not superadded to an emotional "feminine" nature in order to create educational possibilities. Instead, arguments for women's education came from simultaneously assuming their natural potential for reason and the possession of a feminine instinct for mothering. A "knowledge" that would both augment femininity and correct its failures was considered both desirable and possible. There was a demand therefore for a gender differential in the content and purpose of women's education that, however, was to contain certain universal elements.

The women reformers' participation in the themes of reason and nature shows that they believe the principle of reason to be an attribute of human nature and women's possession of reason as a mark of their general humanity. Thus they perform a reconciliatory gesture by overcoming a duality and implanting reason in nature, intellect in the senses. This is evident in the way they conceptualize the educational growth of the child as a composite growth. They claim that women are indeed "natural" but that "reason" itself is a sex-neutral, "natural" gift made by nature to both men and women.

Krishnabhabini Das develops this approach further in her polemic with an anonymous male critic of her essay "Shikshita Nari" ("The Educated Woman"). In "Shikshita Nari" she addresses a pseudo-scientific biological argument for barring women from higher education due to smaller brain sizes. While her acceptance of "scientific education" makes her unable to challenge the initial premise, she introduces a critical dimension from her social perspective on the relationship between biology, history, and consciousness. She believes that social and mental activities have an effect on the body, just as the latter shapes the mind:

The smaller brain size among women is caused by the absence of education from the primitive times to now. There is no doubt that if women received the same education as men, from the time of the creation to the present, then their brains would have developed equally with men.[52]

In her reply she also introduces the theme of nature, in a way

that is advantageous to women, succeeding in denaturalizing arguments against women's education by giving once more a critical social dimension to the current position. She concedes the value of
"feminine virtues" advocated by her male critic but also says:

*No thinking person can deny that woman's gentleness, innocence, mod-
esty etc. are admired everywhere. But no one respects a woman's ignorance. For this reason, a true education can only improve these virtues of
woman, rather than degrade them.*

Therefore, when a critic of the magazine *Sadhana* says that nature
has particularly vested woman with a special function, an instinct
and a drive, and made her "a denizen of home"—who would
disagree with him? But, on the other hand, who would deny that
though nature has made woman a home-dweller, she has not en-
dowed her with the instincts of a cage-dweller, or made her a creature who is permanently incarcerated? Therefore, when everywhere
in the world, using this excuse of natural weakness, men wholly rob
and control women, and continue to argue whenever the topic of
women's education and independence is raised, then it does not require much intelligence to recognize the male selfishness and tyranny that lie at the bottom of women's incarceration. It is possible to
torture people by inflicting on them both starvation or physical force,
by preventing the natural exercise of their physical faculties or by
repressing their emotional needs. A powerful group or a race can
oppress another in both ways.[53]

Krishnabhabini claimed that some special provisions for
women notwithstanding, the fundamental educational basis for
both sexes should be the same. For her, "Education is equally healthy
for both sexes. Knowledge, and its pursuit, which fill a man's mind
with good thoughts and intentions, are equally healthy for women."[54]

Swarnakumari Debi's positive view of women's education in
general encompasses both the earlier form of *andarmahal* education
as well as that introduced by her father. She corroborates
Krishnabhabini's overall position.

*Young, newlyweds, married daughters learnt from the Baishnabi, but
the unmarried girls went together to the gurumahashay's "pathshala." It*

may not have done much else, but laid the foundations for learning for
girls and boys on the same principle.[55]

She speaks with great admiration about the serious interest of one of
her grandmothers (her mother's aunt's) in philosophical and classical education. This is consistent with her admiration for her "es-
teemed" father, who brought male teachers and classical education
into their *andarmahal,* and not content with the *zenana* education
provided by pundits and white governesses, sent his daughters to
Bethune School. She particularly prizes the fact that he

enriched his family's store of learning, especially by polishing the intelli-
gence, knowledge, and religiosity, of the inhabitants of the women's quar-
ters, by advising them on "true" religion, spirituality, conduct, and at
times by speaking about science in a simple language.[56]

These details point toward a reliance on the universality of reason and knowledge, while showing the specific use women make of
these for self-development and a practical, domestic contribution.

Many are unwilling for women to learn affairs of administration. Ac-
cording to them, habits of work are needed only for shopkeeping and
running offices. There is [supposedly] no need for that kind of education
in the little lives of women in their little homes. But if we pause awhile,
we see that management, habits of accounting etc. are indispensable in
smaller and larger affairs of life. . . . In this there is no difference be-
tween running a home or an office or a shop. This can not be done with
little knowledge and intelligence. Like all other serious responsibilities
running a home requires controlling family affairs, maintaining order
and accuracy, hard work, thrift, frugality, skill and judgement.[57]

This passage argues that an education meant for males and economic viability are also needed for organizing the *griha* or home.
This brings or integrates motherhood and the home with the world
of instruction, which is a public domain. It reinterprets and reworks
the social and practical implications of the concepts of motherhood
and *griha* as seen by the male intelligentsia. To begin with, the re-
quirement of self-education for good motherhood extends women's

task of humanizing or civilizing children *(manush kara)* first unto themselves. Krishnabhabini Das expanded the notion of women's and family's betterment or improvement by introducing the concepts of "women's freedom" *(shri swadhinata)* and economic freedom and claimed them as integral to the educational process of humanization and civilization. Though the great injunction of the Bengali primer, which warns that "only those who study diligently will ride in carriages or horses [that is, have a career]" does not apply to women at this stage, writers such as Krishnabhabini see education as essential for a women's survival and dignity in times of penury. Economic viability is considered as essential to a woman's moral and social independence and as a direct display of her capacity. Thus Hironmoyee Debi in "Newnham College" and Krishnabhabini Das in "Ingraj Mahilar Shiksha O Swadhinatar Gati" ("English Women's Progress in Education and Independence")[58] speak about the importance of Western and Indian women's career development. Of course, they are always careful to link this achievement with a better motherhood and a better home.

It is easy to see, then, why these women educators or reformers did not find the mother goddess figure of Bengali nationalism useful. Since their project was both practically ethical and social, they could not look to this asocial, unpractical, mythic figure for any direction in concrete terms of social reproduction and everyday life. This "mother figure" after all is not a "mothering" one. She is a goddess of war with weapons, rather than a madonna with a child in her arms. It is understandable that a writer such as Sarala Debi, with her concern about national politics rather than a daily politics of reproduction, found the heroic, aryan version of the "mother goddess" congenial, while the others in these magazines hardly allude to this goddess-mother in any significant way.

The central concern of women reformers is the family, the home, and child-raising, in a daily and practical rather than a symbolic or metaphoric way. Thus the symbolism of a mother figure of martial power, which swept the world of male cultural nationalism, had little impact on these Bengali women. The quasi-secular aestheticized version of the mother goddess, in the figure of *Bangamata* (mother India) did not fare any better. It is perhaps the more domestic and essentially sentimental figure of *Bangamata* (mother Bengal) that

shares an affective base of mother love with the new Bengali sentimental teacher-mother. But the critical, educative, and practical requirements of the latter allow for only a partial convergence between
the two figures, which requires the incorporation of a set of urban
domestic social codes rather than rural domestic virtues. The ideal
figure is thus reflective of some of the cultural and daily features of
its creators. It combines "feminine" intuitions or insights with principles of universal reason and humanism along with that of a practical agenda for domesticity and child education.

We can recognize here a Victorian "femininity" and an equally
Victorian utilitarian reform tradition at work. Many of the abovementioned themes, such as "the individual," "the child," "sentimental education," "mother educator" and so on, are found in English
literature and discourse of social reform, from the late eighteenth
century through the nineteenth century. Romanticism undergoes
various developments that are expressed as continuous but unsettled
relations between reason or rationality and emotions or intuition.
Dickens's *Hard Times* is a powerful statement of this, while Mill in
his essay on Coleridge and Bentham expatiates on his notion of a
whole human being by adding Coleridge (emotion/intuition/imagi-
nation) to Bentham (rationality/utility/practicality). The influence
of these social thoughts on the colonial intelligentsia can not be
precisely measured, but readings from contemporary literature or
official documents of Bengal all indicate a wide dispersion and absorption of romantic and Victorian sentimental discourse and forms.
To quote Gauri Visvanathan, "The gestures of enlightenment and
reform co-existed or existed through colonial forms."[59] As Bengali
women expressed themselves often through the patriarchal indigenous modes of middle-class cultural hegemony, so they relied on
certain "colonial" discourses and attitudes, some of which are also
present in the writings of the male intelligentsia.

But to dismiss these women simply as a colonized intelligentsia
does not do justice to the real complexities and contradictions implied in their ideological positions, or the nature of class formation
and class consciousness in Bengal. Class consciousness anywhere in
the world relies on available cultural symbolic presences and social
relations in a given environment. To read the material in the magazines as forms of colonial discourse has limited value, except to indi-

cate English bourgeois thought as a common cultural denominator of the male and female intelligentsia of Bengal. The women form a different category from the men insofar as they are ambivalent or negative with regard to the wisdom of patriarchal Victorian England, just as they are to indigenous male-stream social thought. They are simultaneously molded by and resistant to both of these forms of consciousness.

Images of Victorian gentlewomen are often present in the works of women writers. Figures of reformers, intellectuals, and economically successful women and homemakers of England and the United States provide examples and points of discussion. European women are seen to manifest the possibilities for all middle-class women that lie in the new social relations of bourgeois society. Bengali women writers point to the complexity and necessity of the women intelligentsia's participation in class formation, both as active agents and colonized interpreters. Their use of these reference points and inspiring anecdotes of the freedom of women elsewhere is simultaneously an expression of their own desire for freedom as women, as well as an acknowledgment of a colonial status.

Thus Victorian notions of womanhood were discerningly adapted and absorbed by the Bengali women reformers, and there was always a double edge to their adaptive strategies. The Victorian "feminine sensibility," replete with notions of refinement and sentiment, was both advanced and undercut by themes of reason and practical, utilitarian reform. The version of the ideal woman as a practical homemaker, in conjunction with a typology of an asexual mother-wife and educator (for whom conjugality or mothering is less a pleasure than a duty), together express the Victorian reform influence most effectively. This sentimental utilitarian familial mode does not allow for any emotional excess, especially for women. Deprived of any passionate or "heroic" gesture, it is indicative of a general emotional and sexual repression.

Domesticity, the hallmark of the affective social space of *griha*, or the home, is its typical social form, with which the women intelligentsia seem to be in a constant struggle. On the one hand they treat domesticity and *griha* as an extension of themselves, on the other seek to go beyond domesticity and *griha* in their arguments for women's social and economic independence and engagement with

reason. They use the utilitarian/enlightenment discourse and Western examples, less as gestures of the colonized's self-castigation, but
more as ways to combat both local and colonial forms of patriarchy.
In essays on the progress of European women, there is no hint of
any inherent inferiority or disability on the part of Bengali or Indian
women. The Western-educated, economically active women stand
as examples of capabilities of all women, but not as their invariable
ideal expressions.

The nationalist male intelligentsia of Bengal criticized some of
these writers, especially Krishnabhabini Das, as being colonial. Their
demand for "women's freedom" *(stri swadhinata)* and criticism of
indigenous patriarchy were interpreted as betrayals to the nationalist cause. In response to this accusation one can only point out the
men's self-serving patriarchal nature and the basically orientalist and
colonially patriarchal nature of Bengali cultural nationalism itself.[60]
Even through the many ideological transferences and inversions,
Bengali nationalism was largely inflected by colonial discourse. But
this in itself did not create any self-criticism among the male intelligentsia, whereas the use of European ideals of women's emancipation and equality by Bengali women writers earned them the epi-
thets of "antinational" and "antipatriotic" from their male
counterparts. It is clear that bourgeois nationalism (colonial or otherwise) does not have the capacity ultimately to express or contain
the feminist aspirations of women reformers anywhere, in spite of
the initial support for women's education or their "improvement."
A conflict continues to rage, on grounds of patriarchy and gender,
against the very terms and conditions of emancipation. A greater
complexity is introduced by the colonial context itself, where the
fragile masculinity of Bengali middle-class males, "feminized" by
the colonial relations and discourse, was fundamentally threatened
by the epistemologies, social views, and demands of reforming
women intelligentsia, who were perceived as emasculators as much
by male reformers as by conservatives.[61]

This threatened response is in the end quite predictable, given
that women used the available European material selectively. They
chose antipatriarchal ideas and practices and as often pointed out
the gender struggle in the colonizer's society. They showed little admiration for Victorian codes of chivalry and social refinement. These

codes never formed the core of their adaptation of utilitarian or enlightenment ideas of education, self-improvement, and home-making. The resentment against the misogyny and private patriar-chal malpractices of male nationalist figures or reformers is not there-fore a proof of a colonized nation's admiration for customs of their foreign masters and mistresses.

There is obviously a tension between becoming a subject in and through an ideology that is both inspirational and circumscribing. *Stri swadhinata* (women's emancipation) is part of the call for national emancipation, but at the same time the same discourse of *swadhinata-paradhinata* (emancipation-subjugation) encourages the women's gender struggle.[62] To respond to the call of the nation [male], to be socially and nationally useful, to be the "mother of the hero," the "mother of the race," coincides with women's need for an active social agency. And yet, as the word *freedom* is increasingly foregrounded, it becomes apparent to women how concepts such as *satitta* (chastity) and *matrittwa* (motherhood) can bring women back into the patriarchal fold. There remains always a tension between achieving full subjectivity as women and as class members. Nation-alism, with its gender codes and patriarchal relations, though newly configured, activates the moral-cultural code of class hegemony.

Conclusion

From the turns and twists of adaptive and negotiatory strategies sketched above, it is clear that we cannot establish one single, uni-fied consciousness for each class. Mental spaces are constructed from countless invisible but powerful sources, re-created and created in various forms and contents, and a class itself is always fragmented. Whereas each fraction within the class may hold the same relation to the means of production, or a place in the ruling apparatus, its subjective and objective social existences are not coterminous. Bengali nationalism reflects these numerous fragmentations, negotiatory containments, and formative strategies.[63] The ideological range extends from secular economic and utilitarian liberalism to hindu revivalism, where secularists can coexist with or participate in reli-gious cultural forms, and hindu revivalists can use positivism to present their argument and support economic liberalism.

In the world of post-1793 (Permanent Settlement) Bengal,

imperfect class differentiation, divisions between country and city, the colonial and the indigenous, popular and elite, interface and contribute to divergent class subjectivities, which compete and seek to dominate each other. As a corollary to this indeterminacy, there is the peculiar nature of the propertied classes in Bengal which are, like Janus, two-faced—ruled and ruling. Whereas the coercive aspect of the colonial rule and its discourses are undeniable, one should also note that in a society with such a highly developed hierarchy in mental and manual labor as in Bengal, the local elite discourse also "voluntarily" took to a foreign elite discourse. Thus there was a convergence of aims and views, which were not simply "imposed" on the colonized or imitatively adopted. A society that was hierarchical (caste/class), patriarchal, and used to empires and the military, with developed forms of commercial capital, with an organized elite (both hindu and Muslim), did not exactly need to be coercively inducted into "the command of language and the language of command."

Since the consciousness of women writers in colonial Bengal is elaborated in the same terrain as that of men, it shares the same common sense of absorption, submission, resistance, and subversion. But what is significant about women's writings is the added dimension of resistance to patriarchy, while accepting the relegated responsibility of putting the class's homes in order. It is this "difference" that marks their acceptance of "motherhood," wifehood" and "femininity," while their existence as literate colonized people marks the way they manipulate colonial cultural elements. This double relation always inflects their social agency, and textures the organization of their thought.

Social subjectivities of both the male and the female intelligentsia are compounded as much of indigenous values and social-cultural forms as of the cultural and social lineaments of the colonizers. Of course the values, symbols, and epistemologies that are thus culled and reorganized do not fuse perfectly. Signifiers continue to have their lives in the domain from which they are culled, unless undercut and mixed thoroughly in the new project. They can, and do, often pull away in unintended directions. Various components of bourgeois womanhood so pervasively present in the elite cultural world can and do overdetermine the construct of the Bengali *bhadramahila*. But what is of greater importance to us is the general direction through which (not to) this educational ideological venture moves.

There is a fine tension between speaking as and for a (gendered) class, and as "women." Gender codes are redefined, expressing new relations of social reproduction of the colonial middle classes while striving toward a relative autonomy for women through concepts such as "individual freedom." The project as a whole is held in place by the use of the notion of "humanization," which provides a legitimation and a destination for women's education. In this interpellated ideological form neither patriarchy nor gender division of labor is discarded, but they are redefined and displaced in such ways as to mediate the emerging new social relations and to form a new ideological cluster. As class agents, the summoned subjects, the women intelligentsia, are active "modernizers" and inventors of "tradition." Their domain, however, is social reproduction, rather than social production, and they help to crystallize an ideology of "home," "femininity," and "motherhood," all of which are complex social and emotional signifiers, replete with desires and practical needs.

In their ventures of self-creation, which involve both discovery and compromise, writers such as Swarnakumari Debi, Gyanadanandini Debi, and Krishnabhabini Das construct social topics in current symbolic and conceptual terms that enable expanding circles of women to speak to each other in at least partially meaningful ways. An example of this is the overlapping discursive worlds of the middle-class hindu and Muslim women. Writers such as Begam Rokeya, for example, in such magazines as *Nabanur*, speak to the same topics, using the same discursive apparatus as their Brahmo or hindu counterparts, though with a specific concern for the realities of Muslim women's lives.

The ideological success of this social reform enterprise, initiated a long time ago, in terms of hegemonizing the consciousness of the present-day hindu Bengali middle classes, can be best guessed if we look at the moral and ideological substructures of current welfare policies and practices regarding women in modern Bengal. Much of the paraphernalia of women's education, social work, or even some aspects of present-day feminist politics and thought, both in Bengal and India as a whole, rely on the same typology, subjectivity, and form of agency constructed by this female intelligentsia in the pages

of these eminently perishable Bengali magazines at the turn of the
century.

Endnotes

This paper is reprinted with permission from the *Journal of Historical Sociology*, Vol. 5,
No. 1, March 1992. This paper is the first of a series that I have undertaken to write in
order to display the gender organization of class, and the ideological construction of
subjectivities and agencies of/for women implied in the social reform projects in colonial Bengal. This project has been very kindly sponsored by the School of Women's
Studies, Jadavpur University, Calcutta, which has offered me the most vital necessi-
ties for research, namely encouragement and an access to original material. I must
especially thank Abhijit Sen of the school, who has most painstakingly and discerningly
copied out by hand articles from magazines that are literally on the verge of extinction.
These articles, until Abhijit rescued them, hardly saw a reader since their first appearance. Abhijit's collection is working toward the publication of volumes of an anthology
with an introduction, a project also sponsored by the School of Women's Studies. I
should also take the opportunity of thanking Professor Jasodhara Bagchi, the director
of the school, herself a scholar in the area, for her unflagging support of the project
and the valuable discussions we had. In the citation of journals, the first year given is
Western; the second is Bengali. All translations within this text, unless otherwise
mentioned, are done by me.

1.   See Sumit Sarkar, *A Critique of Colonial India* (Calcutta: Papyrus, 1985).
2.   Kumkum Sangari and Sudesh Vaid, in "Recasting Women: An Introduction," say
     something similar: "Middle-class reforms undertaken on behalf of women are
     tied up with the self-definition of class, with a new division of the public from the
     private sphere and of course with a cultural nationalism." Kumkum Sangari and
     Sudesh Vaid, eds., *Recasting Women, Essays in Indian Colonial History* (New
     Brunswick, New Jersey: Rutgers University Press, 1989), p. 9 (first published by
     Kail, 1989).
3.   Here the term "common sense" is used in the sense that Antonio Gramsci for-
     mulates in *The Selections from the Prison Notebooks*, ed. and trans. by Quentin
     Hoare and Geoffrey Nowell Smith (London: Lawrence and Wishart, 1971). See,
     for example, his use in "The Study of Philosophy," pp. 323–333. This is consid-
     ered by Gramsci as the general state of consciousness in the everyday sense,
     prescientific, preideological. It is a kind of "political unconscious."
4.   See Meredith Borthwick, *The Changing Role of Women in Bengal, 1849–1905*
     (Princeton, New Jersey: Princeton University Press, 1984), pp. 60–108, on
     women's education and the role of magazines in this process.
5.   Sumanta Banerjee, *The Parlour and the Streets* (Calcutta: Seagull Books, 1989),
     especially the chapter on "Elite Culture in Nineteenth Century Calcutta," pp.
     147–148.
6.   Krishnabhabini Das, "Shinkshita Narir Pratibader," *Sahitya* (1881).
7.   Louis Althusser, *Essays on Ideology* (London: Verso, 1984), pp. 44–51. While
     presenting how ideology interpellates individuals as subjects, he says, "I shall
     then suggest that ideology 'acts' or 'functions' in such a way that it 'recruits'
     subjects among individuals (it recruits them all), or 'transforms' the individuals
     into subjects (it transforms them all) by that very precise operation I have called
     interpellation or hailing and which can be imagined along the lines of the most
     commonplace everyday police (or other) hailing, 'Hey, you there!'" (p. 48).
8.   See Partha Chatterjee, "The Nationalist Resolution of the Women's Question,"
     in Sangari and Vaid, eds., *Recasting Women*, pp. 233–253.
9.   See Philip Corrigan and Derek Sayer, *The Great Arch* (Oxford: Basil Blackwell,
     1985). This book offers an extremely useful demonstration of the moral

dimension of state formation. But this same approach is useful for class aspirations to hegemony as well.

10. See Gauri Visvanathan, *Masks of Conquest: Literary Studies and British Rule in India* (London: Faber and Faber, 1990), pp. 8–9. She uncovers the hegemonic and thus moral design in something seemingly so innocuous as the teaching of English literature in India.

11. Borthwick, *Changing Role*, p. 61.

12. Visvanathan, *Masks*, p. 68.

13. Krishnabhabini Das, "Shikshita Nari," *Sahitya* 1881 (B. S. Savin, 1298), pp. 286–291.

14. Krishnabhabini Das, "Jatay Jiban O Hindu Nari," *Sahitya*, 1881 (B.S. Savin, 1298) pp. 301–315.

15. Corrigan and Sayer, *Great Arch*, p. 4.

16. See Partha Chatterji, *Nationalist Thought: A Derivative Discourse* (London: Zed Books, for the United Nations University, 1986), p. viii: "It is in the shifts, slides, discontinuities and unintended moves, what is suppressed as much as what is asserted, that one can get a glimpse of this complex movement, not as so many accidental disturbing factors but as constitutive of the very historical rationality of its [nationalism's] process."

17. Corrigan and Sayer, *Great Arch*, p. 6.

18. Tapan Raychaudhury, *Europe Reconsidered: Perceptions of the West in Nineteenth Century Bengal* (Delhi: Oxford University Press, 1988), pp. ix–x.

19. Tanika Sarkar, "Hindu Conjugality and Nationalism in Late Nineteenth Century Bengal" in *Indian Women: Myth and Reality*. Paper No. 9, p. 1, National Seminar Papers, School of Women's Studies, Jadavpur University, Calcutta, 1989.

20. *Indian Women*, p. 8. See also Sumit Sarkar, "The Women's Question in 19th Century Bengal," in Sangari and Vaid, eds.,*Women and Culture* (Bombay: SNDT Somen's University, 1985), pp. 157–172. See also Ghulam Murshid, *The Reluctant Debutante: Response of Bengali Women to Modernization 1849–1905* (Rajshahi, Bangladesh: Rajshahi University Press, 1983).

21. Swarnakumari Debi, "Sekele Katha," earlier printed as "Amader Griha Antahpur Shiksha O Tahar Samskar," *Pradip* 1899, pp. 314–320 (reprinted in *Bharati*, [1916], Year 39, pp. 1114–1124, B.S.).

22. Debi, "Sekele Katha."

23. Debi, "Sekele Katha."

24. Debi, "Sekele Katha."

25. Debi, "Sekele Katha."

26. Gyanadanandini Debi, "Stri Shiksha," *Bharati*, 1882 (B.S. Asvin, 1288). See also her "Samaj Samskar O Kusamskar," *Bharati*, 1884 (B.S. Asad, 1290, Year 7).

27. Krishnabhabini Das, "Kindergarten," *Bharati* 1890 (B.S. Agrahayan, 1297).

28. Das, "Kindergarten."

29. Das, "Kindergarten."

30. Sarala Debi, "Amar Balya Jibani," *Bharati*, 1886 (B.S. Baisakh, 1312, Year 29, 1st issue).

31. Swarnakumari Debi, "Strishiksha O Bethune School," *Bharatio Balak*, 1888 (B.S. 1294, Year 11).

32. Krishnabhabini Das, "Striloker Kaj O Kajer Mahatya," *Pradip*, 1892.

33. See "Bamaracana" Competition, "Edeshe Stri Shiksha Samyak Prachalit Na Howatai Ba Kiki Apakar Haitechhe?" *Bamabhodhini*, 1866 (B.S. 1292).

34. Krishnabhabini Das, "Amader Hobe Ki?," *Sahitya*, Kartik Chaitra, 1890.

35. Krishnabhabini Das, "Swadhin O Paradhin Narijiban," *Pradip*, 1888.

36. Das, "Amader Hobe Ki?" See also "Samaj O Samaj Samskar," *Bharatio Balak*, 1891 (B.S. Poush, 1297, Year 14).

37. Das, "Amader Hobe Ki?"

38. See Gulam Murshid, *The Reluctant Debutante*.

39. Das, "Kindergarten." See also "Sandare Shishu," *Sahitya*, 1893, (B.S. Ashad, 1299, Year 3, No. 3).

40. Das, "Kindergarten."
41. Das, "Kindergarten."
42. Das, "Kindergarten."
43. Rammohan Roy. See "A Second Conference between an Advocate for and an Opponent of the Practice of Burning Widows Alive," *Calcutta*, 1820, p. 126. "At marriage the wife is recognized as half of her husband, but in after-conduct they are treated worse than inferior animals. For the woman is employed to do the work of slave in the house, such as, in her turn, to clean the place very early in the morning, whether cold or wet, to scour the dishes, to wash the floor, to cook night and day, to prepare and serve food for her husband, father, mother-in-law, sister-in law, and friends and connections."
44. See Rasasundari Debi, *Amar Jiban*, (Calcutta: College Street Prakashani, 1987).
45. J. Bagchi, "Representing Nationalism: Ideology of Motherhood in Colonial Bengal," *Economic and Political Weekly* (October 20–27, 1990), pp. 65–71.
46. Bagchi, "Representing Nationalism."
47. Das, "Amader Hobe Ki?"
48. Das, "Amader Hobe Ki?"
49. Das, "Amader Hobe Ki?"
50. Das, "Amader Hobe Ki?"
51. A discussion on these different aspects of "motherhood" and their ideological implications is presented in Bagchi's article: She notices an invention and continuity of motherhood of different kinds. She also points out something that is equally tenable for the construct I deal with, that these are "public" politico-symbolic enterprises, not "private" existing realities.
52. Das, "Shikshita Nari."
53. Krishnabhabini Das, "Shikshita Narir Pratibader Uttar" n.p., n.d.
54. Das, "Shikshita Narir Pratibader Uttar."
55. Swarnakumari Debi, "Sekele Katha."
56. Debi, "Sekele Katha."
57. Das, "Shikshita Narir Pratibader Uttar."
58. Krishnabhabini Das, "Ingraj Mahilar Shiksha O Swadhinatar Gati," *Bharatio Balak*, 1891 (B.S. Sraban, 1297, 14).
59. Visvanathan, *Masks*, pp. 68–93.
60. Here we need to look at Uma Chakravarty's essay in Sangari and Vaid, eds., *Recasting Women;* "Whatever Happened to the Vedic Dasi?" pp. 27–87. On page 50 she speaks about identity formation for "the nationalist cause," and the difficulty of constructing an "alternative identity" for women, "given the need for a different kind of regeneration that was necessary in her case."
61. See Tanika Sarkar on this threat to masculinity in "Hindu Conjugality" in Jasodhara Bagchi, ed., *Indian Woman: Myth and Reality* (Hyderabad: Sangam Books, 1995). She shows how hindu men perceived the hindu marriage (by extension of family) as the "last unconquered space," and "how sensitive and fragile this structure was."
62. Sarkar, "Hindu Conjugality."
63. See Asok Sen, *Ishwar Chandra Vidyasager and the Elusive Milestone* (Calcutta: K. P. Bagchi, 1977) on class formation and forms of consciousness and ideology, V. C. Joshi, ed., *Rammohan Roy and the Process of Modernization in India* (Delhi: Vikas Publishing House, 1975).

Chapter Ten
"Loyally Confer through the Regular Channels"
Shaping Political Subjectivity of and for "Women" in Early Twentieth-Century Toronto

Kari Dehli

On a Saturday afternoon in February 1916 a group of women and men met at the University of Toronto. The meeting was well publicized and many people attended, "asked questions, [and] discussion was keen."[1] Four members of the Education Committee of the Toronto Local Council of Women had planned the event. They came prepared with a proposal to establish a new organization, and the following motion was approved by those present:

Whereas the Education Committee of the Local Council of Women stands for the education of the whole boy and girl; and whereas the Home and School clubs are proving such an important archive of usefulness in the co-operation of home and school and state matters; therefore be it resolved that there be formed at once a central organization known as the "Toronto Home and School Council."[2]

Ada Mary Brown Courtice, a longtime crusader for social and educational reform and women's suffrage in the province, was elected president of the new organization. Born into a Quaker family in eastern Ontario, Ada Brown married a Methodist minister who became editor of the *Christian Guardian,* a widely circulated magazine influential in the 1890s. Together they started a small private school for girls, where the curriculum centered on art, literature, music, and physical fitness. When her husband died in his early fifties, Ada Courtice continued to operate the school until she began to dedicate most of her time to social and educational reform, and particularly to the task of organizing women as voters and parents.[3]

In addition to Ada Courtice, those who formed the leadership of the Toronto Home and School Council in the ensuing twenty-five years were, with few exceptions, women of the city's growing "British" professional and middle classes. A small number of single women were active in the council's affairs, particularly school principals, teachers, social workers, nurses, and physicians. However, most of the leaders were married women—wives of businessmen, professionals, school principals, university professors, physicians, engineers, civil servants, and the like. Ida Siegel, a Jewish social activist who had moved with her parents from Pittsburgh to Toronto in the 1890s, was one of the few exceptions to this pattern. I will return to Siegel's attempts to organize a mothers' club among Jewish working-class women, since the fate of that club offers an illustration of how "Home and School" came to be seen, and saw itself, as an Anglo-Canadian and middle-class organization, in spite of its frequent public claims to speak for all parents and all mothers.

During the first few years of its history, the Toronto Home and School Council advocated for child welfare and health care provision, water purification and sanitation, and, especially, for better and more "progressive" schooling. While on the one hand arguing for increased public expenditures on social services, health, and education, the Council joined other middle-class reform groups to demand greater financial "efficiency" from local governments and to hold them accountable for how property taxes were spent. At times the council joined in coalitions with other organizations, including the Toronto Local Council of Women, the Big Sisters and Big Brothers associations, the Board of Trade, the Bureau of Municipal Research, as well as the Toronto Trades and Labor Council, to influence the Board of Education and municipal and provincial governments.

The leadership of the Home and School Council worked very hard to establish itself as the representative of "parents" in educational decision-making. The council tried, with mixed success, to mobilize parents, and in particular newly enfranchised, middle-class, Anglo-Canadian women, to take active interest in the public affairs of the Board of Education and City Council. The organization called on women to vote, and another strategy was to endorse and organize in behalf of candidates running for elected positions on the school board and City Council.[4] During the period discussed here, the right to vote and run in municipal and school board elections was tied to ownership or rental of property, and both voters and candidates also had to be either Canadian-born or "British subjects." Coinciding with the struggle for women's suffrage, women had obtained the right to vote in local elections in Ontario in 1913, provided, of course, that they fulfilled the requisite property and citizenship qualifications. Several women, including Ada Courtice and Ida Siegel, were elected for several terms to the Board of Education between 1914 and 1940. In addition to such election efforts, council members also made deputations before local and provincial government committees to press for changes in social and educational policies and practices, and they sent a regular observer to Board of Education meetings.

The council also engaged in educational activities of a different, although interdependent, sort: they worked to transform and "improve" childrearing and homemaking practices among working-class families, with a focus on women and children who were new to the city and to Canada. In this they collaborated with teachers, attendance officers, social workers, and public health nurses to seek out women who, in their view, ought to be educated in the ways of "Canadian" homemaking, cooking, and childrearing. In council newsletters and minutes, these efforts were described in terms of "good" and "intelligent" mothers imparting their knowledge to "less fortunate" women.

Finally, Home and School clubs provided a source of voluntary female labor for many schools, organizing graduation ceremonies, sewing costumes for school plays and pageants, chaperoning school trips, and raising money for libraries, musical instruments, artwork, and the like. Over time, the image of "Home and School" and "the P.T.A." became synonymous with tireless "bakesale" organizers, women who could be called on to cheerfully serve schools with their "voluntary" labor. These organizations have become fixtures of middle-class Anglo-Canadian neighborhoods, providing local venues for women to socialize with each other, get to know the local teachers, and especially to support their children's schooling. I have argued elsewhere that it is precisely through such (apparently) mundane and daily service activities that middle-class women contribute to the ongoing and intergenerational organization of class relations.[5]

I am interested in how notions of "good" and "intelligent" mothering came to be worked up and represented in the Toronto Home and School Council's organizing and educational activities during the first fifteen years of the Toronto Home and School Council's existence, from 1916 to 1930–31. The council leadership made strenuous efforts to be taken seriously by school officials as representatives of "organized parenthood." In pursuing this goal they sought to show that they were keen to "do good" for schools and "be good" for children, and that they possessed the required "intelligence" to take part in educational decision-making. Eventually the council was rewarded for its efforts and won recognition as an "inside" organization with the Toronto Board of Education.

Between 1916 and 1930, the Home and School Council and its leaders sought to shape a version of political subjectivity of and for women in the domain of local educational politics, recently opened up for women. It is impossible to make sense of this group's organizational and political work without attending to their involvement in processes of class formation. This was a period when professional, administrative, and white collar employment was rapidly expanding in businesses and government, and these jobs required forms of knowledge imparted through formal education. Thus, for middle-class families, in particular, schooling became ever more central to their children's ability to secure future careers. The early decades of the century were also a time of large-scale migration to urban centers such as Toronto, and of migration to the North American continent. The end of World War I saw major social upheavals in Europe and North America, with workers and women organizing to press for individual and collective rights, including the rights of citizenship and the right to organize trade unions. Although it would be wrong to argue that these changes had an immediate and uniform effect on schools, it is clear that school systems expanded dramatically to accommodate increased numbers of students, especially in secondary schools, to develop a more differentiated curriculum, and to reorganize and professionalize school management and governance according to principles of fiscal accountability and functional efficiency.[6]

It has become commonplace for North American feminist historians to focus on relations of power, inequality, and "differences" among women.[7] In this paper I will take up some themes from this literature to explore tensions in the Home and School leaders' efforts to position themselves and their membership as "good" and "intelligent" women and mothers. I will show that their organizational activities and public representations not only presumed and effected their difference from and superiority over "other" women, but that their work also involved concerted attempts to shape and regulate the conduct and identities of their own members, of themselves. These self-forming and self-regulating activities are the topic of this paper. I will argue that the organizational work of the Home and School Council—its public and political representations, its educational work among members, and its management of member groups—was as much about regulating the conduct of Home and School women themselves as it was about controlling and regulating "others." These activities were interrelated, and can be seen as practices of moral regulation.

In a 1981 article, Philip Corrigan drew on the sociology of Emile Durkheim and the sociolinguistics of Basil Bernstein to suggest that investigations of moral regulation can direct our attention to the ways in which formation of social individuality or subjectivity is both constrained and constructed in and through social relations and through the disciplinary powers and practices of the state.[8] In another context Corrigan (with Derek Sayer) described moral regulation as "a project of normalizing, rendering natural, taken for granted, in a word 'obvious,' what are in fact ontological and epistemological premises for a particular and historical form of social order."[9] Corrigan traces (through historical and sociological inquiry) the organization of, and links between, forms of rule, forms of expression, and the formation of social identity:

Moral regulation . . . concerns forms and contexts, determining thus the realization of utterance, display, gesture, indication, action—in a phrase, proper forms of expression which are always-ever far more than lingual. It is not simply that meanings are context-linked but that the structured means of expression are already "valued," providing not simply . . . the illocutionary along with the locutionary but a variety of other indicators. These moral repertoires are what establish social identity, or rather . . . identities.[10]

Seen thus, moral regulation is "about" organized, repetitive, and often mundane practices and relations that privilege certain forms of expression and behavior, all the while rendering other forms as marginal, contained, illegitimate, or immoral.[11] Two kinds of questions emerge in studies of moral regulation: how, why, and from where do moral repertoires and regimes emerge, and how do they become effective? The first question directs attention to socially structured and institutionally organized relations and practices. The second concerns how human subjectivity is formed and embodied in relations and practices of moral regulation. Both questions are versions of the "classic" debates in sociology and history about structure and agency, social and individual, order and change.

Corrigan framed his exploratory 1981 paper on moral regulation as an alternative to the work of social theorists who argue that people's apparent complicity with patterns of order can be explained either by way of shared values or by the obvious appeal of some inherent system of logic. On the other hand, and as a critique of many fellow Marxists, he rejects those accounts of social relations that conceptualize power as a possession of a particular class, gender, or "race," or as (only) an externalized, constraining, and controlling force acting on human beings as though they were passive victims or objects. Rather, he suggests that power is both constraining and constructive.[12] Such a conception of power draws on Michel Foucault's account of modern disciplinary power.

Foucault argued that modern forms of power work most effectively through discourses and institutional practices (or technologies), especially those discourses that are implicated in knowing the social and the individual, and those forms of discipline that work through self-regulation.[13] These are disciplinary knowledges which, in Foucault's terms, form "regimes of truth" that are always also regimes of power with the capacity to produce "the social" and "the subject" as their effects. Here the capacity to effect change appears to be located within disciplinary practices and discourses which, in turn, enable the production of subjects as their "effects." I will not enter into a discussion here about whether this position reduces human subjectivity to an effect of discourse(s), or if it is precisely through a conception of subjectivity as socially and discursively constituted that it is possible to imagine agency and alternative forms of subjectivity and sociality. Feminist writers have been among the most vociferous participants on many sides in these debates.[14] For example, while Nancy Hartsock warns that Foucault's notion of power, discourse, and subjectivity would render feminism without political capacity to act to end the oppression of women, Judith Butler argues that "to claim that the subject is constituted is not to claim that it is determined; on the contrary, the constituted character of the subject is the very precondition of its agency."[15]

These issues are relevant to my questions about the work of middle-class women's organizations in educational reform and local politics in Toronto in the first half of this century. It seems to me that although it is crucial to recognize the productive effects of knowledge, power, and discourse, I am not convinced that much is gained by rejecting the constitutive capacities of human subjects altogether. (It is another question whether the latter position follows from a misreading of Foucault's writings on power and the subject, and perhaps, from a lack of clarity in the use of the terms "individual," subject and subjectivity, agency, and experience.[16]) In this paper I try to show the ongoing interrelation and frequent tensions within and between the formative and productive effects of discourses of the "good" and "intelligent" mother, and the self-constituting activities and capacities of women in Home and School associations, who both "took up" and exceeded, and challenged, these discourses and their effects. I will illustrate my arguments through three examples that show how women in Home and School groups very actively sought to position themselves in, and also to challenge and transform, existing discourses on motherhood, femininity, class, race, and citizenship. Moreover these discourses were and are always embedded in and organized through social relations and institutional practices of power.

The women who formed the leadership of the Toronto Home and School Council between 1916 and 1930 were initially very active and interested in broad-based social and educational reform work. Ada Courtice's vision was that the new organization would provide a decentralized but well-integrated movement that could organize, unite, and represent the interests of parents in school matters. She had a vision of a social movement based in local neighborhoods and centered around schools that would unite the purposes of teachers and parents, men as well as women. It was understood that such an organization would work in the interests of children.

It proved difficult to recruit men and to sustain their interest in the daily affairs of Home and School clubs. Activities such as meetings with teachers at the local school and attending lectures on child welfare, schooling, and childrearing were seen as extensions of women's childrearing and domestic labor. At the same time, many of the "experts" who were brought in to lecture for Home and School members were men: school principals, administrators, trustees, judges, journalists, and professors in education and in the emerging social and psychological sciences. For these men the council offered an appreciative audience for their views as well as occasional alliances in pursuit of reform initiatives or in defense of school programs. At other times, the council or some of its member clubs came into conflict with the male-dominated educational "establishment."

The council sought to create a place for themselves among middle-class social and educational reform groups in Toronto, and its leadership also established contacts with Home and School or parent-teacher organizations across Canada and in the United States.[17] These relationships were maintained through correspondence, magazine subscriptions, and by visiting "sister" organizations. Toronto activists were invited to take part in annual meetings of the National Congress of Mothers in Washington, for example, while the congress sent delegates who, in turn, spoke at Toronto council meetings.[18] Council leaders in Toronto also sought out women's organizations in smaller towns and rural areas of Ontario, particularly women's institutes, which had taken an active interest in school affairs since their inception at the turn of the century. Three years after the formation of the Toronto group, Ada Courtice launched a Provincial Federation of Home and School Associations during the 1919 convention of the Ontario Educational Association.[19] The Toronto Home and School Council had been invited by the O.E.A. to organize a session during its annual meeting. The new federation was immediately accepted as a section of the Elementary School Department of the O.E.A.[20]

Membership in the O.E.A.—an influential federation of school administrators, teachers, education "experts," and elected officials—provided the nascent Home and School movement with some legitimacy among school people. The O.E.A. circulated reports of its yearly convention to hundreds of Ontario teachers, principals, inspectors, and school trustees. The inclusion of the Home and School Federation's deliberations among those of teachers and inspectors might suggest to educators that parent organizations were important to the educational enterprise. At the same time members of the Home and School Federation would be able to follow and learn from developments in educational debates and practices of the day by reading O.E.A. annual reports. O.E.A. membership also provided the federation with much-needed organizational resources. Printing and distribution of annual meeting records across the province helped in "getting the word out" to local leaders and members, provided a link among member organizations, served as an organizational tool, and introduced member groups to worthwhile topics for discussion at their local meetings. Thus, the formal connection to the O.E.A. forged a relationship between the leadership of the Home and School movement and a well-established public sphere of educational debate.

One key assumption of Home and School organizations was that a unity of interest should and could be created between principals, teachers, and parents, and that these local neighborhood clubs, linked together into a broad social movement, could be of great benefit to teachers and principals, as well as to parents. The appeal to teachers and mothers was made both in terms of moral rightness and practical organization and "efficiency." In a speech to the Elementary Teachers' section of the O.E.A. in 1918, Ada Courtice pleaded with the audience:

In order that the process of education should have its cultural and practical results, parents and teachers must naturally think and work together and must have a common meeting-place from which to send out their vision and their effort.[21]

It was this double appeal to the immediate and the general, the practical and the ideological, combined with promises of immediate benefits to children's schooling, that attracted large numbers of middle-class women to the new organization. The Toronto Home and School Council grew quickly. By 1921 thirty-three associations were federated with it; ten years later there were seventy member clubs; and in 1935 there were eighty Home and School clubs in Toronto.[22] Local clubs provided a way for women to meet each other in their neighborhoods and to get to know their children's teachers. Accounts of the early years of individual clubs emphasize their social functions as much as their educational benefits. From annual reports we get glimpses into groups of women—twenty to sixty members seemed common—getting together for fund-raising efforts, entertainment and teas, meet-the-teacher nights, and educational lectures for "social uplift."[23]

Most clubs reported that their working meetings were held in the afternoon, usually toward the end of the school day, between two and four o'clock. Public events to which male experts or fathers were invited were held during the evening. Organizational activity during the afternoon presumed that mothers of schoolchildren were free to attend meetings at such times. This practice excluded most men and women who were engaged in wage labor, and women with small children at home. There is no indication in the council records that childcare was provided, or that children were brought along to meetings, unless they were providing entertainment or serving tea with their mothers. Daytime gatherings assumed a gender division of household and childrearing labor in which women were expected to be full-time mothers and homemakers. Such arrangements also presumed that teachers had no domestic responsibilities, by requiring their attendance at school meetings after the end of the school day.

The goals of the Home and School movement centered on Christian notions of character, virtue, femininity, and masculinity. Ada Courtice argued that parents and teachers shared the objective of educating children and "building strong, good character and a healthy body, training the mental faculties, and cultivating the virtues that constitute Christian manliness and womanliness."[24] A handbook circulated by the council to member clubs in 1927 or 1928 again emphasized virtue, as well as service, patriotism, and citizenship. At the same time, that handbook drew attention to the appropriate conduct of Home and School clubs by pointing out important distinctions between acceptable and unacceptable activities:

The guiding principles of the association are the embodiment of social service, civic virtue and patriotism, maintaining, as it does, that it is not "a means of entertainment, or charity or criticism of school authority, but a co-operative, non-political, non-sectarian, non-commercial effort to produce Canadian citizens who shall be capable of perpetuating the best which has been developed in our national life."[25]

Here the pursuit of citizenship, patriotism, nationalism, and so forth is given a practical content by attending to and attempting to regulate the daily affairs of local Home and School clubs. A great deal of effort was required to manage these affairs. Several times during the early years of its existence, the Home and School Council found itself in situations where it had to "handle" tensions between women's new role as citizens and their position as mothers, between (some) women's desire to be taken seriously as "intelligent" participants in school affairs, and their subordinate servicing status as "good" helpers supporting teachers' work.

Mothers vs. "the Lady Principal"

In 1921 a conflict between the Home and School Council at John Ross Robertson School (in an upper-middle-class Toronto suburb) and a school principal made newspaper headlines in Toronto for several weeks. Having simmered for several months, the troubles became public when a letter written by the president of the club, a Mrs. McGregor, to the chief inspector of the Board of Education was released to the school trustees and to the press. In the letter McGregor asked for the resignation of the principal, Miss Cullen.[26] The club members complained that Miss Cullen had blocked their access to school space for club events, and their letter referred to "a series of unpleasant situations existing between the club and the principal."[27] According to newspaper accounts, the divisions had become so deep that some parents had taken their children out of the school, while the principal had convened a competing mothers' club, of which she herself was president.[28] Toronto papers delighted in sexualizing the protagonists in the conflict and detailed every bit of tension and accusation between "the Lady Principal" and "warring factions" of "North Toronto Mothers." In the midst of the controversy a male school trustee called a meeting of fathers, which sixty

men attended. According to several newspaper reports the men resolved to apologize "to the Board of Education for the annoyance
caused the trustees" by their wives.[29] This intervention was treated
as a good-natured and humorous resolution to the issue, in which
men demonstrated their greater capacity for reason by correcting
the excesses and emotionality of women. Some male school trustees
proclaimed outrage that a group of women would dare to criticize a
principal and even request that she resign. At the same time, this
public expression of indignation did not prevent the same trustees
from launching an inquiry into the "disciplinarian and academic
qualifications of female principals."[30]

   This was a difficult matter for the Home and School Council.
One of its member clubs was a key protagonist, and Mrs. McGregor,
who wrote the offending letter, was on the executive of the Ontario
Federation of Home and School Associations and was a friend of
Ada Courtice. In spite of these connections, several complications
made it difficult for the council to take a clear position in the conflict, however. The presence of two competing clubs of mothers at
the same school threw into question the goals of harmony and collaboration. In addition, some of the "old" club's members were
women whose children no longer attended the school. As the story
was told in the newspaper, it turned out that some of the most vocal
members of the John Ross Robertson School Home and School Club,
including Mrs. McGregor, had taken their children out of John Ross
Robertson and enrolled them in private schools in the area because
of the tensions in the school caused by the conflict. The "second"
club, presided over by the principal, raised the question of who could
legitimately represent the interests of parents. An executive member
of this club stated in a speech to the Board of Education:

*We represent the parents whose children attend the school. The Home
and School Club do not represent the parents. We are the stronger
league and have made more money for the school than the other side.
We have no feelings against the Home and School, but we are all
mothers of children attending the school and are consequently very
busy looking after their welfare. Our efforts are confined to this particular school whereas the work of the Home and School Club affects
various schools.[31]*

While claiming the right to speak for "parents," this statement also makes visible that the proper role of a Home and School club is to support the school, through fund-raising efforts, for example. The speaker continued, saying that it seems the first club not only failed to reach the same standard in this regard, but also had exceeded the boundaries of proper conduct for Home and School clubs by criticizing the school's staff: "Parents are beginning to ask if it is right for outsiders to come in and demand the resignation of a teacher, . . . We have never attempted to dictate, . . . We have never had the slightest friction." The impropriety of mothers questioning and criticizing the performance and conduct of teachers and principals was at the heart of the dispute in this wealthy neighborhood.

Ada Courtice, who was then organizing secretary for the Ontario Federation of Home and School Associations, declined to publicly support either club. When the John Ross Robertson "affair" was discussed by the Toronto Home and School Council in January 1922, the executive decided not to take any action. They were waiting for the Board of Education to review its policies regarding the use of school space. The rationale for not intervening in the conflict was that "the Council is hopeful that the Board would recognize H. & S. Clubs as 'Inside Organizations' and this in a great measure would solve the difficulty of permits and fees."[32]

As "inside organizations" the council and its clubs would not be required to obtain individual permits for use of school space, nor pay fees for each event they wished to organize in school buildings. This would save substantial work, money, and time, and "inside" status would also provide much-wanted legitimacy and recognition from trustees, administrators, and teachers for the fledgling organization. On the other hand, such status could not be obtained unless a group could demonstrate that its purposes and practices were supportive of and compatible with those of the school. A publicized request from a member club for a principal's resignation was hardly conducive to the Home and School Council's obtaining the practical advantage and symbolic privileges attached to "insider" status. The John Ross Robertson School affair could not have come at a less propitious moment.

The final difficulty was that the principal concerned was a woman. Her gender was played up by the Toronto press and by male trustees, who insisted on referring to Miss Cullen as a "lady principal" and drawing attention to complaints about her performance. In December 1921 the Board of Education voted to launch an inquiry into the qualifications of all female principals. At this point the Toronto Home and School Council was not silent. Its president was outraged at the attempt to judge "women in general . . . based on one local incident." She added that she was certain that women had made "great successes as school principals."[33] Since its inception the council had supported women teachers in their efforts to open up administrative positions and principalships to women. We can therefore imagine their frustration that an issue involving one of its member clubs would cause the Board of Education to question the abilities of women as school managers.

Finally, it is not coincidental that this issue was played out in an affluent area of the city, where mothers were likely to consider themselves socially superior to women teachers and principals. It may well be that women in such neighborhoods expected teachers of their children to comply with their wishes, and were frustrated to find school staff who instead considered their involvement in the school as rather meddlesome interference.[34] That they would criticize a principal to her superiors moved them further beyond the pale of good conduct expected by Home and School members. In terms of class and gender relations, this incident—and the school board's, the press's, and the Home and School Council's responses to it—suggest that Home and School groups, with their presumption of mothers' happy cooperation with and subordination to teachers' better judgment, were not well suited to organize upper-class and wealthy women's relations to schooling.

An Un-British Affair

In 1921 members of another Home and School club found themselves in conflict with the Toronto Board of Education. Parents of children attending Brown Elementary School wanted their children to learn French. French was not included as a subject in the elementary school curriculum, so the parents hired one of the school's teachers to instruct the children in a classroom after regular school hours. In order to pay for the teacher's services, the club charged a fee from those parents whose children participated. A permit was needed to use a classroom for such a purpose, and it was first obtained without much ado in September 1921. It was when the club approached the board's Management Committee in January 1922 to renew the permit that problems arose. After a bitterly fought election, the new board was for the second year in a row dominated by opponents of "fads and frills," several of whom owed their political fortunes to the city's business community and the Orange Lodges. Rather than treat Brown Home and School club's application as a routine request, some trustees seized upon the issue as an unpatriotic "threat" to Toronto's Britishness. In an intriguing line of reasoning that anticipated arguments against multicultural programs fifty years hence, trustee Wanless charged that the Brown Home and School club's request for a classroom in which to teach French stirred up a "racial" issue:

The attempt to develop a racial issue is unpatriotic, un-British and calls for the condemnation of all true citizens. If French is granted in these primary schools, what is to be done if classes are requested also in Italian, Hebrew, Finnish and Bulgarian and where is the money to come from? This is an English-speaking city and provision must first be made for Anglo-Saxons.[35]

It was, in Wanless's opinion, an unfortunate oversight that the first permit had been issued. The Management Committee would ensure that it would not happen again.

There was more to this matter than WASP trustees mouthing racist and anti-French opinions and asserting the dominance of the English language and anything "British" in Toronto's public schools. The parents of Brown school children were not advocating for French language teaching as a matter of minority rights. Although some of their supporters, such as Professor C. B. Sissons of the University of Toronto, used arguments of the schools' responsibility to foster understanding between the English and French in Canada, that was not the main concern of the parents.[36] The issue had rather more to do with class relations, and with securing a middle-class and professional future for their children. Trustee McClelland, who spoke in favor of the Brown Home and School club, explained their case:

*The boys and girls who wanted to go higher did not like to take the
fourth form in that school because they could not get the languages.
Then when [the boys] went on to U.C.C. and St. Andrew's, they had to
step back a full year. It was to remedy this situation and build up the
fourth form that it was decided to hold special classes.[37]*

In other words, teaching of French would help the children to get
on better in private, secondary schooling. As if to underscore the
opposing class investments in this issue, another trustee characterized the Brown parents, and the Home and School delegation, as
a "highbrow" group who sought to take advantage of the public
schools in order to provide their children with special privileges. He
contrasted them with the "poorer schools like York Street" in his
constituency.[38]

In contrast to the members of the John Ross Robertson club,
the Brown Home and School group did obtain strong public support from the council. They mobilized an impressive and influential
range of groups and individuals, including the Collegeview Heights
Ratepayers (from the area surrounding Upper Canada College), several university professors, some school principals, and even the chief
inspector of schools, Robert Cowley. Toronto middle-class and
professional educational reform "intelligentsia" confronted "ward
politicians," who in this instance claimed to speak on behalf of "ordinary" parents and taxpayers.[39]

In their opposition to the Brown parents' request for the use of
a classroom in which to teach French, some trustees tried to undermine the Home and School delegation by racializing the issue, as we
have seen above, and by sexualizing those who supported it.

*These women arrogate to themselves the right to sit in judgment on the
qualifications of the trustees, to formulate and direct the educational
policy of Toronto, overlooking or forgetting the fact that the
board . . . represents the concentrated selection of citizens and is made
up of medical men, business men, lawyers, clergymen, contractors and
educationists . . . The board will not allow any group to usurp its pre-
rogatives by any amount of fussing and feathering, but will be at all
times willing to give a courteous hearing to any group of citizens who
loyally confer through the regular channels.[40]*

While several men had joined the Home and School Council on this occasion, it was the presence of and presentations by women that angered these and other trustees. "Fussing and feathering" was a pejorative and dismissive description that could hardly be applied to men. Again women were called to task for presuming that they could "sit in judgment," this time over the qualifications of trustees. The permit to teach French at Brown School was denied.[41]

Occurring around the same time as the John Ross Robertson controversy, this dispute also brought out tensions between the more political and servicing aims of the Home and School Council and its member clubs, between their claims to comprise "intelligent" parenthood, and their position as subordinate, feminine supporters of school managers. In this case, however, there were tensions among school administrators and elected trustees. Those trustees who opposed the teaching of French in Brown used racist and anti-French arguments to their advantage and undermined the credibility of their opponents by reminding women of their "proper place" in school affairs.

The Language of Patriotism

Although most Toronto Home and School clubs were formed in Anglo-Canadian and middle-class neighborhoods, the council's records detail much concern with schools in "foreign" and working-class districts. One such school was Elizabeth Street School, later named Hester How School, located in "the Ward," a downtown area composed of busy streets, shops, and small rental flats. The area provided the cheapest housing in the city, and many immigrants found housing there when they first arrived in Toronto. Among middle-class observers in the early twentieth century, the area had a reputation as morally and physically dangerous and unsanitary, and it was described by one observer as "the festery sore of our city life."[42]

Ida Siegel, a social democrat and activist in Toronto's Jewish community, helped teachers organize a Mothers' Club (another, earlier name for a Home and School club) at this school as early as 1912.[43] The purpose of the club was twofold: to foster closer cooperation between mothers and teachers, and to build citizenship and patriotism among "foreign" families. Indeed, Hester How School was designated by the Board of Education as a school with potential to make "good Canadians" out of "newcomers."[44] In their English classes, children prepared invitations for their mothers to attend club meetings. Most of the women who attended the club were Jewish, recent immigrants from Eastern Europe who spoke little English. The club was used to instruct mothers in English and introduce them to a "Canadian way of life."[45] Through talks (in English) on topics such as childcare, hygiene, and nutrition, school nurses and teachers attempted to transmit "Canadian values" to its members.[46]

As president of the club, Ida Siegel did not oppose the goals of promoting cooperation, citizenship, and patriotism among Jewish women. However, she opposed every attempt to Christianize Toronto's Jewish children and adults. In this regard her agenda was quite at odds with that of the Hester How teachers, and she used unconventional strategies in her work with Jewish women. She was able to change the practice of writing invitations to mothers and conducting meetings entirely in English. Invited speakers occasionally addressed the Mothers' Club in Yiddish, or Ida Siegel would interpret from English to Yiddish. Moreover, she and the mothers spoke among themselves in their own language during the social portion of the meetings. Over time it seems that the school staff became more and more unhappy with Ida Siegel's conduct of the club's affairs. Relations between mothers, the teachers, and principals began to change, as the mothers gained some small measure of control over how the meetings were organized, what should be discussed, and, particularly, the language that was spoken.

At the end of 1918 the teachers and a school nurse resigned from the club. In a letter to Chief Inspector Cowley, they accused Ida Siegel of being a "non-Ward resident," and therefore an "outsider" with no legitimate status in the school. It especially angered them that she had relegated them, in their minds the club's "legitimate" leadership, to a secondary and supportive role. Finally they charged that the use of Yiddish on school property was unpatriotic and ought not to be permitted.[47] Inspector Cowley and the majority of board trustees concurred, some of them arguing that such behavior was tantamount to "Bolshevism."[48] The board passed a motion that only the English language could be used during events held in city schools.[49]

How could a small group of women meeting to talk about cook-ing, childrearing, and health, and speaking in their own language, come to be seen as a threat to social order? In her retelling of these events in an interview taped in 1976, Ida Siegel described how she thought of herself as having no "political" intentions in her work with the Hester How Mothers' Club. She talked about the anti-Semitic accusations leveled against her and about how she could not fit the mundane activities of the Hester How Mothers' Club with the hysterical reactions they caused among teachers, trustees, and the press. She also recalled that such hostility against Jews in Toronto was uncommon neither during this period nor in later years.

In retrospect, she remembered that the Toronto Home and School Council and women trustees were among the few who supported her in her battle to be "exonerated."[50] Ada Courtice was an elected school trustee at this time. She voted against the En-glish-only motion in the board meeting, arguing that it was "not the way to assimilate them as Canadians."[51] Her difference with other trustees was not based on opposition to assimilation of "for-eigners," nor did she argue that Mothers' Clubs should not be used to achieve such ends. On the contrary, she feared that the prohibi-tion of "other" languages would turn away from the schools the women who spoke them. She felt that a more flexible and moder-ate approach would be more successful in the long run. The friendly, neighborly contacts between women that were established through Home and School Clubs could offer much-needed practical sup-port to women and foster a stronger, more enduring patriotism, citizenship, and democracy. In a speech to the Ontario Educational Association a year earlier, she had declared: "If we want a demo-cratic country the best type of democracy will come from a chain of democratic groups of neighborhoods."[52]

Although Ada Courtice supported Ida Siegel in her capacity as a school trustee, there is no written record of the council's backing in its documents. During the few months when this particular con-flict was fought, the minutes of the Toronto Home and School Coun-cil make no reference to the issue. There is no record in school board minutes to indicate that the council intervened publicly in behalf of mothers at Hester How School when the board made the decision to bar their meetings. This does not necessarily mean that they provided no support, although it might suggest that their efforts were informal and personal rather than public and official.

It was unusual that contradictions between the Home and School "idea" and working-class and immigrant life would come to the attention of the school board in this way. However, the difficulties encountered at Hester How school in 1919 were by no means isolated. In June 1917 a committee had been established "to study the question of interesting the Non-English speaking parents in H. & S. Work."[53] Nothing further was reported from this committee until November 1919, several months after the board had passed its English-only motion. It turned out to be difficult for the council to organize and maintain clubs in schools in working-class and "foreign" districts. This was not for lack of effort. Both school officials and council leaders alike agreed that it was in these schools that Home and School clubs would be of the greatest benefit. For the few clubs that were established in working-class neighborhoods, only scant records are available. Some appear to have lasted for only short periods, and those that did survive more than a few months were consistently "represented" at council meetings by school principals.

An investigative report on another school located in "the Ward" (York Street School), written in March 1920 by the Bureau of Municipal Research, proposed that parents' associations in "finer districts" should adopt downtown schools and donate works of art to them so that "prevailingly foreign" children could be exposed to "proper" Canadian culture.[54] Some hesitant attempts were made by the council in this direction. A report of the work of the council's Extension Committee in 1928 explained that its duties were "to visit schools where there are difficulties in the way of forming a Home and School Association, and with the co-operation of the principal and teachers to arrange a meeting."[55] *Home and School* was a failed attempt to produce a regular magazine for and by the Toronto Council. Only one issue was ever published. Instead members received the *Home and School Review,* published by the Ontario Federation of Home and School Associations and edited by longtime Toronto teacher and activist Lillian Payne. The report goes on to describe how meetings and social gatherings were organized in a few schools, where a "short address on some pertinent topic is combined with a programme of music and reading, followed by refreshments. The latter are always much appreciated."

A few associations were formed in working-class schools as a result of this committee's work, although its purpose was only to "bring the aims and ideals" of Home and School before parents and teachers, and it was "not meant for organization purposes."[56] Another account of the "extension" work reported on "programmes put on in downtown schools, where it seemed impossible or inadvisable to have Associations."[57] This suggests that Home and School clubs, in spite of the council's public claims to represent all parents, were not seen as a vehicle where working-class or "foreign" women might act in their own behalf in school matters. Rather, it is clear that these organizations were created to suit the lives of middle-class mothers, and that women who could not (or would not) "fit in" to these groups were positioned beyond the public sphere of local educational decision-making.

Conclusion

One result of these early controversies surrounding Home and School clubs was that both trustees and Home and School leaders agreed that they ought to chart rules that would regulate relations among community groups, school administrators, teachers, and trustees. One issue was to define how, by whom, and for what purposes school buildings could, or could not, be used. This work had begun in December 1921. To help define what constituted proper conduct, the board established detailed guidelines for any group seeking to use school space for its activities. According to a lengthy article in the *Daily Star*, these guidelines permitted discussion of "civic and educational" topics, but without "partisanship" and with safeguards as to "the loyal nature of any meeting held in the schools." "Political and religious" activities were explicitly prohibited, and regulation number one stated: "Any utterance of a seditious or disloyal nature will automatically revoke this permit, and will disqualify the parties from holding any further meetings in school buildings."[58] The article, whose headline acknowledged that the new rules were "rigid," went on to assure "the public" that

no revolution-breeding gatherings will be countenanced, . . . One of the significant rules of the board is that lectures, addresses, etc. are to be given only in the English language. No bilingualism for Toronto trustees.[59]

Moreover, persons signing the permit application had to be "British subjects" and "bona fide ratepayers." Edith L. Groves, who was very active within the Home and School Council, and who was first elected to the Board of Education in 1920 with enthusiastic council support, chaired the committee that drew up these regulations. Subsequent records of the Toronto Home and School Council and the Board of Education indicate that the council worked hard to ensure that its members and member clubs adhered to these rules.

Early twentieth-century discourses of education reform were closely intertwined with rhetorics of civic virtue, citizenship, and national efficiency. In these discourses mothers were positioned as a critical link in the great project of nation- and empire-building. The Canadian minister of trade and commerce, the Honorable Sir George E. Foster, put it this way when he spoke to the Ontario Educational Association in 1915: "Woman power is one of the subtlest and most powerful instrumentalities in making nationality and building Empire. . . . The home is the cradle of the Nation."[60] As I have tried to show here, the tropes of nationhood, and imagined and real threats to it, were frequently invoked as some women began to enter the public arena of school politics. At the same time the success of schools began to be measured by new criteria. It was no longer sufficient to count the numbers of pupils who passed (or failed) their "entrance," nor to point to schools' ability to "keep children off the streets." Equally important was the extent to which schools and school boards (as well as municipal administration and public services generally) were being run according to "scientific" business principles. The women who became active in Toronto Home and School clubs set out to learn about these methods, and to become versed in the latest theories of pedagogy and child development. They sought both to be taken seriously as informed and "intelligent" political actors speaking on behalf of women, and to be seen as "good" and supportive members of local school communities.

Although resourceful in many ways, middle-class women encountered much opposition. They were constantly watched, and their behavior was the subject of sexist comments by male colleagues on the school board as well as pundits in Toronto newspapers. When they supported women teachers' campaigns for equal pay and access to promotions, for example, Home and School leaders were accused of bringing "sex politics" into the school board. An editorial in the *Telegram* charged in 1925:

> *The game of sex politics is already played out in the educational civic affairs of this city. . . . "The women of Toronto" are not represented or controlled by the busybody organizations that represent nobody outside of the ranks of an extremely limited membership.*[61]

The chairman of the board, on his part, charged: "The only time politics is introduced is when a lot of women's organizations start interfering and try to control the board."[62]

Different groups of women fared quite differently in their attempts to influence programs and personnel in the schools their children attended. The Jewish women of the Hester How Mothers' Club were viciously attacked for wanting to speak their own language among themselves, and while they received some support from individual Home and School leaders, their cause was never championed with the vigor that benefited the Brown Home and School Club's campaign for French courses. On the other hand, the affluent and Anglo-Saxon members of John Ross Robertson Home and School Club received even less support from the council. That particular case touched on much broader issues and relations in which the council was engaged, specifically the use of school space, the position of women principals, and more generally, a definition of boundaries of Home and School activities in relation to schools and the school board.

Over time, women in Home and School associations became important contributors to the day-to-day running of many schools, through fund-raising events and organization of trips, theater nights, and meet-the-teacher events. Criticism and "political" activities were explicitly discouraged, while schools assumed and came to rely on the unpaid support and caring labor of women in the family and in local clubs and organizations such as the Toronto Home and School Council. While visible political achievements may be few, the long-term relations that Home and School associations facilitated between middle-class women and schools in Toronto are, in my view, far more significant. Through these relations, middle-class women not only shaped school practices that were advantageous to their own children, but also helped to develop programs that aimed to restructure the relations of other women and children to schools and schooling as well.

Women's work in Home and School associations fit into a wide range of moral reform projects in English Canada. Through organizing, writing, public speaking, electioneering, deputizing, and so on, these women sought to represent and regulate the good and intelligent mother in relation to school governance. Successful claims to "goodness" and "intelligence" relied on moral regulation, self-regulation of proper conduct, and visible displays of knowing and following rules of public, political interaction. At the same time, adult women were offered, and took up, different positions as subjects in Home and School discourses and institutional practices of schooling. Claiming an essential capacity for nurturing that could be "made conscious" through concerted educational activity, some women were able to argue for particular pedagogical practices in the name of femininity, and to enter a broader public sphere of social, moral, and educational reform as "good" and "intelligent" mothers.

The council and its members and leadership continued to be marked, and represented themselves, as gendered participants in school affairs, and to be assigned to areas in the political and practical division of educational labor that were (and are) considered feminine, subordinate, and marginal. However, they worked within and attempted to push beyond the gendered boundaries of that space, as the council sought to establish itself as the political voice and representative of "good" and "intelligent" motherhood. Their relative and variable success in this effort depended upon their ability to mark their difference from, but also their professed concern for, women who were not included in those categories. My account of Home and School women's relation to "other" women is quite conventional and joins that of many other recent feminist attempts to revise the historiography of different women's engagements with and positions in early twentieth-century social and educational reform in North America. However, I have tried to focus here on the ways in which Home and School women sought to regulate their own behavior and conduct, how moral regulation worked to shape an appropriate political subjectivity of and for women.

Endnotes

1. Lola Burgoyne, *A History of the Home and School Movement in Ontario* (Toronto: Charters Publishing, 1935), p. 2.
2. Toronto Home and School Council, Minutes, February 12, 1916, Toronto Board of Education Archives, C7-4, 375 (Box 1 of 9). Hereafter Toronto Home and School Council will be cited as T.H.S.C., the Toronto Board of Education Archives as T.B.E.A. In the text I will often refer to the Toronto Home and School Council as "the council."
3. Terry Crowley, "Ada Mary Brown Courtice: Pacifist, Feminist and Educational Reformer in Early Twentieth-Century Canada," *Studies in History and Politics*, 1980, pp. 75–114.
4. Schools in Ontario are governed by the provincial Ministry of Education and locally elected boards of school trustees. The election boundaries of school boards overlap with those of municipal and county councils, and elections for boards of education are held at the same time as those for city, township, and county councils.
5. Kari Dehli, "Women and Class: The Social Organization of Mothers' Relations to Schooling in Toronto, 1915 to 1940." Ph.D. diss., Ontario Institute for Studies in Education, Toronto, 1988.
6. Robert M. Stamp, *The Schools of Ontario: 1876–1976* (Toronto: University of Toronto Press, 1983); Raymond E. Callahan, *Education and the Cult of Efficiency* (Chicago: University of Chicago Press, 1962).
7. See, for example, these excellent collections: Franca Iacovetta and Mariana Valverde, eds., *Gender Conflicts: New Essays in Women's History* (Toronto: University of Toronto Press, 1992); and Ellen Carol DuBois and Vicki L. Ruiz, eds., *Unequal Sisters: A Multicultural Reader in U.S. Women's History* (New York: Routledge, 1990).
8. Philip R. D. Corrigan, "On Moral Regulation: Some Preliminary Remarks." Chap. 3 in Corrigan, *Social Forms/Human Capacities* (London: Routledge 1990).
9. Philip R. D. Corrigan and Derek Sayer, *The Great Arch: English State Formation as Cultural Revolution* (Oxford: Basil Blackwell, 1985), p. 4.
10. Corrigan, "On Moral Regulation," p. 102.
11. See Mariana Valverde, ed., *Studies in Moral Regulation* (Toronto: Centre for Criminology, University of Toronto, 1994), also published as a special issue of the *Canadian Journal of Sociology*, Vol. 19, No. 2, 1994; Mariana Valverde and Lorna Weir, "The Struggle of the Immoral: Preliminary Remarks on Moral Regulation," *Resources for Feminist Research/Documentation sur la recherche feministe*, Vol. 17, No. 3, 1987, pp. 31–34.
12. Corrigan, "On Moral Regulation," pp. 122–23; see also chap. 4, "Towards a Celebration of Difference(s): Notes for a Sociology of a Possible Everyday Future," in *Social Forms/Human Capacities*.
13. Michel Foucault, *Power/Knowledge: Selected Interviews and Other Writings, 1972–1977*, edited by Colin Gordon (New York: Pantheon Books, 1980).
14. Among the huge number of recent collections and books, see for example, Irene Diamond and Lee Quinby, eds. *Feminism and Foucault* (Boston: Northeastern University Press, 1988); Nancy Fraser, *Unruly Practices: Power, Discourse and Gender in Contemporary Social Theory* (Minneapolis: University of Minnesota Press, 1989); Linda J. Nicholson, ed., *Feminism/Postmodernism* (New York: Routledge, 1990); Jana Sawicki, *Disciplining Foucault: Feminism, Power and the*

Body (New York: Routledge, 1991); Lois McNay, *Foucault and Feminism* (Boston: Northeastern University Press, 1992); Caroline Ramazanoglu, ed., *Against Foucault: Explorations of Some Tensions between Foucault and Feminism* (New York: Routledge, 1993).

15. Nancy Hartsock, "Foucault on Power: A Theory for Women?" in Nicholson, ed., *Feminism/Postmodernism*, pp. 157–175; Judith Butler, "Contingent Foundations," in Judith Butler and Joan W. Scott, eds., *Feminists Theorize the Political*, (New York: Routledge, 1992), p. 12.

16. See for example the debate between Joan Scott and Laura Lee Downs in *Comparative Studies in Society and History:* Laura Lee Downs, "If 'Woman' Is Just an Empty Category, Then Why Am I Afraid to Walk Alone at Night? Identity Politics Meets the Postmodern Subject"; Joan W. Scott, "'The Tip of the Volcano,'" (reply to Laura Downs); and Laura Downs, "Reply to Joan Scott," all in *Comparative Studies in Society and History*, Vol. 35, No. 2, April 1993, pp. 414–451. See also Joan W. Scott, "Experience," in Butler and Scott, eds., *Feminists Theorize the Political*.

17. Steven Schlossman, "The Formative Era in American Parent Education: Overview and Interpretation," in Ron Haskins and Diane Adams, eds., *Parent Education and Public Policy* (Norwood, N.J.: Ablex Publishing, 1983), pp. 7–39.

18. Mary E. James, *The First Fifty Years: Toronto Home and School Council, 1916–1966* (Toronto: Toronto Home and School Council, 1966), p. 11.

19. The O.E.A. held its convention each year in Toronto. For an account of the centrality of this organization in Ontario school history and educational debate, see Edwin C. Guillet, *In the Cause of Education: Centennial History of the Ontario Educational Association, 1861–1960* (Toronto: University of Toronto Press, 1960).

20. T.H.S.C., Minutes, n.d., April 1919; *Ontario Educational Association Proceedings,* 1919, pp. 55–60. Hereafter these *Proceedings* will be cited as *O.E.A. Proceedings*. They were published in Toronto by the O.E.A. following its annual convention.

21. Ada Courtice, "The Value of Home and School Clubs," *O.E.A. Proceedings,* 1918, p. 166.

22. T.H.S.C., *The Story of the Toronto Home and School Council through the Years 1916–1936* (Toronto: Toronto Home and School Council, 1936), pp. 44–46.

23. See, for example, Margaret Evans, "The Home and School Club," *The School,* Vol. 11, No. 4, December 1922, pp. 262–263 (an address given at a meeting of the Ontario Federation of Home and School Associations, held at the Normal School Building, Toronto, October 11 and 12, 1922).

24. Courtice, "The Value of Home and School Clubs," p. 166.

25. "Home and School Club Sets Forth Aims in New Handbook," T.B.E.A., T.H.S.C., Cab. 8–1, File: Clippings, n.s., n.d., but probably 1927 or 1928.

26. *Telegram,* October 28 and 29, November 4 and 24, and December 8, 1921; *Toronto Daily Star,* October 28, November 1 and 2, December 16 and 17, 1921, and January 24, 1922; *Mail and Empire,* December 6, 1921.

27. *Telegram,* October 28, 1921.

28. "Ask Principal's Removal," *Evening Telegram,* October 28, 1921; "Blames Principals for Lack of Harmony," *Toronto Daily Star,* November 1, 1921; "Principal Caused Trouble," *Evening Telegram,* November 1, 1921; "Knock Insane Ideas Out of the Children's Heads," *Evening Telegram,* November 24, 1921.

29. The *Toronto Daily Star* headline of this meeting ran: "Fathers Settle It. Mothers Keep Silent. More or Less Humour in Meeting of Dads of J. R. Robertson School Pupils. Approve Principal. 'The Female of the Species Is More Deadly Than the Male,' Is Quoted." *Toronto Daily Star,* November 2, 1921. See also "Parents Rally beside Teacher," *Globe,* November 2, 1921; "Fathers Back School Principal. Rebuff for Club Complainers," *Evening Telegram,* November 2, 1921; "Woman Principal of School Upheld," *Mail and Empire,* November 2, 1921.

30. "Come to Defence of Lady Principals," n.s., December 8, 1921, T.B.E.A., News clippings, Microfilm Reel 2, 1916–1921.
31. "Jealousy the Cause of Big School Row," *Toronto Daily Star,* October 28, 1921.
32. T.H.S.C., Minutes, January 10, 1922.
33. "Come to Defence of Lady Principals," n.s., December 8, 1921, T.B.E.A., News clippings, Microfilm Reel 2, 1916–1921.
34. For a brief account of relations between women teachers and middle-class women's organizations in Toronto, see Alison Prentice, "Themes in the Early History of the Women's Teachers' Association of Toronto," in Paula Bourne, ed.,*Women's Paid and Unpaid Work; Historical and Contemporary Perspectives,* (Toronto: New Hogtown Press, 1985), pp. 97–121, especially 107–110.
35. "Home and School Club Tries to Be Dictator," interview with Trustee Wanless, *Toronto Daily Star,* January 24, 1922.
36. C. B. Sissons, "Little Men and Big Issues," *The Canadian Forum,* Vol. 2, 1922, pp. 522–524.
37. "Trustees Vote 9 to 7 against French Class," *Toronto Daily Star,* February 3, 1922. U.C.C. refers to Upper Canada College, which along with St. Andrew's was, and still is, among the most exclusive private schools for boys in Canada.
38. Trustee Berlis, quoted in "Trustees Vote 9 to 7."
39. For a detailed history of urban reformers and ward politicians on Toronto's city council, see John C. Weaver, "The Modern City Realized: Toronto Civic Affairs, 1880–1915," in Alan Artbise and Gilbert A. Stelter, eds., *Planning and Politics in the Modern Canadian City* (Toronto: Macmillan 1979).
40. Wanless, "Home and School Club Tries to Be Dictator."
41. "No French in Brown School. Board Refuse Permit to Club," *Telegram,* February 3, 1922.
42. Rev. H. S. Magee, cited in Michael J. Piva, *The Conditions of the Working Class in Toronto,* 1900–1921 (Ottawa: University of Ottawa Press, 1979), p. 126; see account of Hester How School by Donald Jones, "Teacher 'Aunt Hessie' Inspired Juvenile Courts and Day Care," *Toronto Star,* June, 12 1982, p. F14.
43. Ida Siegel, taped interview by Don Nethery, May 31, 1976, T.B.E.A. Vertical Files, Biographies, Siegel; T.H.S.C., *The Story,* p. 44; Stephen A. Speisman, *The Jews of Toronto: A History to 1937* (Toronto: McClelland and Stewart, 1979), pp. 146–152, 181, 319–320.
44. Weaver, "The Modern City," p. 45.
45. Luigi G. Pennacchio, "In Defence of Identity: Ida Siegel and the Jews of Toronto versus the Assimilation Attempts of the Public School and Its Allies, 1900–1920," *Canadian Jewish Historical Society Journal,* No. 9 (Spring 1985), pp. 41–60.
46. T.H.S.C. Minutes, June 11, 1917; November 17, 1919.
47. T.B.E. Minutes, December 19, 1918, p. 246; "Must Use English Tongue," *Telegram,* December 21, 1918.
48. "Bolshevism in Schools? Idea Riles Trustees," *Telegram,* January 9, 1919.
49. "Bolshevism in Schools;" and T.B.E., Management Committee, Minutes, January 8, 1919.
50. Siegel, interview, 1976.
51. "'English Only' Is Rule for Students," *Toronto Daily Star,* January 17, 1919.
52. Ada Courtice, "The Value of Home and School Clubs," in *O.E.A. Proceedings,* 1918, p. 167.
53. T.H.S.C. Minutes, June 11, 1917.
54. Bureau of Municipal Research, *Biographies of Individual Schools under the Toronto Board of Education, 1. York Street School* (Toronto: Bureau of Municipal Research, March 1920), pp. 19, 8.
55. Jean E. Tedman, "Extension Committee," *Home and School,* Vol. 1, No. 1, December 1928, p. 11.
56. T.H.S.C., *The Story,* p. 20.
57. Ibid., p. 20.

58. "Rigid Rules to Govern the Use of the Schools," *Toronto Daily Star,* December 17, 1921.
59. Ibid.
60. "Women as Empire Builders," in *O.E.A. Proceedings,* 1915, p. 82.
61. *Telegram,* editorial, January 2, 1925.
62. Trustee McBrien, quoted in *Toronto Daily Star,* October 9, 1925.

Chapter Eleven
What Do "They" Want from Us?
Moral Regulation Gets Real in England and Wales in the 1990s

Philip R. D. Corrigan

Dedicated to Jane Brown, Head Teacher, Kingsmead School,
Borough of Hackney, London, England, for her calm courage.

> *It isn't polite to talk about class these days.*
> > —*Andy Croft, "The Silver in the Stone,"*
> > *BBC Radio 4, August 5, 1993*

> *By people I mean the white people the Black people the female people the lonely people the terrorized people the elderly people the young people the visionary people the unemployed people the regular ordinary omnipresent people who crave grace and variety and surprise and safety and one new day after another. Democratic anything presupposes equal membership in the body politic.*
> > —*June Jordan, "Waking Up in the Middle of Some American Dreams"* [1]

In this chapter I seek to focus some general arguments on a highly specific, localized situation—that of the material textual consequences of educational politics in England and Wales from 1993 to 1994. Given the rapidity of changes within schooling policies and politics, it should be noted that the data base for this chapter ceases on July 1, 1994. Every single theme sketched here—and "morality" issues in particular—was returned to the political and media stage at least twice since that date. What follows is thus very empirical, but not, I hope, empiricist. I attempt here a sort of social ethnography—an ethnography that attends to the contradictions of social forms and human capacities. How do attempted, and relatively successful, state-imposed changes in the shape, space, structure, weight, and consequence of the social forms of schooling alter the meaningful resources of cultural production within what we have been taught to call, quite falsely, education? If their purpose is to restrict dissonance, ambiguity, contradiction, and the more open play of this semiotic system, does that work?

Such a sketch has implications beyond the located situations of England and Wales. I think of Canada, the USA, Australia, New Zealand, France, Germany, Italy, and Japan—those countries that have all re-formed their schooling systems from the mid-1970s onwards. In each and every case, we need to open the categories (part of a strategy I have called "making the contradictions sing") to attend to the connected contradictions of "education" politics, policies, programs, and practices in relation to the differential historical experiences of teachers, staff, students, pupils, and parents/guardians. We must keep in mind that politics "x" does not necessarily eventuate in policy "x," program "x," and practice "x"; and even if such an unlikely event occurs, there remains the meaning-making of teachers and students/pupils.

This, then, is a focusing of some of my own earlier arguments and those of others.[2] From the different strands of my work on state formation and forms, on the elementary forms of schooling, and on the cultural contra/dictions of meaning-making, I am trying to make sense of one of the most coherent restructurings of institutionalized space, time, and textuality. To do so I concentrate on one national state form, in one year, in official (state-provided or state-regulated) schooling.

It is probably unnecessary to indicate not just that capitalism is in crisis, but that the form of these crises is violently contradictory regarding such schooling systems. Education as both solution and problem is a recurrent trope in England and Wales, from the 1830s if not earlier. The centrality of educative practices which form proper and correct subjectivities, through varieties of focused moral regulation, are constant from the late eighteenth century. The "Enlightenment" project was both occidentalist and a class and gendered and racialized/ethnicized project for the re-making of the population, first and foremost into respectable and rational male members of "the Public" and secondarily, into diligent and skilled workers through occupational training. State-regulated and -provided schooling systems have always referred to the "children of other classes," and not those of the very school promoters, politicians, and state servants who designed the schooling for other people's children. The recent fearful revivals of social Darwinism and eugenics, the values of virtue and civics, along with the defenses of inequality, are very ancient tropes of ruling. Note how former U.S. Secretary of Education William J. Bennett's *Book of Virtues* (1993) remains—after seventy-five weeks—in the top fifteen of the *New York Times* 's "Book Review" hard-back nonfiction list.

None of this denies a split or contradiction within ruling state groups between the proportional importance of the moralization project versus the occupational skilling project. Strung between an economism and a culturalism, strategies for schooling map the eventuation of politics which is a commonplace in O.E.C.D./G7 countries: parents (note, not students/pupils) are made over both as consumers of a production system and as unpaid adjunct teachers.

While I focus on the politics of schooling I hope to make visible some of the general features of the coherent attempt at fashioning moral regulation as a key aspect of the revolution in governance underway in England and Wales since the mid 1970s. It is a form of moral regulation that does not argue from principles but from appeals to a sort of "realism" and "necessity." A more detailed account would accentuate the phasing in of this revolution and demonstrate the connectivity of reforms within schooling to the wider moral revolution currently in progress. Throughout the major modality is that of accounting, entailing as the central state form fiscal policing. Evidence of this is that one of the major legislative "targets" has been the reform of local governance and a related shift in the modality and means of state relations.[3]

This point, in turn, needs connecting with the fact that governance here since the mid-1970s has been massively legislative. Besides the quantity of new statute law we must add two other forms of delegated legislation: that of U.K. law and that of European laws entering into U.K. law. Thus, ignoring the current education bill in process, there have been some 800 pages of new statute law regarding education since 1979, but at a conservative estimate perhaps ten times that in delegated legislation, all of which carries the full force of law. Adding to this the separate 144 acts regarding local government, you can begin to see the deluge through which teachers, among many others, have been living.

Still, nobody can say for certain exactly what state policy is concerning schooling, since shifts and variations are announced daily. As one teacher at a primary school phrased it, "I have noticed, over the past four years, that my primary colleagues are arriving earlier and earlier and leaving later and later. Why? Simple: The National Curriculum."[4]

In what follows I consider only the most explicitly evidential projects of moral regulation in and through schooling: religious instruction, sports, and sex education. My analysis centers on England and Wales, and my remarks, in the main, apply only to state schooling and not to the "public" (that is, private) schools, to which some 7–8 percent of the children of Britain go (but which "produce" about half the entrants to Oxford and Cambridge, for example).[5] I also want to say something about both teachers and parents and guardians, insofar as they have been interpellated in terms of an explicit morally regulatory project, and provide a brief sketch of how the moral means being argued as necessary within education relate to the wider projects of revolution in governance and cultural revolution.

Morality, in a General Sort of Way

In October 1993, a morality slogan arrived in the U.K. and other capitalist states: "Back to Basics," which had some of the qualities of the earlier "Victorian Values." In both cases only some of the "Values"/"Basics" were to be restored or encouraged: noticeably not those of public institutions and social assets. Alas, the slogan coincided with a phantasmagoria of "revealed" immoralities by significant Conservatives.[6] It was also inextricably intertwined with discussions of what constitutes "Britishness." As David Starkey commented, defining "Back to Basics" was a "campaign to 'remoralize' society. This morality, whatever its proponents may say, has almost nothing to do with religion and everything to do with social control."[7] There was a lot of noise and gossip, and then David Hargreaves, professor of education at University of Cambridge, wrote:

The problem of Britain as pluralistic society is how to find some social cement to ensure that people with different moral, religious and ethical

values, as well as social, cultural and linguistic traditions can live to-
gether; and to discover what part the education system should play in
generating social cohesion.[8]

Ignoring differences of embodied realities such as gender, sexual
orientation, race, ethnicity, and class, Hargreaves relied upon a very
ancient conception of morality as "agreed upon values," discussed
by Mary Warnock in a *Sunday Times* lecture called "The Rebirth of
Ethics":

Despite all we know about the different cultures within our society, there
exists far more unanimity about what social values must be upheld than
might first appear. Most people prefer the rule of law to its opposite,
prefer democratic processes, however tedious, to the usurpation of power.
It is important, indeed crucial, that this unanimity, a consensus moral-
ity based on shared sentiment, should be built up, and passed on to
children from the earliest age.[9]

Resisting the temptation to subject this quotation to the
deconstruction it deserves, let me simply note the contradictory
claims about *shared values* and how they must, in spite of unanimity
and consensus, be *taught.* Suddenly, as part and parcel of the fact
that radical conservative monetarist imperatives have begun to
affect the professional middle classes, various perspectives and terms
that were more or less erased in the 1980s have been argued back
onto the agenda. Centered here are terms like "civic," "civil," and
"community."

In early January 1994 the secretary of state for education issued
261 pages of detailed guidelines that were summarized in the *Sunday Times:*

Teachers will be expected to emphasize moral values by ensuring chil-
dren learn the difference between right and wrong—the so-called "five
Rs"—reading, writing, arithmetic, right, and wrong.[10]

The imperatives and values in these 261 pages are in marked contrast to other possible definitions of "citizenship" education (for example, "civics") not least because the general Citizen's Charter

initiative (of which the Parent's Charter forms a part) in a general strategic sense regrammatizes citizenship as a form of clientism/consumerism: being a citizen is coming closer and closer to being a customer. Here, however, the modalities of English rule were accentuated, disciplining the subordinates to know (and accept) our place in a hierarchy (and a range of choices) that we do not define.

Not content with this, the "independent" inspectorate took on new duties from February 1994, and as part of their statutory duty under the Education Act of 1992, the "ethos" of the school had become a legally relevant subject of inspection. This later eventuated in a questionnaire, sent to 25,000 schools, on spiritual, moral, social, and cultural development.[11] Cultural development concerned schools within local authorities that have been systematically starved of funds for books, or of the cost of transport for visits. Writing about the most popular tourist attraction in England, the Tower of London, and the likely ending of its free educational services, Diana Spencer pointed out, "It is short-sighted to charge for anything that inducts a child into British culture."[12] I think the Tower of London and all it stands for is rubbish, but I am pointing to massive contradictions in their terms of their own features and forms of moral regulation.

The problem with this vapid doctrinal morality is how it once again attempts to enforce a moral model. But this moral model is viciously harmful and cruel. It implies that a certain modality of social living is possible by efforts of will, independent of the massive material social relations and structures that are not universally available to support such lifestyle mores. During this period of massive moral regulation there was at exactly the same time actual and threatened social punishment for marginal and out-groups. I mean nothing more, but nothing less, than the persistence of enormous subordinations, exploitations, oppressions, and life-threatening, indeed, life-taking structures and relations, which are related to the dominant motor of this social formation: capitalism. Far from experiencing the beneficent "trickle down" effects of a "booming" economy, working classes and the nonworking poor have experienced a bloody deluge, a flood, a nightmare. And of course that, too, is part of the social curriculum that those subject to official schooling cannot fail to have learned.

If we sum up, the targeted groups who are wholly or partially "Enemies Within," blots on the "fact" of society, marginal and unwanted, we come close to some 30 percent of the population. Here is an economic, political, social, moral, spiritual, cultural set of messages that say to "these people" that *they are unwanted.* Worse, that they are a drain on society. What most angers me is the smugness in which old methods are reapplied as if morality were more than, stronger than, materiality; as if ideological sloganeering could in fact deny collective historical experience.[13]

Morality Specified: Christianity, Competition, and Controlled Copulation

One difficulty in any adequate discussion of "morality" and "moral regulation" is the absolutely pervasive way (itself a product of the middle phase of capitalism's cultural revolution) that acts, behaviors, styles, modalities of dress and address, familial forms, forms of living, communication, affection, and coupling—let me be very plain, "unacceptable" forms of loving and solidarity—are negatively moralized. Negative morality has a very thin literature, or seemingly so. In fact, without some sense (sensation) concerning it, all the known movements against the dominating norm would have been impossible.

Given that the majority of the population are so "well regulated" by the ferocity of violence of "business as normal," that is the labor market, why has the moral regulation machinery increasingly been turned into full revolution since the mid-1970s, during the most significant post-1974 crisis of capitalism? Within that blaring noise and searchlight attention, education has been centered in a way that is unlike any period other than that of the nineteenth century. It is as though—dare I risk this naiveté?—capitalism is being re-made comprehensively again.

This is to argue that the historical materialism of moral regulation has to be better spelled out. Those who are rich are structurally related to absolute majorities who barely survive. This has absolutely nothing to do with a "cake theory" of wealth and income (and demanding a larger slice) but with the materiality of how cakes (like bread) come to be "available" and for whom. Between the 1830s and 1870s, English state forms aided existing educational provision, through a variety of means, to organizations that were essentially religious. Initially organizations representing the Established Church of England and other Non-Conformist Protestant Christians were the dominant groups. Later other Non-Conformists, Roman Catholics, and Jews were added to those organizing schooling who could receive grants-in-aid from the state. With state schooling proper (after 1871) it was the form of a generalized but definite *Christianity* that was made central. This was reemphasized in the 1944 Education Act, which was essentially a compromise between Conservative and Labour passed during the period of the "National Government," often called "the Butler Act."[14] That centrality of Christianity within state school curricula has not been shifted by the Education Act of 1988 or any subsequent legislation. It is moreover of the greatest importance that the one group who have been refused legitimacy/ state grants-in-aid (as semi-state schools, "voluntarily aided" as they are called) have been Muslims.[15]

Issues about this feature of moral regulation through schooling connect to other, wider discussions, including the royal family,[16] and arguments about and within the Established Church of England.[17] That is to say, as is entirely expected, this state politics has been caught up within "wider fields of force" concerning what is to constitute "Englishness" (I must again accentuate how there are significant variations regarding Wales, Scotland, and, rather expectedly, Northern Ireland). This has an inward (other religions in England) and outward effect (there remains a major image, quite empirically false, of a socially Catholic Europe, focused and figured into visibility by Jacques Delors, the Catholic/socialist president of the European Commission from 1984 until 1994). Other religions index the religions of "the Other."

The struggles here, within schools, within educational authorities, within curriculum design and assessment, within state inspection, are all very indicative of the general shifting frontiers and borderlines within a religiously focused form of "moral regulation." As the *Times Educational Supplement* editorialized:

Christianity has become a key element in that shapeless longing for the past now traveling as a Back to Basics policy. It has not gone unnoticed that the simpler, safer past full of Christian folk is probably also white.[18]

This editorial goes on to remark how this governmental "regime . . . has suppressed five inconvenient HM Inspectorate reports on religion in the last eight years." This is a general pattern, which should not go unremarked in relation to various chartering initiatives encouraging the new citizen-consumer to complain. In a continuing contrast to the *TES* (both being part of the Rupert Murdoch empire of News International), the *Times*, arguing that the "new Teacher Training Agency," passed by Parliament, "should ensure that a reasonable number of teachers are able to" conduct a simple act of collective worship, editorialized,

In seeking to strengthen the role of religion in school . . . Mr. Patten has chosen a tough battle-ground. But he deserves credit for having made an early contribution to the merging debate on citizenship and morality.[19]

This, along with the unmentioned and yet statutorily required emphasis on Christianity, was answered in advance, as it were, by the *TES* editorial: "RE [religious education] is only one of the subjects that can contribute to such [personal] development. English, science, history, and geography must also confront questions of morality, certainty, belief, tolerance and responsibility."[20]

Before moving to the theme of competitive sports and sex education, both of which link to "muscular Christianity," class, and gender, it is crucial to recall the general context of these initiatives, centrally those of a statutorily enforced national curriculum and tests. Since the latter were almost uniformly rejected and boycotted by the teacher unions and the National Association of Head Teachers in 1992–93, a special commissioner, Sir Ron Dearing, was appointed to review both the national curriculum and the tests, as chairman-designate of the new School Curriculum and Assessment Authority (SCAA). The Dearing Review "slimmed" the national curriculum (proportions of teaching time) and "simplified" modes of assessment to be marked by external assessors and examiners.[21] Thus, "religious education" was allocated a proportion of time, and subject committees then provide and revise the content, for final approval by the SCAA and the secretary of state.

Despite the Dearing Review changes, the National Union of Teachers (unlike the National Union of Schoolmasters and Women

Teachers or the Association of Teachers and Lecturers) voted to continue its boycott of tests in April 1994.[22] This vote produced some of the most "violent" editorials since the 1980s miners' strike.[23]

Play Up and Play the Game: The Right Kind of Basic

It is in the context of the "permanent reform mania" that the *TES* editorialized regarding some leaked proposals of Ian Sproat, the minister for sports, under the title, "The Wilder Shores of Sproat!"[24]

From the point of view of schools and young people, Mr. Sproat's ideas might be thought ill-judged, inappropriate and out-dated at the best of times; coming, as they do, at the most delicate stage of the biggest curriculum battle of all time they are a piece of ill-timed lunacy that might be dangerous if they were not so farcical.[25]

The leaked Sproat proposals came a month after an earlier statement from John Patten to encourage schools to specialize, for example, in sport (or art and music; or business and languages).[26]

Competitive sports were already compulsory to the age of fourteen and physical education continues through the ages fourteen to sixteen. What is crucial here is the way discussion of competitive sports, health and efficiency, fitness and physical education take on a strongly, albeit metaphorical, moral element. But involved here is also a very material element, concerning profitable property, no less. The *Times* editorialized,

The sporting tradition in the nation's schools has been undermined in two quite separate ways. First hundreds of schools have sold off their playing fields in order to raise cash quickly. About 5,000 playing fields are estimated to have been bought from schools in the last 12 years, often for rapid redevelopment. Pupils' access to basic sporting facilities has been severely curtailed. Mr. Sproat's proposal to employ some of the proceeds of the national lottery to help buy them back is admirable.[27]

Meanwhile, since many schools have problems supplying both safe and weatherproof buildings, pencils, paper, and—above all—both textbooks and an adequate library; since the curriculum has so fully packed the teaching week; and since not only are students terrorized into test and examination success, but schools are placed in "League Tables" in terms of "their" exam "successes," the language of the *TES* editorial, "The Wilder Shores of Sproat!", is perhaps too mild.

Let's Talk about Sex

Of all the subjects thus far discussed, sex education perhaps most obviously (if often in very contradictory ways) is linked to the wider projects, modes of imagery of state in/formed moral and legal regulation.[28] But here there is a quite material, corporeal issue of "the facts"—for example, those needed to avoid "unwanted pregnancies," say—versus not encouraging sexual activity. Views and moralities differ about sex outside of the "holy state of marriage"; before the statutorily defined ages of sixteen (for heterosexuality), and eighteen (recently reduced from twenty-one) for male homosexuality (there being no law regarding lesbians); about female homosexuality; about sex only for procreation and not for pleasure.

We now need to spice up this whirling supernova of moral confusions and prejudices by adding both issues around contraceptives and AIDS. At the moment, for example, there is a comprehensive doubtfulness about various laws regarding teachers and the provision of sexual information and advice to children below the age of sixteen (and presumably below the age of eighteen in relation to male homosexuality) without parental permission, whereas nurses and doctors are seemingly protected through a significantly different definition of "professionalism" from legal action in this area. Whirling in and through all this is the 1989 Children Act, which "came into force" in 1992. The *TES* editorialized under the title of "Statutory Values":

From next September [i.e., 1994] sex joins religion as the only subjects on the curriculum over which parents have a veto [that is, they can require that their children are not taught it/do not attend the act of collective worship]. If parental responsibility means anything, it is probably right that, in the absence of complete freedom to choose schools, they should be allowed to withdraw their children from lessons promulgating values they abhor.[29]

They go on to allude to a number of recent incidents and statements, first, John Patten's argument that sex education had to be defined within a "family values" morality.[30] Here Patten draws from a clause in the Education Act of 1986 inserted following a revelation that an inner London teachers' library contained a book called *Jenny Lives with Eric and Martin.*[31] Second, "sex education" most comprehensively triangulates the necessity for allowing "ideological struggle" to enter in, with the student carrying the consequences.

It is clearly intended that the teacher as superior "moral agent" will "correct" the "bad" lessons to be learned from "bad" parents. This is called breaking the vicious circle of deprivation, degeneracy, and dependency. Yet other parents who know their schools must have the right to exempt their children from teachers who are themselves deemed immoral.

Then, as indicated earlier, this matter of sex education in schooling is not to be separated from the wider health initiatives regarding the centrality of knowledge, advice, help, treatment, and support for anyone in need. Alas, John Patten's draft circular on sex education curriculum and pedagogy appeared in the midst of a series of "sex scandals" involving members of the Conservative Party, and some of the highest in the land. Then, in the following months there were a series of other shock and horror stories, like the discovery that a nurse discussed oral sex—a discussion initiated by the pupils—with a class of ten ten- to eleven-year-olds, the growing specter of children's watching television and "having access" to pornographic videos, and the booklet *Your Pocket Guide to Sex,* published by the Health Education Council.[32] Meanwhile, an Exeter University study of twenty thousand pupils, aged eleven to sixteen, found they relied on friends, television, and film for their sex education but that they wanted parents and teachers to provide more information.[33]

The intra-state clashes can be summed up in terms of morals in their narrow sense and thereby fall within that crucial contrast between rights and values-and-duties-and-obedience, which historically are such solid modalities of social normality and ruling in England. In no other country is there such a smothering, a sort of moral fog, of any direct statements concerning the massive forms of difference and inequality.

Do Your Duty, Police Your Children! Parents as Teachers

Here I will address the ways in which parents and teachers have been increasingly rendered as "moral agents" within the new modalities of this revolution in governance. Again, these tropes are not new but their interweaving with other focuses and forms I have mentioned is important. Some slippage has occurred around the ancient mode of *in loco parentis* insofar as parents are now argued to be doubly responsible, in the home and for the school. The balance has swung, complicatedly, in two directions at once. Parents now have an increased range of responsibility to the school, first, in delivering the "educable" children to the school; second, in monitoring the children when doing school work at home; and third, in policing and monitoring the school's performance and value. But teachers also, as I have noted above, have responsibilities that are closer and closer to those of the "parental," and tests, as we shall see, are really a way of policing teachers, along with the more frequent inspections, along with local management of schools. And, finally, there has been an unprecedented de-democratization of schooling through a massification of the central state power and control, which is part and parcel of a general de-democratization and engrossing that dates from the mid-1970s.

The maelstrom through which teachers, along with all public service employees, have lived in England and Wales, has been both excessively documentary and extensively legislative. In two important senses, the reach of moral regulation has been extended and intensified. What has happened here, and very rapidly, has been the ability, or at least the attempt, of the central state to shift blame and change the "common sense" of the questions that should be asked. I do not mean the working classes have been successfully subordinated in a new "social cement" of hegemony. There is now more class hatred, and a degree of class violence, than there was in the 1960s: I do not recall, then, the stealing of trucks, bottles, gasoline, and the Molotov cocktail–firing of five schools in one night, for example. I mean the mores and means of both the intensification of what I want to call the labor of being held responsible of parents and teachers and the extensification of the fact that Schools are the Solution/Schools are to Blame double bind.

Sir Christopher Ball argues the need for a "triangle of care":

parents, professionals, and the community, working together. But "parents must be the apex of the triangle." It is hardly news to remark how parenting-in-general has an extensive set of politics, hence debates, organized around it: "the family" has broken down, broken up, decayed, withered, is under threat, and so on. In a House of Lords debate in December 1993, Baroness Young spoke of "a kind of breakdown in the fabric of society," arguing that now a first generation of schoolchildren were growing up "without a moral framework"; the Bishop of Ripon, quoting the Archbishop of York, spoke of a "progressive breakdown in the structure of moral relationships"; and Lord Jakobovits (a former chief rabbi) spoke of how marriage had become a "disaster area."[34] As the *Sunday Times* editorialized, "Society needs both a revaluation and remoralization of marriage."[35]

A month later, Roy Chapman, chairman of the Headmasters' Conference (the major association of private schools), argued that "pupils are crying out for guidelines. Whatever they may say, pupils want to know where the lines of behavior should be drawn."[36] But it is his remarks on parents I wish to quote:

And what about the role of parents in education? That contribution cannot be overestimated, not only in supporting what is offered in schools, but also in their personal example in the standard that they set and the attitudes that they adopt. In recent years, there has been a tendency for some parents to opt out and leave everything to do with education to schools and teachers. Unfortunately, at the same time, teachers have sometimes opted out, bewailing the lowering of standards of behavior and blaming the parents, government and social conditions. But there can be no return to basics unless parents can be won over to play their own part with conviction, again by actions and example rather than by their words.[37]

The logic of this is to be found not only in the Parent's Charter but in a new clause added by the home secretary to the Criminal Justice Bill, which would compel parents to pay fines "for the misdeeds of their children," as the *Times* editorialized under the heading of "Parental Duty." It went on:

But, in the current atmosphere of moral inquiry, Mr Howard's plan is particularly significant. It hints at a political discourse in which civic responsibility will be as important as civic rights. The example of parents' control over their children's education has increased enormously. They have gained new rights of appeal against admissions decisions taken by schools and access to an unprecedented supply of information about their relative performance. But it is right that this welcome process of empowerment should be matched by legislation obliging parents to fulfill their responsibilities.[38]

One month later, the *Times* editorialized about how delinquent street culture perverts the meaning of the word *respect* with regard to the kicking to death of Les Reed by four youths.

Mr Reed's tragedy was that he tried to reason with people in what he thought was the common language of social values. Showing respect for your neighbours meant, for him, accepting their legitimate desire to live in peace, free from the threat of anti-social behavior and pointless destruction. But his assailants' code of conduct had a lexicon of its own in which the word "respect" had a perverse, inverted meaning.[39]

Soon after, while addressing the Institute of Directors, the home secretary denied any causal connection between rising unemployment and crime. Instead, he spoke of "the failure of some parents to give children proper values and the ability to discern right from wrong; the failure of some schools to instill discipline and respect." The princess-royal, on the same day, discussed "anti-social behavior" in similar terms.[40] In a very extensive column, on the same day, Janet Daley spoke of a time before the 1960s when there was a "comfortable relationship between police, parents, teachers and courts" that "was a function of the general agreement about what it was to be righteous."[41] And so it goes, going on.

At the 1993 Conference of the Professional Association of Teachers (PAT), teachers argued that the Children Act of 1989 was being exploited by pupils to make false allegations against teachers. Eric Forth, minister for schools, in supporting their concerns, told the conference, "I think the attitude of a lot of parents is becoming a problem." An official of PAT went further, arguing that parents must

be "legally required to take greater responsibility for children's behavior by enforcing curfews and paying fines imposed by the court."[42]

Some of the proposals of Sir Christopher Ball's "Start Right:
The Importance of Early Learning" report were headlined as "Bid to
Yoke Benefit to Good Parenting," where parents could lose Child
Benefit if they failed to attend parenting classes.[43] Prime Minister
John Major said, "As and when resources are available we shall
move towards further nursery education, towards universal nursery
education."[44]

It is in the context of all of this that we should locate the second
edition of the Parent's Charter, delivered to some twenty million
households in June 1994. One news summary said that parents
should ensure that pupils arrived at school, properly dressed, on time,
and after a good breakfast. On television, radio, and news bulletins,
the various criticisms of this "glossy pamphlet" were both accurate
and well made, as they were in the general press coverage.[45]

Surveillance in the Streets

Columnist Barbara Amiel sees the February 1994 measures on truancy from the Department for Education as likely to "weaken the
family." She then proceeds:

*Logically, we could separate parents into groups; first, competent normal
parents who can look after their own affairs. They would decide on the
degree of "truancy" permitted and bring up their families within their
autonomy reinforced by the state. The second group would be declared
incompetent and the state take over the care of their children. The third
group might be those competent parents with dysfunctional children;
there is no question of the parents' competence, but the children require
psychiatric, or psychological care. There might be a fourth group for
super-competent parents in which the parents' achievements clearly indicate that they ought to be allowed to devise any system of upbringing
they wish, and the onus of challenging their authority on the courts.*[46]

From February 2, 1994, onwards, another set of draft guidelines emerged that in two quite distinctive ways reduced parents and
guardians' powers and authority. Parents' letters of explanation for
pupil absences were no longer prima facie justifications for such

absences: only the school can approve absences, not parents. Secondly, a long-standing right for parents and guardians to remove children in term time for up to twenty-one days in any one year was abolished, including that of parents and guardians to take familial holidays in term time.[47] This is crucially important for those on lower income, given the higher cost of vacations in school holidays.

Under the misleading headline "Patten Launches £14M Crackdown on School Truants," John Patten announced how some £500,000 (of this £14 million) would be spent on "truancy watch" schemes. While acknowledging that "we certainly don't want a prying and spying society, but I do think we want a society that actually cares," John Patten urged members of the public to cooperate with police and schools by questioning any seemingly school-age human being found on the streets outside of the normal school holidays.[48]

On February 8, 1994, John Patten had said "I am concerned about the link between truancy, poor academic performance and crime." On March 1, 1994, two charities for children published "School's Out," which detailed how schools were "excluding"— meaning expelling— pupils at a faster rate. Between 1991 and 1992 exclusions rose by almost a third, to reach four thousand. They linked such exclusions to a rise in juvenile crime. From September 1994, the state will fine every state school that excludes a pupil.[49] In February 1994, John Patten announced that further information would be included in the 1994 tables, covering both "authorized" and "unauthorized" absences by pupils.[50] If a school is to be judged on its examination success and its lack of truants, it makes sense to exclude those who are both unlikely to pass examinations and who by their presence disrupt the lessons for all the others. Little of this is new as a "moral panic," but what is new are the modalities of surveillance, visibility, and parent/teacher blaming.[51]

Teachers Being Tested to the Limit

Among targeted negative groups, teachers have been searchlit for much of the last twenty years, caught within that double bind of School as Cause/School as Solution. Aside from the whirling maelstrom of specified schooling reforms, it is teachers and their training that are being tested. As Peter Millar observed of all the new national tests, the "real purpose is to test the teachers, whom we suspect are not doing their job properly."[52] John Patten himself, in a chronology of what the Education Acts have meant, argued similarly: "Now the 1994 bill will reform teacher training which, with 20–20 hindsight, is exactly where we should have started 15 years ago. We aim to give more say to schools, weed out the unnecessary and dated ideology in too many training courses and lay emphasis on subject knowledge and practical classroom skills."[53]

That bill establishes the Teacher Training Agency, and removes teacher training from any necessary contact with any higher educational institution.[54] Teachers will be radically deprofessionalized and placed in training situations within schools through mentoring and apprenticeship relations.

But teachers have other concerns. First, one prediction suggests a shortfall of 20,000 teachers by the year 2000, which should not be disconnected from the Catch-22 established by the governments granting a 2.9 percent salary increase to teachers without any extra funding, the new money to be found from what is so pervasively now called "efficiency savings"—that is, the sacking and retiring of teachers.[55] Moreover, many teachers are now leaving anyway because of "health reasons." In 1983–84, 2,449 teachers left for health reasons; in 1993–94 the figure was 5,535. Much of this is because, to use a headline, "Curriculum Chaos Damaged Morale."[56]

Here one particular incident is entirely to the point, not least because it shows not only, to paraphrase Raymond Williams, "society is always already inside schooling," but also the glaring mediamania spotlighting particular individuals. In late 1993, the press began to report on one Jane Brown, head teacher of Kingsmead School in Hackney, London, England, who had, so the story ran, refused to take up what was reported as a "free" offer for some of her pupils to attend a performance of *Romeo and Juliet* on the grounds of this play's heterosexist bias. It was quickly, and in a very ugly way, established that Jane Brown was a lesbian. But Jane Brown received an overwhelming vote at a parents' meeting for her to stay in her post, and under the new government's local management of schools policies the governors voted five to one against a recommendation from the education officer of the London Borough of Hackney that Jane Brown be suspended. Gradually, the various reasons Jane

Brown had opposed the trip to *Romeo and Juliet* became apparent, including transportation and staffing costs, and the way the play was structured around "gang warfare."[57]

Such events send out very powerful messages to all teachers that add to their labor-process-related insecurities. This also relates to guidelines issued by various trade unions to teachers concerning likely actions under the Children Act of 1989, including reports on the sustained violence against teachers now being experienced in schools.[58] In another vector, the pressure on teachers to give sufficient or extra help and time to their "gifted pupils" adds another strain in terms of classroom management.[59] This has led to, thus far, inconclusive discussions about changing teachers' contracts with regard to both the length of the teaching week and of the school year.[60]

The delegitimation of teachers has been one of the more negative outcomes of the last twenty years' "revolution in governance" and reminds us of the linkage between the words *moral* and *morale*. In the managerial and military metaphors so beloved by the English male elite, it is significant that almost no attempt has been made to cooperate, consult, or collaborate with teachers or to ensure that proposals have some realistic consultation period. No, the normal model has been a bloody deluge, from above, of guideline after guideline, curriculum change after curriculum change, testing methodology after testing methodology. In this, if more violated, teachers have not, of course, been alone: the bloody deluge has fallen upon all groups of workers within social institutions, in the public service, and it should never be forgotten, upon those employed within private capitalist enterprises, not least those in privatized institutions formerly part of the public realm. That the majority of teachers are women seems as relevant a point as that the majority of the Conservative government (the cabinet and the surrounding noncabinet ministers, for example) send their children to private schools. As teachers, nurses, social workers, librarians, and secretaries everywhere—as with civil servants, retail trade workers, homeworkers, and so many others—hugely disproportionate numbers of women workers have had their lives doubly (at least) disrupted by the fierce impositions of this current form of moral regulation, since so many of them work that double-shift typical of their gender.

Conclusion

Editorializing about the National Union of Teachers conference in 1994, under the heading "Barbarians by the Blackboard," the *Sunday Times* mentioned the "proletarianization of the [teaching] profession" as being far advanced, and added:

The barbarians are no longer at the gate; they are inside our classrooms. The fact that these people have responsibility for our children's education must be deeply worrying to parents up and down the land.[61]

In addition to the negative description of teachers, the editorial then involves a different moral lexicon of competition. Clearly, competition exists in many schooling practices. Teaching to the test, with a relatively stable "normal" distribution, has been practiced for long periods of time. But the other senses of competition are equally important: competitiveness within workplaces, between enterprises, and, of course, between countries. The latter entails what seems to be a discussion about how we need a highly skilled labor force of brain workers, if we are to survive in the modern information age.

Within these moral rhetorics, regarding what now seems to be called "labor force participation," are other features of a moral rhetoric of order. A collaborative, not confrontational, disciplined workforce is also required: one that is not troubled by trade unions, strikes, and other "industrial actions." That there needs to be yet more of this discipline has recently been argued by the head of policy at the Institute of Directors, Ann Robinson:

The distinction between capital and labor has become blurred in modern capitalist economies. . . . There is no longer the sharp distinction between capital and labor which lies at the heart of the "them and us" school of labor relations. We are all "us" today.[62]

There is nothing new about directors opposing strikes. What is new is that capitalism's promises are now being severely qualified by those in governance. What is now commonplace are recognitions that "the best social system ever devised"—resting uneasily on "the" market, democracy, and "the" rule of law—is in fact one of violent oscillations out of control. Capitalism, as they now argue, can "no longer" provide either "the goods" or "the good life." It can no longer, quite centrally, provide lifelong employment.[63] "Flexibility" and being "lean and mean" are now to be *social* characteristics, features of *social* living, not (as formerly) restricted to an imagery of production modes and labor regimes. The earlier massive reduction in industrial and manufacturing employment is now being followed by equally large proportional reduction of employment in the service institutions, whether residually still "public" or fully privatized. These are already involving professionals and middle, and even upper, managerial posts. Finally, what work there is partakes of short-term/part-time or otherwise insecure, and above all else, low-paid work.[64]

So the rhetoric that blames teachers and parents about "us" needing high-skill people does not relate, except at the top end of the labor market and especially among accountants and management consultants, to a high-wage economy. Many of the new jobs are being filled by women or migrant labor; the jobs which are disappearing are white male, working-class, both skilled and semi-skilled. Even many university students now leave the university with significant debts, and something like 12 percent of students remain unemployed in the December following their July graduation.[65]

All of this is conducted in a specific language code (discursive regime and image repertoire) that centers on the word *realism*.[66] A necessitarian logic (the language of necessity) names what is "reality" and hence what is "realistic." Hence my subtitle about moral regulation "getting real." This connects to notions of globalized production and the "real world order" (with Realpolitik logics thereby involved), and it entails a meta-moral regulation, one that rules out in advance any forms of critique energized by a morality that is not isomorphic with the system named as "real," "realistic," and so on. Hence critiques can be denied by two connected rebuttals: the deflation of the critique for its being "old-fashioned," out of date, silly, hysterical, passionate, and all of that; or being utopian, unrealistic, not "living in the real world." There is almost no space to indicate how Their Order has disordered us.

I have been resolutely descriptive, staying very close to the social texture of the shifts and reforms as they happened. I have cited very little literature critical of this or that reform (including important texts on the 1988 Education Act or the working of the National

Curriculum Council, to take but two examples). In part I wanted to give some sense of what "it" feels/felt like. It is the heat and hurt of almost daily documentation falling onto the heads of teachers and thereby, more than like uncelebratory confetti, on the children and youth they teach, that I wanted to indicate, if only for the very limited period of November 1993 through June 1994. And now to remind you that this deluge started in the mid-1970s, we are talking about twenty years of undeclared war, one of many within different capitalist formations. I wished to indicate the rather evidential way in which They had not "Got It Right!," that "Getting It Right" turns out to be a rather complex phenomenon, and hence the belated rediscovery from the Right, that "civic," "civil," and "community" are necessary terms in any social grammar, not least that which wishes to understand "the Market."

Under the contrasting banners about various and often very contradictory moral revolutions (remoralizations, rebourgeoisifica-tions, and so on), what is going on is brutally simple: *they* are trying to make *us* afraid. Ignore talk of skills, attend more to the multiply-ing media of *blaming*, thus involving of course, *naming*. *Blame-names* unspeak human beings from the fully and properly social. We become semi-unpersons, half-here and half-not: Enemies (or terri-fyingly for Them, Others) within. To live in a society of the ex-cluded who, it is increasingly implied, do not belong, is a form of social schooling, in which to learn (and be tested time and time again) a social curriculum that teaches Us that the real "barbarians" in the classroom are Them. This is England in the 1990s.

Endnotes

1.   June Jordan, "Selected Political Essays: Waking Up in the Middle of Some American Dreams," in June Jordan, *Technical Difficulties* (New York: Pantheon, 1992), p. 19.

2.   Philip Corrigan and Derek Sayer, *The Great Arch: English State Formation as Cultural Revolution* (Oxford: Blackwell, 1985); and Philip Corrigan, "On Moral Regulation," *Sociological Review*, Vol. 29, 1981, pp. 313–337; and Philip Corrigan, "In\Forming Schooling" in David Livingstone, ed., *Critical Pedagogy and Cultural Power* (South Hadley, Mass.: Bergin and Garvey, 1989).

3.   These complex relations are crucial to any understanding of state formation and thus the regulatory ethos of the educational state. Apart from Corrigan and Sayer, *The Great Arch*, chap. 6, see Kari Dehli, "Creating a Dense and Intelligent Community: Local State Formation in Early 19th Century Upper Canada," *Journal of Historical Sociology*, Vol. 3, 1990, pp. 109–132; and Bruce Curtis, "The Canada 'Blue Books,'" *Canadian Historical Review*, Vol. 74, 1993, pp. 535–565.

4.   C. Byrne, "Let's Have No Truck with the Reforms," *Times Educational Supple-ment* (hereafter *TES*), June 10, 1994, p. 47, col. 1.

5. Stephen Yeo, *Access* (Leeds: University Press, 1993), pp. 11–12.

6. See "Basics? What Basics," *Economist* (henceforth *Econ*), November 13, 1993,
    p. 43; "Major Turns Spotlight," *Times* (henceforth *T*), November 15, 1993, p. 1;
    "The Basic Issue," and "Er, Basically, Your Majesty," *Econ,* November 20, 1993,
    pp. 13, 24; "Back to Basics" *T* (editorial), January 7, 1994 (and editorials, January
    8, 10, 11, 17 and 18, 1994); "Basic Instinct," *Sunday Times* (henceforth *ST*)
    January 9, 1994, pp. 1.10–1.13; "Major Defies . . ." *T,* February 14, 1994, p. 1;
    "Alliterative Abuse," *Econ,* January 15, 1994, p. 22.

7. David Starkey, "A State without a Church," *T,* December 10, 1993, p. 16; and
    "Back to Basics—and Forwards," *Independent,* December 4, 1993, p. 17.

8. David Hargreaves, *The Mosaic of Learning: Schools and Teaching for the Next
    Century* (London: Demos, 1994). Extracts were published in *TES,* June 24,
    1994, pp. 4–5.

9. Mary Warnock, "Facing up to Morality," *ST,* "The Culture," April 10, 1994, pp.
    10.4–10.5 (the quotation is p. 10.5, cols. 4–5).

10. "Teachers Told to Crack Down on Unruly Children," *ST,* February 2, 1994, p. 1.

11. School Inspectors . . . ," *T,* February 26, 1994, p. 9; "Inspectors . . . ," *TES,* March
    4, 1994, p. 5; J. Adley, "Education without Morals . . . ," *T,* March 10, 1994, p. 16;
    P. Cordingley, "Framework for Moral Message," p. 18 and T. Wragg, "Get Out the
    Shredder . . . ," p. 88, both in *TES,* March 25, 1994.

12. *TES,* August 13, 1993, p. 8, col. 4.

13. "Blair to Keep Tory Education Reforms," *T,* June 27, 1994, p. 2; "Blair . . . ," *TES,*
    July 1, 1994, p. 7. On the overall moral/meaning of the project since 1979, see J.
    Patten (Secretary of State for Education), "Class Room Reform Is Vital for Brit-
    ain," *ST,* June 12, 1994, p. 6.14, a crucial strategic text.

14. Cf. P. H. J. Gosden, *Education in the Second World War* (London: Methuen, 1976);
    "The 1944 Act: 50th Anniversary," Special Supplement, *TES,* May 6, 1994.

15. But see K. Wilson, "Moral and Spiritual Values," NCE Briefing, September 19, 1993;
    TES, Extra(s) "Religious Education," December 10, 1993, and February 25, 1994.

16. Cf. for example, E. Norman, *T,* January 26, 1994. p. 16; June 28, 1994, p. 20; B.
    Amiel, *ST,* January 30, 1994, p. 4.5.

17. "Carey Attacks the Shameful Gap," *T,* April 4, 1994, p. 2; "Why Dr. Carey Is
    Wrong," *T,* April 7, 1994, p. 18.

18. *TES,* January 21, 1994, p. 16, col. 1.

19. *T,* June 1, 1994, p. 17, col. 2.

20. *TES,* August 13, 1993, p. 11, col. 2.

21. *T,* January 6, 1994, p. 5; *TES,* January 7, 1994, pp. 8–11 and editorial, p. 18;
    TES, March 18, 1994, pp. 8ff. See also *The Dearing Report—How Will It Affect
    Teachers?* (DFE, 1994); *1994 Assessment Arrangements* (SEAC, 1993); *Na-
    tional School Tests in 1994* (DFE, 1994).

22. "NUT Votes. . . ," *T,* April 4, 1994, p. 1; for the NUSM/WT, ATL decisions to cease
    their boycotts, see TES, April 8, 1994, p. 14.

23. "Teach Them a Lesson: The Nation's Schools Should Not Be Run by the Unions,"
    T (editorial), April 5, 1994, p. 17; "Barbarians by the Blackboard," *ST,* April 10,
    1994, p. 18; J. Daley, "Teaching Has Become the Last Bastion of Militant Left-
    wing Entryism," *T,* April 7, 1994, p. 18.

24. *T* (editorial), April 8, 1994, p. 17. On Major as "umpire" or "referee" between
    Sproat and Patten, see *T,* April 9, 1994, p. 7; *TES,* April 15, 1994, p. 8.

25. *TES,* April 15, 1994, p. 20, col. 2.

26. *T,* March 23, 1994, pp. 11, 18.

27. *T,* April 8, 1994, p. 17, col. 1.

28. For one example, "The Essence of Sexual Attraction," *T,* September 11, 1993,
    p. 3.1.

29. *TES,* December 10, 1993, p. 14, col. 1.

30. "Patten Puts Morality at the Heart of Sex Education," *T,* December 7, 1993, p. 2.

31. *TES* (editorial), December 10, 1993, p. 14, col. 2.

32. "When Trouble Starts Young," series in *New York Times* (henceforth *NYT*), May 15, 1994, and onwards. See especially, "2 Boys, a Debt, a Gun, a Victim," *NYT*, May 16, 1994, pp. A1, C10–11; "Author Defends," *T*, March 25, 1994, p. 6; "Work on Sex Education Suspended," *T*, April 18 1994, p. 2; "What Did You Learn at School Today . . .? A Lot of Very Confusing Things about Sex," *ST*, March 27, 1994, p. 1.12 (and "The Age of Innocence," editorial, p. 4.5), but see also R. Koenig, "Teach the Whole Child," *ST*, March 27, 1994, p. 1.11.

33. "Teenagers," *T*, March 28, 1994, p. 5, summarizing the report "Young People in 1993" (Exeter, England: Exeter University, 1994).

34. "Cradle of Civilisation," *ST*, December 12, 1993, p. 4.3.

35. "Diminishing Divorce," *ST* (editorial), December 12, 1993, p. 4.5.

36. Roy Chapman, "When Actions Speak Louder than Words," *T*, January 31, 1994, p. 27, col. 3; see also the Secretary of the Headmasters' Conference, Vivian Armstrong, "Discipline the Parents First," *T*, February 14, 1994, p. 35.

37. *T*, January 31, 1994.

38. "Parental Duty," *T* (editorial), February 4, 1994, p. 17. See also p. 1 of the same issue.

39. "Showing 'Respect,'" *T* (editorial), March 23, 1994, p. 19, col. 2.

40. "Howard Lays Blame for Crime at Parents' Door," *T*, April 27, 1994, p. 2.

41. Janet Daley, "Why Can't You Behave?", *T*, April 27, 1994, p. 14 (illustrated with "the perfect family back in the 1950s"). See also T. Wright, "Trampling on a Moral Freedom," *T*, July 17, 1993, p. 8, who discusses how "the generation of the 1960s and 1970s" became the "tramps and the tourists of the moral sphere."

42. "Parents Break Teachers' Grip on Discipline," *T*, July 29, 1993, p. 7.

43. *TES*, March 4, 1994, p. 1. The report is summarized fully in *TES*, March 18, 1994, pp. 4–5; and p. 18 (editorial); *T*, March 18, 1994, pp. 2, 19; "Some Parents Never Learn," *ST*, March 20, 1994, p. 1.13. One member of the advisory group for Ball's report, Gillian Pugh, disagreed in an article called "Training Parents or Social Control?", *TES*, March 18, 1994, p. 18; see also *TES*, same date, sect. 2, p. 11.

44. *T*, March 18, 1994, p. 2, cols. 3–4.

45. *T*, June 14, 1994, p. 8; *T*, June 15, 1994, p. 7; "Chart a bold course," *T* (editorial), June 17, 1994, p. 21; *TES*, June 17, 1994, p. 14, and "Chartered Accountability" (editorial), p. 20.

46. Barbara Amiel, "Welcome, Children, to the Ant Heap," *ST*, February 13, 1994, p. 4.4.

47. Parents . . . ," *T*, February 2, 1994, p. 2; "Unions Reject . . . ," *TES*, February 4, 1994, p. 16; "Nothing New," *TES*, February 18, 1994, p. 21 (a letter from the Association of Chief Educational Social Workers, once known as "School Board Men" or "Truancy Officers").

48. *T*, February 9, 1994, p. 6. Nine days later the same John Patten refused to renew a grant to a Manchester scheme, involving police, youth-workers, teachers, and education welfare officers, exactly organized to combat truancy. *TES*, February 18, 1994, p. 1.

49. "School Expulsions Feed Crime," *T*, March 2, 1994, p. 2.

50. *TES*, "In Brief," February 25, 1994, p. 2; John Patten, *T*, February 25, 1994, p. 27; "Time to Slow the Tables," *TES* (editorial), February 25, 1994, p. 20.

51. For one historical sociological rooting/routing I commend the work of Fiona Paterson. See her *Out of Place* (London: Falmer 1989); "Schooling the Family," *Sociology*, Vol. 22, 1988, pp. 331–350; "Measures of Schooling," *Journal of Historical Sociology*, Vol. 1, No. 3, 1988, pp. 278–300.

52. Peter Millar, "Putting Class Back into the Classroom," *T*, April 6, 1994, p. 14, col. 2. Cf. letter, *T*, April 15, 1994, p. 17; and F. Abrams, "Teachers," *T*, February 17, 1994, p. 31.

53. Patten, "Class Room Reform . . . ," *ST*, June 12, 1994, p. 6.14, cols. 3–4.

54. "Delayed Bill . . . ," *TES*, July 1, 1994, p. 7. Cf. "Learn by Example," *T* (editorial), May 3, 1994, p. 17; "Patten vows. . . ," T, May 4, 1994, p. 4.

55. Shortfall of 20,000 Staff Looms," *TES*, June 18, 1994, p. 4.; "Teachers' Pay

Rise . . . ," *T,* February 15, 1994, p. 5; "Schools Caught . . . ," *TES,* February 25, 1994, pp. 1, 5; *T,* March 7, 1994, p. 31; "Sackings . . . ," *TES,* April 8, 1994, p. 11; "5000 Teachers . . . ," *T,* May 30, 1994, p. 1.

56. "More Teachers Quitting," *T,* June 27, 1994, p. 8; "Curriculum Chaos Damaged Morale," *TES,* June 24, 1994, p. 8. Cf. M. Hewitt, "Back and Forth with the Basics," *TES,* April 1, 1994, p. 13; and M. Harrison, "Time to Debunk the Glorious Past," *TES,* June 24, 1994, p. 5.

57. This is best approached by the superlative account of R. Picardie, "Two Women of Hackney," *Independent,* Vol. 3, February 3, 1994, p. 23. But see "Media Watch," *TES,* January 4, 1994, p. 5; "After Romeo," *T* (editorial), February 28, 1994, p. 15; "Who Is Really in Charge?" *T,* January 31, 1994, p. 27; and, importantly, "Union Leaders Back Head in Ballet Bar," *T,* April 5, 1994, p. 2.

58. "Class Conflict . . . ," *T,* April 8, 1994, p. 3.

59. "Drive to Help Gifted Children," *T,* August 9, 1993, p. 1, 27.

60. "School Tests . . . ," *T,* November 26, 1993, p. 5.

61. *ST,* April 10, 1994, p. 4.5., col. 2.

62. Ann Robinson, "Last Croak of the Dinosaur," *ST,* June 26, 1994, p. 4.16, cols. 2, 3.

63. *T,* May 15, 1994, p. 9, col. 1. See also recognitions of massive structural contradictions (that is, slow, patchy, reversible, and jobless growth!) in G. Searjent, *T,* April 11, 1994, p. 38; May 9, 1994, p. 38; D. Wright, *ST,* May 8, 1994, p. 5.2.

64. For two contemporary "snapshots" of all this and consequences, see Alex Bryson and Stephen McKay, eds., *Is It Worth Working?* (Policy Studies Institute, 1994, especially chapter by Huw Beynon, "Changes in the Experience of Work") the research report by Alice de Wolff, *Strategies for Working Families* (Toronto: Ontario Coalition for Better Child Care, 1994), and *Job Loss and Entry Level Information Workers* (Toronto: Ontario Training and Adjustment Board, 1995). For a valuable and general overviewing critique and rebuttal, see *Socialist Register, 1994,* on "Globalism," especially chapter by M. Bienefeld (pp. 94–129).

65. See issues of the *Times Higher Education Supplement* 1992 through 1994, plus the data summarized in Yeo, *Access.*

66. For further discussion on the most recent waves of downsizing see Corrigan, "A Dose of Realism? The Social Grammar of Globalism," in Ted Schrecker, *Surviving Globalism* (New York: St. Martin's Press, 1997), pp. 239–252 and de Wolff, *Job Loss and Entry Level Information Workers.* Both texts extend the discussion begun here, detailing the changes of the social context that make possible and extend corporate strategies into schooling.

Chapter Twelve
Conclusion
New Perspectives on Moral Regulation and Schooling

Kate Rousmaniere, Kari Dehli, and Ning de Coninck-Smith

We entered this project with a shared understanding that formal schools are organized around the creation and maintenance of disciplinary boundaries and moral norms that reinforce normative beliefs about good and bad, right and wrong, and the very definition of good schooling, good teaching, and good parenting. Inside schools, students, teachers, and parents have (apparently) embodied these norms in their daily practices, assumptions, and social relations. Moral regulation works in ways that render some forms of expression, conduct, and behavior obvious, natural, and normal. That is, some ways of saying, doing, and being human are privileged over others, rendering other ways deviant, dangerous, marginal, or unacceptable. By their very taken-for-grantedness, dominant moral norms appear to live a secret, invisible, and effortless life. Only in conflict does their constructed and pervasive character become visible, when students, teachers, administrators, and parents challenge, question, and subvert the norms that structure the lives of schools. It is in such moments of challenge that we can begin to glimpse the enormous apparatus devoted to shoring up the dominant normative order. When students, teachers, administrators, and parents have challenged, questioned, and undercut these norms, they bring to light the otherwise (again apparently) quietly assumed values of schooling.

The perspective on schools as sites of moral regulation has opened up a broader and multidimensional view on the history of education. Schools of the past have been described as silent shells of administrative authority, the passive recipients of policies and programs of school reformers, government officials, and educational professionals. Rarely have historians been able to tell the historical tale of students' experiences in schools: the anxieties of an examination, the fear of a teacher's discipline, the self-consciousness of trying to conform to the norm of a classroom. Nor have we been able to understand the experience of being a teacher in the past: the frustration of conforming one's own visions of good teaching to school expectations, the exhaustion and humiliation of teaching a bad class, and the self-reprimanding and self-blame of losing control over a class of dozens of energetic children crammed into a small room. The authors in this collection have chronicled how moral regulation works, and how it should not be seen as an intrusive or simply controlling power of the state, the school board, or the church, but rather a dialectical and dynamic force that is interwoven inside daily school practice. Children are subjects of socialization programs, but they are also active respondents to those programs. Teachers and parents are moral regulators of children, but they are also subjects of moral regulation in their own work.

Our common interest in what we call the interiority of schools, the formations of identities and behaviors, of social norms and moral standards, and the ways in which these norms are regulated is part of a growing field of interpretive examinations of the experience of state schooling. Two areas of focus are emerging in the research. First, each of the studies here either implicitly or explicitly refers to the role of schooling in state formation: schools are state directed and tax funded, and in many countries attendance is compulsory and the rules and regulations of the school are established by governmental fiat. The school is a state agency that sits between the private and the public, between the state and civil society, and to that extent, the regulatory powers of schools have been particularly significant in the dual process of subject formation and state formation. Moral regulation draws attention to how state formation is not simply about laws, roads, taxes, administration, government buildings, and so forth. It involves also, and centrally, the shaping and reshaping of political identities—often labeled as civics—and the reformation of individuals' very conception of their role in society. Moral regulation involves also the shaping and reshaping of civic identities, and the reformation of individuals' very conception of their role in society. These histories look under the skin of broader structural change and investigate how people not only were formed to adjust to new structures, but also how people contributed to that process. Central to this process was the school, which functioned as both the agent of and the object of state interests. Inside schools, students and teachers were active, if often unwilling and unintentional participants in cultural formation and reformation.[1]

A second line of historical research has focused on the local and often individual expressions and experiences of moral regulatory practices inside schools. These histories draw on new methodological approaches designed to investigate and narrate the everyday educational reality of individuals in schools of the past.[2] The guiding question in these studies is how to reconstruct the experiences of schooling in the past, and how to make meaning out of those experiences. The question of how to accomplish these explorations of the interior landscape of schools has encouraged the use of new sources, and the asking of new questions of those sources. Educational historian Geraldine Jonçich Clifford has proposed that historians need to rethink what they have assumed to be the "data" of history by investigating not only public events, but also "the meanings people attach to their experiences; their sense of what drives or limits their actions; the victories and defeats of their lives; what builds them up and what wears them down; the struggle within as well as the struggle without."[3] These historians have taken on a search for the everyday reality of schools of the past, to look behind traditional institutional histories and identify and interpret the meanings of schooling and teaching in the past.

It is no coincidence that feminist historians have been especially interested in the interiority of schooling, and in the everyday experiences of those who populate schools. In many ways, this interest coincides with feminist attempts to make the "private" public, to give voice to those who have been silenced, and to make visible that which has been excluded, marginalized, and forgotten in more "mainstream" histories of education. At the same time, however, there are many historians (and others) who question how stories of or from experience are told. It is not so much that historians should avoid talking about experience (be it their own or that of others), but rather that they ought not to treat "experience" as a foundation of truth or knowledge. That is, histories of experiences interior to schooling, for example, must be mindful of the socially and historically constructed character of experience. In context of this book, we would argue that moral regulation offers a strategy for dealing with this question, because it draws attention to how social and discursive repertoires—the ways in which we conduct our experiences and tell stories about ourselves—provide, and often privilege, certain ways of making sense of our world.

The authors in this volume have used a variety of sources in their research, including photographs, diaries, governmental documents, legal testimonies, and community reports, daily news accounts, educational texts, popular essays, and fiction. They have identified public disputes about student discipline, teachers' classroom practices and social behavior, and the moral and legal expectations of parents and teachers. Such disputes are moments of conflict that offer some of the few documented accounts of moral assumptions, and the contestation over those assumptions. The authors have also asked unusual questions of their sources, searching for the missing people in the photograph, questioning the presumptions and generalizations of the official texts, and extending the meaning of their findings both outside into the public sphere of school management and state politics and inside into the private experiences of individuals. As these authors have shown, schooling is not merely a formal place where explicit curricula are transmitted, nor a fixed event in people's lives, but a whole series of experiences over time. Schooling is rich with personal dynamics, social relations, and individual perceptions; schooling is a fluid and complex phenomenon that bleeds inside people's lives, affecting their sense of self and shaping both their material opportunities for the future and their personal potential. Nowhere is this melting of boundaries between school and self, and between school and the social order, more profound than in relations of discipline and moral regulation.

The concept of moral regulation, then, does not refer just to types of events and power relations issuing from a state agency; it also enables a way of seeing and understanding how individuals experience and conduct themselves in the social world. It is our hope that other researchers will continue from here and investigate a range of areas not covered by this publication, including the role of moral regulation in daily pedagogical relations between teachers and students and in the complex labor relations between teachers and administrators; the effect of the broader culture on shaping and confining students', teachers', and parents' experiences of schooling; the elements of control and normalization of colonial education, state schooling of the poor and racial minorities; and the control of teachers' and students' work in periods of significant state reorganization. We also encourage contemporary examinations of moral regulation in schools in a period when public debates about discipline and morality in schools are intricately tied with economic and political objectives. Social change, and also social stasis, continues to rest in the daily practices and teachings of the public school.

Endnotes

1. E. Thomas Ewing, "Discipline and Culture: Soviet Teachers and the Politics of Order, 1931–1939," History of Education Society Annual Conference, Minneapolis, October 1995; David Hogan, "The Market Revolution and Disciplinary Power: Joseph Lancaster and the Psychology of the Early Classroom System," *History of Education Quarterly*, Vol. 29, No. 3, Fall 1989, pp. 381–417; Bruce Curtis, *Building the Educational State: Canada West, 1836–1871* (Sussex: Falmer Press; London, Ont.: Althouse Press, 1988).

2. Mark Depaepe and Frank Simon, "Is There Any Place for the History of 'Education' in the 'History of Education'? A Plea for the History of Everyday Educational Reality In and Outside Schools," *Paedagogica Historica*, Vol. 331, 1995, pp. 9–16.

3. Geraldine Jonçich Clifford, "Marry, Stitch, Die or Do Worse: Educating Women for Work," in Harvey Kantor and David Tyack, eds., *Work, Youth, and Schooling: Historical Perspectives on Vocationalism in American Education* (Palo Alto, CA: Stanford University Press, 1982), p. 225.

Selected Bibliography

Åberg, Göran. *Högre allmänna läroverket i Jönköping 1878–1968*. Uppsala: Föreningen för svensk undervsiningshistoria, 1991.

Ahlén, Abraham. *Mina ungdomsminnen från Skara*. Stockholm: P. Palmqvist, 1911.

Alaimo, Kathleen. "Childhood and Adolescence in Modern European History." *Journal of Social History* 24 (Spring 1991): pp. 591–602.

Albisetti, James C. *Schooling German Girls and Women: Secondary and Higher Education in the Nineteenth Century*. Princeton: Princeton University Press, 1988.

———. "The Feminization of Teaching in the Nineteenth Century: A Comparative Perspective." *History of Education* 22 (1993): pp. 253–263.

Althusser, Louis. *Essays on Ideology*. London: Verso, 1984.

Andersson, Inger. "Formal Education in Reading and Writing and the Formation of a Swedish National Identity." In Ryszard Kucha and Ulla Johansson, eds. *Polish and Swedish Schools in the 19th and 20th Century: A Historical Study*. Lublin: Marie Curie-Sklodowska University Press, 1995.

Annerstedt, Claes. *Idrottslärarna och idrottsämnet. Utveckling, mål, kompetens-ett didaktiskt perspektiv*. Göteborg: Göteborgs Universitet, 1991.

Bagchi, J. "Representing Nationalism: Ideology of Motherhood in Colonial Bengal." *Economic and Political Weekly* (October 20–27, 1990): pp. 65–71.

Bågenholm, Ragnhild. *Min barndom i Majorna*. Göteborg: Ewald Elanders Bokförlag, 1955.

Ball, Stephen J., ed. *Foucault and Education: Disciplines and Knowledge*.

London: Routledge, 1990.

Banerjee, Sumanta. *The Parlour and the Streets*. Calcutta: Seagull Books, 1989.

Bernstein, Basil. *Class, Codes and Control. Vol 3. Towards a Theory of Educational Transmission*. London: Routledge & Kegan Paul, 1975.

Bjerne, Ulla. *Livet väntar dej*. Stockholm: Bonniers, 1955.

Borthwick, Meredith. *The Changing Role of Women in Bengal, 1849–1905*. Princeton: Princeton University Press, 1984.

Britzman, Deborah. "Cultural Myths in the Making of a Teacher: Biography and Social Structure in Teacher Education." *Harvard Educational Review* 56 (November 1986): pp. 442–456.

———. *Practice Makes Practice: A Critical Study of Learning to Teach*. Albany: State University of New York Press, 1991.

———. "The Terrible Problem of Knowing Thyself: Toward a Poststructural Account of Teacher Identity." *Journal of Curriculum Theorizing* 9 (Spring 1992): pp. 23–46.

Burchell, Lawrence. *Victorian Schools: A Study in Colonial Government Architecture 1837–1900*. Melbourne: Melbourne University Press, 1980.

Burgess, Hilary, and Bob Carter. "'Bringing Out the Best in People': Teacher Training and the 'Real' Teacher." *British Journal of Sociology of Education* 13 (1992): pp. 349–359.

Burgoyne, Lola. *A History of the Home and School Movement in Ontario*. Toronto: Charters Publishing, 1935.

Butler, Judith. "Contingent Foundations." In Judith Butler and Joan W. Scott, eds. *Feminists Theorize the Political*. New York: Routledge, 1992.

Chatterjee, Partha. *Nationalist Thought: A Derivative Discourse*. London: Zed Books, for the United Nations University, 1986.

Christie, Nancy. "Psychology, Sociology and the Secular Moment: The Ontario Educational Association's Quest for Authority, 1880–1900." *Journal of Canadian Studies* 25 (Summer 1990): pp. 119–143.

Clifford, Geraldine Jonçich. "Marry, Stitch, Die, or Do Worse: Educating Women for Work." In Harvey Kantor and David Tyack, eds. *Work, Youth, and Schooling: Historical Perspectives on Vocationalism in American Education*. Palo Alto, CA: Stanford

University Press, 1982.

Corrigan, Philip. "Dichotomy Is Contradiction: On 'Society' as Constraint and Construction: Remarks on the Doctrine of the 'Two Sociologies.'" *Sociological Review* 23 (May 1975): pp. 211–243.

————. "On Moral Regulation: Some Preliminary Remarks." *Sociological Review* 29 (1981): pp. 313–337.

————. "In/forming Schooling." In David Livingstone, ed. *Critical Pedagogy and Cultural Power.* Toronto: Garamond, 1987.

————. "State Formation and Classroom Practice: Once Again on Moral Regulation." In Geoffrey Milburn, Ivor F. Goodson, and Robert J. Clark, eds. *Re-interpreting Curriculum Research: Images and Arguments.* Lewes, Sussex: Falmer Press, and London, Ontario: Althouse Press, 1989.

Corrigan, Philip, ed. *Capitalism, State Formation, and Marxist Theory: Historical Investigations.* London: Quartet, 1980.

Corrigan, Philip, Bruce Curtis, and Robert Lanning. "The Political Space of Schooling." In Terry Wotherspoon, ed. *The Political Economy of Canadian Schooling.* Toronto: Methuen, 1987.

Corrigan, Philip and Derek Sayer. *The Great Arch: English State Formation as Cultural Revolution.* Oxford: Basil Blackwell, 1985.

Curtis, Bruce. "The Myth of Curricular Republicanism: The State and the Curriculum in Canada West, 1820–1850." *Histoire Sociale/Social History* 16 (1983): pp. 305–329.

————. "The Speller Expelled: Disciplining the Common Reader in Canada West." *Canadian Review of Sociology and Anthropology* 22 (1985): pp. 346–368.

————. *Building the Educational State: Canada West, 1836–1871.* London, Ontario: Althouse Press, 1988.

————. *True Government by Choice Men? Inspection, Education, and State Formation in Canada West.* Toronto: University of Toronto Press, 1992.

————. "Gender in the Regime of Statistical Knowledge/Power." Paper presented to the ANZHES/CHEA Conference, University of Melbourne, 1993.

Dahlborg, Carl, et al. *Betänkande avgivet utav kommitterade, som utsetts av Svenska Provinsialläkarföreningen för utredning av skolhygieniska spärsmål rörande folk- och småskolor å landsbygden.*

Stockholm: Häggströms boktryckeri, 1914.

Dahr, Elisabeth. *Flickskolor i Jönköping.* Uppsala: Föreningen för svensk undervisningshistoria, 1975.

Davidoff, Lenore, and Catherine Hall. *Family Fortunes: Men and Women of the English Middle Class, 1780–1850.* London: Hutchinson, 1988.

de Coninck-Smith, Ning. "Skolejubi-læ(r)erne. Et bidrag til skolejubilæernes historie." *Historie og Samtid 3* (1989): pp. 69–74.

———. "Internatet, Københavns Kommunes Internat på Vesterfaelledvej, 1879–1905." In *Social Kritik* 17 (November 1991): pp. 56–82.

———. "Paa den mest ryggesløse Maade." *Den jyske Historiker 56* (1991): pp. 71–90.

Dean, Mitchell. "'A Social Structure of Many Souls': Moral Regulation, Government, and Self-formation." *Canadian Journal of Sociology* 19 (1994): pp. 145–168.

———. *Critical and Effective Histories: Foucault's Methods and Historical Sociology.* London and New York: Routledge, 1994.

Dehli, Kari. "Women and Class: The Social Organization of Mothers' Relations to Schooling in Toronto, 1915 to 1940." Ph.D. diss., Ontario Institute for Studies in Education, Toronto, 1988.

Dehli, Kari, and Harry Smaller. "Introduction." *Ontario History* 85(4) (December 1993): pp. 301–310.

Depaepe, Mark, and Frank Simon. "Is There Any Place for the History of 'Education' in the 'History of Education'? A Plea for the History of Everyday Educational Reality In and Outside of Schools." *Paedagogica Historica* (1995): pp. 9–16.

Diamond, Irene, and Lee Quinby, eds. *Feminism and Foucault.* Boston: Northeastern University Press, 1988.

Dinwiddy, J.R. "The Nineteenth-Century Campaign against Flogging in the Army." *English Historical Review* 97 (1982): pp. 308–331.

Downs, Laura Lee. "If 'Woman' Is Just an Empty Category, Then Why Am I Afraid to Walk Alone at Night? Identity Politics Meets the Postmodern Subject." *Comparative Studies in Society and History* 35 (April 1993): pp. 414–451.

DuBois, Ellen Carol, and Vicki L. Ruiz, eds. *Unequal Sisters: A Multicultural Reader in U.S. Women's History.* New York:

Routledge, 1990.

Edquist, Märta. "Sanningen om klostret." In *När jag gick i skolan.*
Skol- och ungdomsminnen från 1800-talets senare hälft berättade
av 34 svenska män och kvinnor. Uppsala: J.A. Lindblads
förlag, 1934.

Ekelund, Herman. "Från Braheskolan i Jönköping." In *När jag gick*
i skolan. Skol- och ungdomsminnen från 1800-talets senare hälft
berättade av 34 svenska män och kvinnor. Uppsala: J. A. Lindblads
förlag, 1934.

Elias, Norbey. *The Civilizing Process.* New York: Pantheon, 1978.

Englund, Tomas. *Curriculum as a Political Problem. Changing Edu-*
cational Conceptions, with Special Reference to Citizenship Edu-
cation. Lund: Studentlitteratur, 1986.

Ewing, E. Thomas. "Discipline and Culture: Soviet Teachers and
the Politics of Order, 1931–1939." Paper presented to the History of Education Society Annual Conference, Minneapolis,
Minnesota, October 1995.

Finkelstein, Barbara. "In Fear of Childhood: Relationships between
Parents and Teachers in Popular Primary Schools in the Nineteenth Century." *History of Childhood Quarterly* 3 (Winter 1976):
pp. 321–335.

———. "Incorporating Children into the History of Education."
Journal of Educational Thought 18 (April 1984): pp. 21–41.

———. *Governing the Young: Teacher Behavior in Popular Primary*
Schools in the Nineteenth-Century United States. New York:
Falmer Press, 1989.

———. "Redoing Urban Educational History." In Ronald K.
Goodenow and William E. Marsden, eds. *The City and Educa-*
tion in Four Nations. Cambridge: Cambridge University Press,
1992.

Florin, Christina. *Kampen om katedern. Feminiserings- och*
professionaliseringsprocessen inom den svenska folkskolans lärarkår
1860–1906. Stockholm och Umeå: Almqvist and Wicksell,
1987.

———. "Social Closure as a Professional Strategy: Male and Female Teachers from Co-operation to Conflict in Sweden, 1860–
1906." *History of Education* 20 (1991): pp. 17–26.

Florin, Christina, and Ulla Johansson. *"Där de härliga lagrarna gro . . . ." Kultur, klass och kön i det svenska läroverket 1850–1914.* Stockholm: Tiden, 1993.

Folkundervisningskommitténs betänkande I:3. Bilagor. Historik och statliga utredningar. Stockholm: Norstedt, 1911.

Förslag till en förbättrad Skol-Ordning, jemte Betänkande och Bilagor, i underdånighet upprättadt af den i nåder tillförordnade Uppfostrings-Comité. Stockholm, 1817.

Foucault, Michel. *Discipline and Punish: The Birth of the Prison.* New York: Vintage Books, 1977.

———. "Nietzsche, Genealogy, and History." In Michel Foucault, *Language, Counter-Memory, Practice.* Ithaca, NY: Cornell University Press, 1977.

———. *The History of Sexuality, Vol. 1.* New York: Vintage, 1980.

———. *Power/Knowledge: Selected Interviews and Other Writings, 1972–1977.* Edited by Colin Gordon. New York: Pantheon Books, 1980.

———. "The Subject and Power." In Hubert L. Dreyfus and Paul Rabinow, eds. *Michel Foucault: Beyond Structuralism and Hermeneutics.* Chicago: University of Chicago Press, 1983.

———. "Governmentality." In Graham Burchell, Colin Gordon, and Peter Miller, eds. *The Foucault Effect: Studies in Governmentality.* Chicago: University of Chicago Press, 1991.

Fowler, Sandra. "The Character of the Woman Teacher during Her Emergence as a Full-Time Professional in Nineteenth-Century America: Stereotypes vs. Personal Histories." Ed.D. diss., Boston University, 1985.

Franklin, Barry M. "Self-Control and the Psychology of School Discipline." In William F. Pinar, ed. *Contemporary Curriculum Discourses.* Scottsdale, AZ: Gorsuch Scarisbrick, 1988.

Fraser, Nancy. *Unruly Practices: Power, Discourse and Gender in Contemporary Social Theory.* Minneapolis: University of Minnesota Press, 1989.

Gemie, Sharif. "The Schoolmistress's Revenge: Secular Schoolmistresses, Academic Authority and Village Conflicts in France, 1815–1848." *History of Education* 20 (1991): pp. 203–217.

Gidney, Robert D., and Wyn Millar. *Inventing Secondary Education: The Rise of the High School in Nineteenth-Century Ontario.* London, Ontario: McGill-Queen's University Press, 1990.

Ginzburg, Carlo. *The Cheese and the Worms: The Cosmos of a 16th-Century Miller.* London: Routledge and Kegan Paul, 1980.

————. "Clues: Roots of an Evidential Paradigm." In Carlo Ginzburg. *Clues, Myths, and the Historical Method.* Baltimore: Johns Hopkins University Press, 1989.

Graham, Elizabeth. "Schoolmarms and Early Teaching in Ontario." In Janice Acton, Penny Goldsmith, and Bonnie Shepard, eds. *Women at Work, Ontario, 1850–1930.* Toronto: Canadian Women's Educational Press, 1974.

Gramsci, Antonio. *The Selections from the Prison Notebooks.* Edited by Quentin Hoare and Geoffrey Nowell Smith. London: Lawrence and Wishart, 1971.

Green, Andy. *Education and State Formation: The Rise of Educational Systems in England, France and the USA.* London: Macmillan, 1990.

Grumet, Madeleine. *Bitter Milk: Women and Teaching.* Amherst: University of Massachusetts, 1988.

Hagen, Ellen. "Ljudlösa steg i Åhlinska flickskolan." In *När jag gick i skolan. Skol- och ungdomsminnen från 1800-talets senare hälft berättade av 34 svenska män och kvinnor.* Uppsala: J.A. Lindblads förlag, 1934.

Hall, B. Rud, ed. *Hågkomster från folkskola och folkundervisning.* Uppsala: Föreningen för svensk undervisningshistoria, 1933.

————. *Minnen från privatläroverk.* Stockholm: Föreningen för svensk undervisningshistoria, 1938.

————. *Minnen från folkskolan och folkundervisning. V.* Uppsala: Föreningen för svensk undervisningshistoria, 1942.

————. *Minnen från folkskola och folkundervisning, VIII.* Uppsala: Föreningen för svensk undervisningshistoria, 1945.

Hamilton, David. "Adam Smith and the Moral Economy of the Classroom System." *Journal of Curriculum Studies* 12 (1981): pp. 281–291.

————. *Towards a Theory of Schooling.* London: Falmer Press, 1989.

Hammerich, Poul. *Skindet på næsen. Første bind af En Danmarkskrønike 1945–1972.* Copenhagen: Gyldendal, 1976.

Hansen, Bodil K. *Skolen i landbosamfundet ca. 1880–1900.* Sorø: Landbohistorisk Selskab, 1977.

Harney, John. "Boarding and Belonging." *Urban History Review* 2

(1978): pp. 8–37.

Hartsock, Nancy. "Foucault on Power: A Theory for Women?" In Linda Nicholson, ed. *Feminism/Postmodernism*. New York: Routledge, 1990.

Hemberg, Eugen. "En nittioårings minnen." *Vandringar i kulturens och naturens tempel.* Malmö: Bokförlaget Scania, 1936.

Herbst, Jurgen. *And Sadly Teach: Teacher Education and Professionalization in American Culture.* Madison: University of Wisconsin Press, 1989.

Hilden, Adda. "Stærk som døden - en uægteskabelig historie fra 1800-tallets slutning." *Historiske Meddelelser om København* (1993): pp. 33–51.

Hilden, Adda, and Erik Nørr. *Lærerindeuddannelse. Lokalsamfundenes kamp om seminariedriften. Dansk læreruddannelse 1791–1991, Vol. 3.* Odense: Odense Universitetsforlag, 1993.

Hogan, David. "The Market Revolution and Disciplinary Power: Joseph Lancaster and the Psychology of the Early Classroom System." *History of Education Quarterly* 29 (Fall 1989): pp. 381–417.

————. "Modes of Discipline: Affective Individualism and Pedagogical Reform in New England, 1820–1850." *American Journal of Education* 99 (November 1990): pp. 1–56.

Hoole, Charles. *A New Discovery of the Old Art of Teaching Schoole.* London: London University Press, 1913 [1659].

Hooper, Carole. "Vision Unrealised: State Secondary Education in Victoria, 1850–1872." *History of Education Review* 19 (1990): pp. 1–30.

Hoskin, Keith. "The Examination, Disciplinary Power and Rational Schooling." *History of Education* 8 (1979): pp. 135–146.

Houston, Susan. "Politics, Schools and Social Change in Upper Canada." *Canadian Historical Review* 53 (1972): pp. 261–283.

Hunter, Ian. *Rethinking the School: Subjectivity, Bureaucracy, Criticism.* Sydney: Allen and Unwin, 1994.

Iacovetta, Franca, and Mariana Valverde, eds. *Gender Conflicts: New Essays in Women's History.* Toronto: University of Toronto Press, 1992.

Jensen, Knud Peder. *Nåden og skammen.* Copenhagen: Gyldendal, 1985.

Jessen, Johs. *C. V. og Ø. Flakkebjerg Herreders Skolehistorie. Blade af den danske Skoles Historie fra ca. 1690 til vore Dage.*

Slagelse, 1938.

Johansson, Ulla. *Att skolas för hemmet. Trädgårdsskötsel, slöjd, huslig ekonomi och nykterhetsundervisning i den svenska folkskolan med exempel från Sköns församling.* Umeå: Umeå University, 1987.

———. "Ordning i klassen! Disciplin och straff i 1800-talets lärda skola." In Stig G. Nordström, et al., eds. *Utbildningshistoria 1990.* Stockholm: Föreningen för svensk utbildningshistoria, 1990.

———. "Historien om likvärdighet i svensk skola." In *Likvärdighet i svensk skola.* Stockholm: Skolverket, 1995.

Johansson, Ulla, and Christina, Florin. "'Where the Glorious Laurels Grow . . . .' Swedish Grammar Schools as a Means of Social Mobility and Social Reproduction." *History of Education* 22 (1993): pp. 147–162.

———. "Order in the (Middle) Class! Culture, Class and Gender in the Swedish State Grammar School 1850–1914." *Historical Studies in education/Revue d'histoire de l'education* 6 (Spring 1994): pp. 21–44.

———. "The Trinity of State, Church, and School in 19th-century Sweden." In Ryszard Kucha and Ulla Johansson, eds. *Polish and Swedish Schools in the 19th and 20th Century. A Historical Study.* Lublin: Marie Curie-Sklodowska University Press, 1995.

Jones, Dave. "The Genealogy of the Urban Schoolteacher." In Stephen J. Ball, ed. *Foucault and Education: Disciplines and Knowledge.* New York: Routledge, 1990.

Jordanova, Ludmilla. "Children in History." In Geoffrey Scarre, ed. *Children, Parents and Politics.* Cambridge: Cambridge University Press, 1989.

Kaestle, Carl F. *Joseph Lancaster and Monitorial Education.* New York: Teachers College Press, 1973.

———. "Historical Methods in Educational Research." In Richard M. Jaeger, ed. *Complementary Methods in Research in Education.* Washington DC: American Educational Research Association, 1988.

Kyle, Gunhild. *Svensk flickskola under 1800-talet.* Göteborg: Göteborgs Universitet, 1972.

Läroverkskomiténs underdåniga utlåtande och förslag angående organisationen af rikets allmänna läroverk afgifvet den 25 augusti

1884, II. Stockholm: P A Norstedt and Söner, 1884.

Larsen, Joakim. *Bidrag til den danske Folkeskoles Historie 1818–1898.* Copenhagen, 1899.

Lehmann, Henrik. *Haandbog i Lovgivningen om den danske Folkeskole.* Copenhagen: Systematisk Fremstilling, 1909.

———. *Haandbog i Lovgivningen om den danske Folkeskole.* Copenhagen: Kronologisk Fremstilling, 1914.

Leloudis, James. *Schooling in the New South: Pedagogy, Self, and Society in North Carolina, 1880–1920.* Chapel Hill: University of North Carolina Press, 1996.

Lewis, Jan. "Mother's Love: The Construction of an Emotion in Nineteenth-Century America." In Andrew E. Barnes and Peter N. Stearns, eds. *Social History and Issues in Human Consciousness.* New York: New York University Press, 1989.

Linder, Gurli. *På den tiden. Några bilder från 1870-talets Stockholm.* Stockholm: Albert Bonniers Förlag, 1924.

Lopéz, Silvano B. "Högre utbildning för kvinnor. En studie av Kungliga Högre lärarinneseminariet." Unpublished essay. Umeå: Umeå University, Department of History, 1993.

———. "The Royal Teacher Training College for Women. The Construction of a Women's Élite." Unpublished essay. Umeå: Umeå University, Department of History, 1994.

Macpherson, C.B. *The Political Theory of Possessive Individualism.* Oxford: Oxford University Press, 1962.

McNay, Lois. *Foucault and Feminism.* Boston: Northeastern University Press, 1992.

Meadmore, Daphne. "The Production of Individuality through Examination." *British Journal of Sociology of Education* 14 (1993): pp. 59–73.

Miller, Peter, ed. *The Foucault Effect: Studies in Governmentality.* Chicago: University of Chicago Press, 1991.

Murshid, Ghulam. *The Reluctant Debutante: Response of Bengali Women to Modernization, 1849–1905.* Rajshahi, Bangladesh: Rajshahi University Press, 1983.

Netzler, Fritz. *Helsingborgsminnen från min ungdom.* Munkedal: Carl Zakariasson, 1985.

Nicholson, Linda J., ed. *Feminism/Postmodernism.* New York: Routledge, 1990.

Nielsen, Hanne Rimmen. "Christian and Competent Schoolmistresses: Women's Culture at the Aarhus Training College for Women Teachers." In Tayo Andreasen, ed. *Moving On. New Perspectives on the Women's Movement.* Aarhus: Aarhus University Press, 1991.

————. "Mine Hvid, Samsø - Den første kvindelige førstelærer." *Den jyske Historiker* 62 (1993): pp. 62–94.

Nielsen, Lisbeth, and Poul Porskær Poulsen. *Kæltringer og skikkelige folk i Gødvad sogn. Et midtjysk sogn og dets mennesker, belyst gennem herredsretten 1858–1890.* Odense: Landbohistorisk Selskab, 1991.

Nielsen, Stinus. "Kampen mod § 8 og § 33. Den danske lærerstands retsstilling gennem 75 år." *Danmarks Lærerforening 1874–1949.* Århus Danmarks Lærerforenings Hovedstyrelse, 1949. pp. 184–194.

Nissen, Gunhild. *Bønder, skole og demokrati. En undersøgelse i fire provstier af forholdet mellem den offentlige skole og befolkningen på landet i tiden ca. 1880–1920.* Copenhagen: Institut for dansk Skolehistorie, 1973.

Nørr, Erik. *Skolen, præsten og kommunen. Kampen om skolen på landet 1842–1899.* Viborg: Jurist- og Økonomforbundets Forlag, 1994.

O'Neill, John. "The Medicalization of Social Control." *Canadian Review of Sociology and Anthropology* 23 (1986): pp. 350–364.

Paterson, Fiona M.S. "Schooling the Family." *Sociology* 22 (February 1988): pp. 65–86.

Pennacchio, Luigi G. "In Defence of Identity: Ida Siegel and the Jews of Toronto Versus the Assimilation Attempts of the Public School and its Allies, 1900–1920." *Canadian Jewish Historical Society Journal* 9 (Spring 1985): pp. 41–60.

Petterson, Lars. *Frihet, jämlikhet, egendom och Bentham. Utvecklingslinjer i svensk folkundervisning mellan feodalism och kapitalism 1809–1860.* Stockholm: Almqvist and Wicksell International, 1992.

Plumb, J.H. "Children, the Victims of Time." In J.H. Plumb. *In the Light of History.* London: Penguin Press, 1972.

Polakow, Valerie. *The Erosion of Childhood.* Chicago: University of Chicago Press, 1982.

Pollock, Linda. *Forgotten Children: Parent-Child Relations from 1500 to 1900.* London: Cambridge University Press, 1983.

Prentice, Alison. "Themes in the Early History of the Women's Teachers' Association of Toronto." In Paula Bourne, ed. *Women's Paid and Unpaid Work: Historical and Contemporary Perspectives.* Toronto: New Hogtown Press, 1985.

————. "Friendly Atoms in Chemistry: Women and Men at Normal School in Mid-Nineteenth-Century Toronto." In David Keane and Colin Read, eds. *Old Ontario: Essays in Honour of J.M.S. Careless.* Toronto: Dundurn Press, 1989.

Prentice, Alison, and Marta Danylewycz. "Teachers' Work: Changing Patterns and Perceptions in the Emerging School Systems of Nineteenth- and Early Twentieth-Century Central Canada." *Labour/LeTravail* 17 (Spring 1986): pp. 59–80.

Prentice, Alison, and Marjorie R. Theobald, eds. *Women Who Taught: Perspectives on the History of Women and Teaching.* Toronto: University of Toronto Press, 1991.

Ramazanoglu, Caroline, ed. *Against Foucault: Explorations of Some Tensions between Foucault and Feminism.* New York: Routledge, 1993.

Raychaudhuri, Tapan. *Europe Reconsidered: Perceptions of the West in Nineteenth-Century Bengal.* Delhi: Oxford University Press, 1988.

Richardson, Gunnar. *Kulturkamp och klasskamp. Ideologiska och sociala motsättningar i svensk skol- och kulturpolitik under 1880-talet.* Göteborg: Akademiförlaget, 1963.

Rousmaniere, Kate. "Losing Patience and Staying Professional: Women Teachers and the Problem of Classroom Discipline in New York City Schools in the 1920s." *History of Education Quarterly* 34 (Spring 1994): pp. 49–68.

Rury, John L. *Education and Women's Work: Female Schooling and the Division of Labor in Urban America, 1870–1930.* Albany: State University of New York Press, 1991.

Sahlin, Einar. "Ett didaktiskt kanon för profkandidater och yngre lärare." *Pedagogisk Tidskrift* (1893): pp. 90–99.

Sandin, Bengt. *Hemmet, gatan, fabriken eller skolan. Folkundervisning och barnuppfostran i svenska städer 1600–1850.* Lund: Arkiv, 1986.

————. "Education, Popular Culture, and the Surveillance of the Population in Stockholm between 1600 and the 1840's." *Con-*

tinuity and Change 3 (1988): pp. 357–390.

Sangari, Kumkum and Sudesh Vaid, eds. *Women and Culture.* Bombay: SNDT Somen's University, 1985.

———. *Recasting Women, Essays in Indian Colonial History.* New Brunswick, NJ: Rutgers University Press, 1989.

Sarkar, Sumit. *A Critique of Colonial India.* Calcutta: Papyrus, 1985.

Sawicki, Jana. *Disciplining Foucault: Feminism, Power and the Body.* New York: Routledge, 1991.

Schelin, Margitta. *Den officiella skolstatistiken i Sverige åren 1847– 1881.* Umeå: Umeå University, 1978.

Schlossman, Steven. "The Formative Era in American Parent Education: Overview and Interpretation." In Ron Haskins and Diane Adams, eds. *Parent Education and Public Policy.* Norwood, NJ: Ablex Publishing, 1983.

Scott, Joan W. "'The Tip of the Volcano,'" and Laura Downs, "Reply to Joan Scott." *Comparative Studies in Society and History* 35 (April 1993): pp. 414–451.

Selleck, R.J.W. *James Kay-Shuttleworth: Journey of an Outsider.* Portland, OR: Woburn Press, 1994.

Smaller, Harry. "Teachers' Protective Associations, Professionalism and the 'State' in Nineteenth-Century Ontario." Ph.D. diss. University of Toronto, 1988.

———. "Gender and Status: The Founding Meeting of the Teachers' Association of Canada West, January 25, 1861." *Historical Studies in Education/Revue d'histoire de l'education* 6 (Fall 1994): pp. 201–218.

Steedman, Carolyn. "Prisonhouses." *Feminist Review* 20 (Summer 1985): pp. 7–21.

———. "'The Mother Made Conscious': The Historical Development of a Primary School Pedagogy." *History Workshop* 20 (Autumn 1985): pp. 149–163.

Steiner, E.E. "Separating the Soldier from the Citizen: Ideology and Criticism of Corporal Punishment in the British Armies, 1790–1815." *Social History* 8 (1983): pp. 19–35.

Strachan, Hew. "The Early Victorian Army and the Nineteenth-Century Revolution in Government." *English Historical Review* 95 (1980): pp. 782–809.

Sundkvist, Maria. *De vanartade barnen. Mötet mellan barn, föräldrar och Norrköpings barnavårdsnämnd 1903–1925.* Linköping: Linköpings Universitet, 1994.

Svedelius, Carl. *Norra real 1876–1926.* Stockholm: P A Norstedt and Söner, 1927.

Svensk författningssamling. *Kongl. Maj:ts nådiga cirkulär till Domkapitlen angående underwisningen i gymnastik och militärövningar wid elementarlärowerken, folksskolelärarsemeinarierna och folksskolorna.* No. 3, 1863.

———. *Kongl. Maj:ts nådiga stadga för rikets läroverk.* No. 53, 1878.

Theobald, Marjorie. "Discourse of Danger: Gender and the History of Elementary Schooling in Australia, 1850–1880." *Historical Studies in Education/Revue d'histoire de l'education* 1 (1989): pp. 29–52.

——— "Women's Teaching Labour, the Family and the State in Nineteenth-Century Victoria." In Marjorie Theobald and R.J.W. Selleck, eds. *Family, School and State in Australian History.* Sydney: Allen and Unwin, 1990.

Torstendahl, Rolf. "Technology in the Development in the Society, 1850–1980: Four Phases of Industrial Capitalism in Western Europe." *History and Technology* 1 (1984): pp. 157–174.

Turner, Johnathan. *The Body and Society.* Oxford: Blackwell, 1984.

Tyack, David, and Elisabeth Hansot. *Learning Together. A History of Coeducation in American Public Schools.* New York: Russell Sage, 1992.

Undersökning af Sveriges högre flickskolor. Underdånigt utlåtande afgifvet den 19 januari 1888 af utsedde komiterade. Stockholm: Norstedts, 1888.

Valverde, Mariana. *In the Age of Light, Soap and Water: Moral Reform in English Canada, 1885–1925.* Toronto: McClelland and Stewart, 1991.

Valverde, Mariana, ed. *Studies in Moral Regulation.* Toronto: Centre for Criminology, University of Toronto, 1994. Also published as a special issue of the *Canadian Journal of Sociology* 19 (2), 1994.

Valverde, Mariana, and Lorna Weir. "The Struggle of the Immoral: Preliminary Remarks on Moral Regulation." *Resources for Feminist Research/Documentation sur la recherche feministe* 17 (1987): pp. 31–34.

Ve, Hildur. "Women's Experience—Women's Rationality." In Inga Elgqvist-Salzman, ed. *Education and the Construction of Gender.* Umeå: Umeå University, kvinnovetenskapligt forum, 1991.

Vick, Malcolm. "Building Schools, Building Society: Accommodating Schools in Mid-Nineteenth-Century Australia." *Historical Studies in Education/Revue d'histoire de l'education* 5(2), 1993: pp. 231–250.

Visvanathan, Gauri. *Masks of Conquest: Literary Studies and British Rule in India.* London: Faber and Faber, 1990.

Walkerdine, Valerie. "It's Only Natural: Rethinking Child-Centered Pedagogy." In Ann Marie Wolpe and James Donald, eds. *Is There Anyone Here From Education?* London: Pluto Press, 1983.

———. "Developmental Psychology and the Child-Centered Pedagogy: The Insertion of Piaget into Early Childhood Education." In Julian Henriques, et al., eds. *Changing the Subject: Psychology, Social Regulation and Subjectivity.* London: Methuen, 1984.

———. *Schoolgirl Fictions.* London: Verso, 1990.

Wallis, Curt. *Om folkskolans hälsovårdsförhållanden och medlen att förbättra desamma.* Stockholm: Fritze, 1896.

Warren, Donald, ed. *American Teachers: Histories of a Profession at Work.* New York: Macmillan, 1989.

Wennås, Olof. *Striden om latinväldet. Idéer och intressen i svensk skolpolitik under 1800-talet.* Stockholm: Almqvist and Wicksell, 1966.

Willis, Paul. *Learning to Labour: How Working-Class Kids Get Working-Class Jobs.* Aldershot: Gower, 1977.

Index